Appreciative Inquiry

Change at the
Speed of Imagination

Jane Magruder Watkins and Bernard J. Mohr

**Forewords by Richard Beckhard
and David Cooperrider**

JOSSEY-BASS/PFEIFFER
A Wiley Company
www.pfeiffer.com

Practicing
Organization
Development

Published by

JOSSEY-BASS/PFEIFFER
A Wiley Company
989 Market Street
San Francisco, CA 94103-1741
415.433.1740; Fax 415.433.0499
800.274.4434; Fax 800.569.0443

www.pfeiffer.com

Jossey-Bass/Pfeiffer is a registered trademark of John Wiley & Sons, Inc.

ISBN: 0-7879-5179-X
Library of Congress Catalog Card Number 00-011522

Copyright © 2001 by John Wiley & Sons, Inc.

Library of Congress Cataloging-in-Publication Data

Watkins, Jane Magruder.
   Appreciative inquiry: change at the speed of imagination /
Jane Magruder Watkins and Bernard J. Mohr; foreword by David
Cooperrider.
        p. cm. — (Practicing organization development series)
Includes bibliographical references and index.
      ISBN 0-7879-5179-X
   1. Organizational change. I. Mohr, Bernard. II. Title. III.
Series.
      HD58.8 .W388 2001
      658.4′06—dc21

                         00-011522

Copyright page continued on page 243.

Acquiring Editor: Matthew Holt
Director of Development: Kathleen Dolan Davies
Developmental Editor: Susan Rachmeler
Editor: Rebecca Taff

Senior Production Editor: Dawn Kilgore
Manufacturing Manager: Becky Carreño
Interior and Cover Design: Bruce Lundquist
Illustrations: Richard Sheppard

Printed in the United States of America.

Printing   10 9 8 7 6 5 4 3

We at Jossey-Bass strive to use the most environmentally sensitive paper stocks available to us. Our
publications are printed on acid-free recycled stock whenever possible, and our paper always meets or
exceeds minimum GPO and EPA requirements.

Contents

List of Tables, Figures, and Exhibits

Foreword
to the Series

ON **1967,** Warren Bennis, Ed Schein, and I were faculty members of the Sloan School of Management at MIT. We decided to produce a series of paperback books that collectively would describe the state of the field of organization development (OD). Organization development as a field had been named by myself and several others from our pioneer change effort at General Mills in Minneapolis, Minnesota, some ten years earlier.

Today I define OD as "a systemic and systematic change effort, using behavioral science knowledge and skill, to transform the organization to a new state."

In any case, several books and many articles had been written, but there was no consensus on whether OD was a field of practice, an area of study, or a profession. We had not even established OD as a theory or even as a practice.

We decided that there was a need for something that would describe the state of OD. Our intention was to each write a book and also to recruit three other authors. After some searching, we found a young editor who had just joined the small publishing house of Addison-Wesley. We made contact, and the series was born. Our audience was to be human resource professionals who spent their time consulting with managers in their development through various small-group activities, such as team building. More than thirty books have been published in that series, and the series has had a life of its own. We just celebrated its thirtieth anniversary.

At last year's National OD Network Conference, I said that it was time for the OD profession to change and transform itself. Is that not what we change agents tell our clients to do? This new Jossey-Bass/Pfeiffer series will do just that. It can be seen as:

- A documentation of the re-invention of OD;

- An effort that will take us to the next level; and

- A practical effort to transfer to the world the theory and practice of leading-edge practitioners and theorists.

The books in this new series will thus prove to be valuable resources for change agents to keep current with the new and leading-edge ideas and practices.

May this very exciting change agent series be most creative and innovative. May it give our field a renewed burst of energy and awareness.

Richard Beckhard
Written on Labor Day weekend 1999 from my summer cabin near Bethel, Maine

Introduction
to the Series

"We must become the change we want to see."

—Mahatma Gandhi

"We live in a moment of history where change is so speeded up that we begin to see the present only when it is already disappearing."

—R. D. Laing

WE CAN EXPECT MORE CHANGE to occur in our lifetimes than has occurred since the beginning of civilization over ten thousand years ago. *Practicing Organization Development: The Change Agent Series for Groups and Organizations* is a new series of books being launched to help those who must cope with or create change in organizational settings. That includes almost everyone.

The Current State of Organization Development

Our view of OD in this series is an optimistic one. We believe that OD is gaining favor as decision makers realize that a balance *must* be struck between the drivers of change and the people involved in it and affected by it. Although OD does have its disadvantages at a time characterized by quantum leap change, it remains preferable to such alternative approaches to change as coercion, persuasion, leadership change, and debate.[1] Organization development practitioners are reinventing their approaches, based on certain foundational roots of the field, in combination with emerging principles to ensure that OD will increasingly be recognized as a viable, important, and inherently participative approach to help people in organizations facilitate, anticipate, and manage change.

A Brief History of the Genesis of the OD Series

A few years ago, and as a direct result of the success of *Practicing Organization Development: A Guide for Practitioners* by Rothwell, Sullivan, and McLean, the publisher—feeling that OD was experiencing a rebirth of interest in the United States and in other nations—wanted to launch a new OD series. The goal of this new series was not to replace, or even compete directly with, the well-established Addison-Wesley OD Series (edited by Edgar Schein). Instead, as the editors saw it, this series would provide a means by which the most promising authors in OD whose voices had not previously been heard could share their ideas. The publisher enlisted the support of Bill Rothwell, Roland Sullivan, and Kristine Quade to turn the dream of a series into a reality.

This series was long in the making. After sharing many discussions with the publisher and circulating among themselves several draft descriptions of the series editorial guidelines, the editors were guests of Bob Tannenbaum, one of the field's founders, in Carmel, California, in February 1999 to discuss the series with a group of well-known OD practitioners interested in authoring books. Several especially supportive publisher representatives, including Matt Holt and Josh Blatter, were also present at that weekend-long meeting. It was an opportunity for diverse OD practitioners, representing many philosophical viewpoints, to come together to share their vision for a new book series. In a sense, this series represents an OD intervention in the OD field in that it is geared to bringing change to the field most closely associated with change management and facilitation.

---

[1]W. Rothwell, R. Sullivan, & G. McLean. (1995). Introduction (pp. 3–46). In W. Rothwell, R. Sullivan, & G. McLean, *Practicing Organization Development: A Guide for Consultants*. San Francisco, CA: Jossey-Bass/Pfeiffer.

What Distinguishes the Books in this Series

The books in this series are meant to be cutting-edge and state-of-the-art in their approach to OD. The goal of the series is to provide an outlet for proven authorities in OD who have not put their ideas into print or for up-and-coming writers in OD who have new, sometimes unorthodox, approaches that are stimulating and exciting. Some of the books in this series describe inspirational concepts that can lead to actionable change and purvey ideas so new that they are not fully developed.

Unique to this series is the cutting-edge emphasis, the immediate applicability, and the ease of transferability of the concepts. The aim of this series is nothing less than to reinvent, re-energize, and reinvigorate OD. In each book, we have also recommended that the author(s) provide:

- A research base of some kind, meaning new information derived from practice and/or systematic investigation and

- Practical tools, worksheets, case studies and other ready-to-go approaches that help the authors drag "theory" to "practice" to make these new, cutting-edge approaches more concrete.

Subject Matter That Will (and Will Not) Be Covered

The books in this series are varied in their approach, but they are united by their focus. All share an emphasis on organization development (OD). Hence, books in this series are about participative change efforts. They are not about such other popular topics as leadership, management development, consulting, group dynamics—unless those topics are treated in new, cutting-edge ways and are geared to OD practitioners.

This Book

As the global village becomes actual, the impact on organization change theory and practice is profound. Models and methods to facilitate change have increased as OD practitioners try to help organizations cope with the rapid and discontinuous shifts in both form and function. But something more is needed. This book is about Appreciative Inquiry, a theory and practice for approaching change from a holistic frame. Based on the belief that human systems are made and imagined by those who live and work within them, AI leads systems to move toward the generative and creative images that reside in their most positive core—values, visions, achievements, best practices. With ever-increasing spread around the globe, AI has been introduced into every possible type of human system with the remarkable possibility that it may be a *philosopher's stone* in the practice of OD—a way to approach human organizing that has the capacity to shape itself to fit any culture.

Series Website

For further information and resources about the books in this series and about the current and future practice of organization development, we encourage readers to visit the series website at *www.pfeiffer.com/go/od.*

William J. Rothwell
University Park, PA

Roland Sullivan
Deephaven, MN

Kristine Quade
Minnetonka, MN

Statement
of the Board

IT IS OUR PLEASURE TO PARTICIPATE in and influence the start up of *Practicing Organization Development: The Change Agent Series for Groups and Organizations.* The purpose of the series is to stimulate the profession and influence how OD is defined and practiced. This statement is intended to set the context for the series by addressing three important questions: (1) What is OD? (2) Is the OD profession at a crossroads? and (3) What is the purpose of this series?

What Is Organization Development?

We offer the following definition of OD to stimulate debate:

> Organization development is a system-wide and values-based collaborative process of applying behavioral science knowledge to the adaptive development, improvement, and reinforcement of such organizational features as the strategies, structures, processes, people, and cultures that lead to organization effectiveness.

The definition suggests that OD can be understood in terms of its several foci:

First, *OD is a system-wide process.* It works with whole systems. In the past, the bias has been toward working at the individual and group levels. More recently, the focus has shifted to organizations and multi-organization systems. We support that trend in general but honor and acknowledge the fact that the traditional focus on smaller systems is both legitimate and necessary.

Second, *OD is values-based.* Traditionally, OD has attempted to distinguish itself from other forms of planned change and applied behavioral science by promoting a set of humanistic values and by emphasizing the importance of personal growth as a key to its practice. Today, that focus is blurred and there is much debate about the value base underlying the practice of OD. We support a more formal and direct conversation about what these values are and how the field is related to them.

Third, *OD is collaborative.* Our first value commitment as OD practitioners is to bring about an inclusive, diverse workforce with a focus of integrating differences into a world-wide culture mentality.

Fourth, *OD is based on behavioral science knowledge.* Organization development should incorporate and apply knowledge from sociology, psychology, anthropology, technology, and economics toward the end of making systems more effective. We support the continued emphasis in OD on behavioral science knowledge and believe that OD practitioners should be widely read and comfortable with several of the disciplines.

Fifth, *OD is concerned with the adaptive development, improvement, and reinforcement of strategies, structures, processes, people, culture, and other features of organizational life.* This statement not only describes the organizational elements that are the target of change, but also describes the process by which effectiveness is increased. That is, OD works in a variety of areas, and it is focused on improving these areas. We believe that such a statement of process and content strongly implies that a key feature of OD is the transference of knowledge and skill to the system so that it is more able to handle and manage change in the future.

Sixth and finally, *OD is about improving organization effectiveness.* It is not just about making people happy; it is also concerned with meeting financial goals, improving productivity, and addressing stakeholder satisfaction. We believe that OD's future is closely tied to the incorporation of this value in its purpose and the demonstration of this objective in its practice.

Is the OD Profession at a Crossroads?

For years, OD professionals have said that OD is at a crossroads. From our perspective at the beginning of the new millennium, the field of organization development can be characterized by the following statements:

1. Practitioners today are torn. The professional organizations representing OD practitioners, including the OD Network, the OD Institute, the International OD Association, and the Academy of Management's OD and Change Division, are experiencing tremendous uncertainties in their purposes, practices, and relationships.

2. There are increasing calls for regulation/certification.

3. Many respected practitioners have suggested that people who profess to manage change are behind those who are creating it. Organization development practitioners should lead through influence rather than follow the lead of those who are sometimes coercive in their approach to change.

4. The field is defined by techniques.

5. The values that guide the field are unclear and ill-defined.

6. Too many people are practicing OD without any training in the field.

7. Practitioners are having difficulty figuring out how to market their services.

The situation suggests the following provocative questions:

- How can OD practitioners help formulate strategy, shape the strategy development process, contribute to the content of strategy, and drive how strategy will be implemented?

- How can OD practitioners encourage an open examination of the ways organizations are conceived and managed?

- How can OD focus on the drivers of change external to individuals, such as the external environment, business strategy, organization change, and culture change, as well as on the drivers of change internal to individuals, such as individual interpretations of culture, behavior, style, and mind-set?

- How much should OD be part of the competencies of all leaders and how much should it be the sole domain of professionally trained, career-oriented OD practitioners?

What Is the Purpose of This Series?

This series is intended to provide current thinking about OD as a field and to provide practical approaches based on sound theory and research. It is targeted for full-time external or internal OD practitioners; top executives in charge of enterprise-wide change; and managers, HR practitioners, training and development professionals, and others who have responsibility for change in organizational and trans-organizational settings. At the same time, these books will be directed toward cutting-edge thinking and state-of-the-art approaches. In some cases, the ideas, approaches, or techniques described are still evolving, so the books are intended to open up dialogue.

We know that the books in this series will provide a leading forum for thought-provoking dialogue within the OD field.

About the Board Members

David Bradford is senior lecturer in organizational behavior at the Graduate School of Business, Stanford University, Palo Alto, California. He is co-author (with Allan R. Cohen) of *Managing for Excellence, Influence Without Authority,* and *POWER UP: Transforming Organizations Through Shared Leadership.*

W. Warner Burke is professor of psychology and education and chair of the Department of Organization and Leadership at Teachers College, Columbia University, New York, New York. His most recent publication is *Business Profiles of Climate Shifts: Profiles of Change Makers,* (with William Trahant and Richard Koonce).

Edith Whitfield Seashore is organization consultant and co-founder (with Morley Segal) of AUNTL Masters Program in Organization Development. She is co-author of *What Did You Say?* and *The Art of Giving and Receiving Feedback* and co-editor of *The Promise of Diversity.*

Robert Tannenbaum is emeritus professor of development of human systems, Graduate School of Management, University of California, Los Angeles; recipient of Lifetime Achievement Award by the National OD Network. He has published numerous books, including *Human Systems Development* with Newton Margulies and Fred Massarik.

Foreword

"Appreciative Inquiry is, in my view, an exciting breakthrough, one that signals a change in the way we think about change. I'm intrigued by how rapidly it is emerging; but it is something substantive, conceptually strong, not like the quick fads. In my view we are looking at something important—AI will be of enduring consequence and energizing innovation for the field. That's my prediction. And that is why we are going to give it more attention in this session."

—*Richard Beckhard*
National Academy of Management Conference, August 1999
Symposium on The Past, Present, and Future of Organization Development

RICHARD BECKHARD, ONE OF THE FOUNDERS of the OD field, had this to say about AI before one of his last presentations at the Academy of Management. And it was a thrill to be there with him. He spoke these words at a meeting he had with Ed Schein, me, and a few others right before the session. The result was a rapid juggling, last minute, in the order and timing of the speakers. In his opening remarks, Beckhard promised everyone "more time for the future." The room was packed. Many had to sit on the floor. And the interest in the emergence of Appreciative Inquiry was palpable. People left the session energized, ready to experiment—some in small ways but others in large ways—and so will everyone who reads this uplifting volume by Jane Watkins and Bernard Mohr.

Jane's great gift, as an experiential educator in corporations and nonprofits around the world, is the ability to draw people into the swirling sea of changes (paradigm shifts) in philosophies of knowledge, some quite abstract, and to help those people emerge with new hope and immediate transformations in practice. When she was chairperson of the NTL Institute for Applied Behavioral Sciences, I witnessed people come out of her workshops redefining directions in life purpose, careers, and perspectives. A bit later, she and Bernard Mohr, a leading thinker in the area of organizational design, teamed up to do the very same thing with their life-changing workshops on Appreciative Inquiry. For Jane and Bernard, good theory, good practice, and good transformation are a simultaneous moment—and it is this generative combination that they keep whole in this volume. Lucky are the people who can do both, that is, enjoy this book *and* engage in their programs.

What makes this volume unique in the rapidly expanding literature on Appreciative Inquiry is the conviction that a new *mental metabolism* is required in our collective journey, beyond the problem analytic or deficit-based theories of change implicated in the machine logic of the 20th Century. The life-centric instinct of AI as a method—it searches continuously for *what gives life to human systems when they are most alive, freeing, meaningful, creative in their ventures and connected in healthy ways to their communities*—depends, say Watkins and Mohr, less on technique than paradigmatic transformation. "We are convinced," they say, "that AI is not centrally a method." They assert that we must all be willing to cross into a dislodgment of certainty from the linear world of the known and mechanistic to a more vibrant, chaotic, holistic world stance that is focused on health, mystery, playfulness, and emergent relationships. What they do, for the first time, is to link the social constructionist meta-theories of AI to the languages, metaphors, and images of chaos theory and the "new sciences"—in ways that serve to inspire and support rather than to obscure practice.

Make no mistake, this is a book that will empower your practice. How would you introduce AI to a senior team of mangers—bottom-line oriented, demanding, and rightfully suspicious of fads that over-promise and under-deliver? You have two hours. What would you do? How do you talk about the shift from problem analysis (what's wrong, deficient, broken, in need of diagnosing, fixing) and illustrate how AI begins and ends in valuing? What research might you cite and link to the world of business that speaks to the *idea* of positive change? For example, how might one mobilize an AI effort by introducing the whole interdisciplinary arena of image theory: the importance of positive images in medicine (placebo research and psychoneuroimmunology); in education (Pygmalion studies); in sociology (rise and fall of cultures); in cognitive studies of healthy people (inner dialogue); and in athletics and learning (positive self-monitoring)?

These are areas in which Watkins and Mohr share *generously* from their time-tested practice and training designs: two-hour introductions to AI; training designs to prepare interviewers; sample reports; steps in the 4-D process; and models for the training of trainers. The concrete, even some minute-by-minute, guides provide solid grounding for experimentation. But in the end Jane and Bernard return to a core message: "AI becomes not a methodology but a way of seeing and being in the world" and it is one they believe will "fundamentally reshape the practice of organizational learning, design, and development—much the same way that the philosophy of *process consultation* reshaped the field of management consulting forty years ago."

Last week at British Airways, Diana Whitney mobilized a major inquiry focused on the organizational dimensions of "outstanding arrival experiences"—reversing decades of repetitive diagnostic work on excessive baggage loss. The same week Ron Fry and I, at one of the nation's largest truck carriers, Roadway Express, led an AI Organizational Summit with almost two hundred dock workers, truck drivers, union leaders, managers, customers, and partners. Their inquiry was for insights and images of "optimizing margins" and "delivering the premium product in the industry." There was not one fishbone analysis, problem-solving diagnosis, or burning platform speech. But monumental changes were envisioned as people searched the positive core of their history—some that could wreak havoc on old stove pipes and challenge industry norms of truck drivers "leaving their brains" at the door. Roadway decided it truly did want a new era and ecology of engagement. A week later, Marge Schiller, speaking at the Cape Cod Institute, told of the recent Catalyst Award story, where the glass ceiling was opened wide at the senior levels of management of the Mexican plant of a Fortune 500 company. It happened not by trying to solve "the problems," for example, of sexual harassment, but by doing systematic inquiry into the highest quality co-leadership moments of equality, respect, and power sharing—"women and men working as a team." The result was what they called a 21st Century organization design.

The illustrations in this book are provocative. They will make people in the deficit-based "change industry" squirm. Think about the assertion, for example, that organizations do not have to be fixed and that problem solving assumptions hold great potential for bringing methods of organization analysis and change to a slow crawl. Imagine letting go *completely* of deficit-based methods, assumptions, and interventions in your work.

This is exactly what Jane Watkins urged me to do about a decade ago. In fact, she was even stronger: "You are still holding on to the old paradigms—let go, trust, trust where the new logic and spirit of constructionist thought is leading." She was a great mentor. The experimentation gifted me with many learnings. Two stand out.

First, not only do the organizations we work with move in the direction of what we study and ask questions about, but also so do *we* as human beings. Simply put, I am not the same person when I am in a discovery mode asking in-depth questions of what leads to "joy, inspiration, and hope" as I am when I do analysis of "low morale" and its causes. Inquiry and change are a simultaneous moment and we ourselves are inescapably "in it," even if the study is "out there." Inquiry intervenes, and it works both ways. I cannot think of a more health-enhancing vocation than doing AI every single day—that is, to be an *agent of inquiry*, a student of the positive core of what gives life to living systems when they are most alive, creative, effective, inspired, and productive.

The second insight, or refreshed learning, is about primacy of relationships. Organizations are, first and foremost, centers of human relatedness, and relationships thrive where there is an appreciative eye—when people see the best in one another, when they share their dreams and ultimate concerns without filters or censorship, and when they are connected in full voice to create not just new futures, but better ones. Nowhere is this more vivid than in today's web world of instant connectivity and net partnerships. You simply cannot treat your partner in deficit-change theoretical terms—as a "problem to be solved." AI involves the deliberate discovery of collectively combined capacities and seeks, as Peter Drucker might say, to create an alignment of strengths in ways that make weaknesses irrelevant.

Think of AI as a new conversation, as a search engine for the positive core of a system, as a convergence zone or "space" creating a multiplier effect in the area of human imagination and intellectual capital. Appreciative Inquiry is about the liberation of capacity. And yes, it makes command-and-control structures squirm. It observably thrives best in settings that are more comfortable with risk than with regulation, where people are connected across stove pipes, and where they are engaged as essential co-creators of whole systems. Full voice, convivial community, rigorous inquiry, shared speculation and dreams, articulation of things that matter, improvisation—these are ingredients that ensure that AI praxis does not devolve into sterile happy talk. Be reminded of this more emergent, wild element of AI as you read about Jane and Bernard's invitation to chaos theory.

The idea of positive change—that co-inquiry into the true, the good, the better, the possible will lead to faster, more democratic and energized change than will deficit-based inquiry into the broken and the problematic—is the suggestive hypothesis I find most intriguing in *Appreciative Inquiry: Change at the Speed of Imagination.* Enjoy this book. Call on it to ignite your own passion and "spirit of discovery." Create. Experiment. And let yourself venture on a new path of positive change with two of the field's finest guides.

David L. Cooperrider
Weatherhead School of Management
Case Western Reserve University
Cleveland, Ohio
September 2000

This book is dedicated to
David Cooperrider,
friend and mentor, who embodies the appreciative life,
and to friends and colleagues, known and unknown, who are
working together toward a positive future for the world.

"Appreciative Inquiry is based on a reverence for life and is
essentially biocentric in character. It is an inquiry process
that tries to apprehend the factors that give life to a living
system and seeks to articulate those possibilities that can
lead to a better future. More than a method or technique,
the appreciative mode of inquiry is a means of living with,
being with, and directly participating in the life of human
systems in a way that compels one to inquire into the deeper
life-generating essentials and potentials of organizational
existence."

David Cooperrider
Positive Image, Positive Action

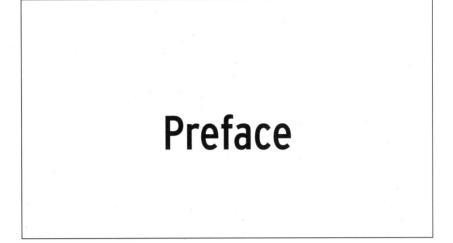

Preface

AS THE GLOBAL VILLAGE BECOMES AN ACTUALITY, the impact on organization change theory and practice has been profound. The number of models and methods available to facilitate change has increased as OD practitioners try to help organizations cope with many of the rapid and discontinuous shifts in both form and function.

But something more is needed.

This book is about Appreciative Inquiry (AI), a theory and practice for approaching change from a holistic framework. Based on the belief that human systems are made and imagined by those who live and work within them, AI leads systems to move toward the generative and creative images that reside in their most positive core—their values, visions, achievements, and best practices.

As the illusion that there can be a "stable" environment fades, organizations are embracing the challenge of thriving in a world of constant change, realizing that change is not a force acting on organizations, but the very water in which organizations swim. A different perspective and new and innovative ways of thinking about and working with human systems are required.

As the new paradigm emerges, the shifts and transformations are stunning. It is not a time of incremental change and evolutionary processes. Organizations feel the call for new ways of working. Hierarchies are flattening; risk taking is desirable; flexibility is essential. A process for enabling agile organizations to engage all of their human capability and technical resources is required. The stability of long-range plans and predictable processes is giving way to the realization that every moment is new, and so new solutions are required.

Appreciative Inquiry is congruent with the emerging paradigm. Grounded in the theory of "social constructionism," AI recognizes that human systems are constructions of the imagination and are, therefore, capable of change at the speed of imagination. Once organization members shift their perspective, they can begin to invent their most desired future.

Appreciative Inquiry is both a world view and a practical process. In theory, AI is a perspective, a set of principles and beliefs about how human systems function, a departure from the past metaphor of human systems as machines. Appreciative Inquiry has an attendant set of core processes, practices, and even "models" that have emerged. In practice, AI can be used to co-create the transformative processes and practices appropriate to the culture of a particular organization.

Our intent in writing this book is to provide information on Appreciative Inquiry as an emerging innovative process for guiding organization transformation. We will focus on using AI as an effective way to work with organizations as organic systems (more like streams than like machines).

In brief, this book will provide organizations and organizational consultants with an understanding of the shifting paradigm in which we work, of the role Appreciative Inquiry can play in enabling organizations to embrace the new paradigm, and of some of the emerging applications of AI.

The organization of the book is as follows: Chapter 1 is an exploration of why there is a need for a new approach to organization change. It examines the emerging paradigm, observable global and organizational shifts, and the impact of the new sciences on our current thinking about how the world functions.

Chapter 2 contains a definition of Appreciative Inquiry and its history, relevance, current state, and relationship to organization change theories of the past. The theory and research on which AI is grounded are covered, as well as social constructionism, the social science research that points to the power of image, the importance of grounded theory, and the five principles that underlie the practice of AI.

Chapter 3 is a presentation of the core processes that are needed to guide organization change from an AI perspective, some methods and examples of applications, and the skills needed for those who want to lead an AI process.

The focus of Chapter 4 is on the first core process: *Focus on the positive.* The process of introducing AI to client organizations and the rationale for a positive focus on organization change are described.

Chapter 5 is about the second core process: *Inquire into stories of life-giving forces.* Here we discuss the interviewing process itself—deciding what to look for, creating an interview protocol, and deciding the process for collecting the stories.

In Chapter 6 we describe the third core process: *Locate themes that appear in the stories.* This chapter describes what a "theme" is and suggests processes for discerning and using them.

Chapter 7 contains suggested ways to approach the fourth core process: *Create shared images for a preferred future.* Ideas are given for ways to encourage and guide the creation of an image for the organization's future.

The fifth core process: *Innovate ways to create the preferred future,* is covered in Chapter 8. We share ideas and examples from our work and from the work of colleagues of ways to work with clients to move the organization toward the articulated preferred future.

Chapter 9 contains a discussion of AI as a new paradigm for research and evaluation. We cite some results reported by organizations that are using it for every kind of OD intervention. The Postscript contains a series of frequently asked questions about AI theory and technique and our answers. The questions were culled from the AI listserv, clients, and colleagues.

To help illustrate the core processes of AI, we have included two case studies at the end of each of the process chapters (Chapters 4 through 8). To collect these cases, we requested examples from consultants who are using AI in a variety of organizations. We selected a wide range of cases so that readers can see the variety and scope of the use of AI. The case stories are brief and descriptive. For more in-depth information, we have provided contact numbers for the person who wrote the case. The cases are presented in the following format:

Client organization	Type of organization; work done; size of total organization; size of target organization
Client objectives	Goals or concerns articulated by the client
What was done	Who did what? A summary of how the AI process was used and what occurred in each phase of the process
Outcomes	Results achieved for the business, for members of the organization, and for customers or other stakeholders
Learnings	What worked especially well and wishes for the next time
Author contact	Ways to contact the author of the case study for additional information
Client contact (optional)	Ways to contact the client

In selecting the cases, we looked for several factors that are in line with the theories and processes of AI that are covered in this book. Although there are many interventions that might be considered informed by AI, cases selected for this book represent more comprehensive AI interventions based on the following factors:

- The case was either a comprehensive 4-D process or a rich description of a discrete part of that process.
- The questions that were asked elicit stories, not facts or opinions.
- Questions focused on the generative and creative moments, the moments of excitement, and the high points of experience.
- Customized interview protocols were co-created by the consultant and members of the client system.
- A significant percentage of interviews done in the system were conducted by members of that system.
- When the consultants left, AI was embedded in the organization so that it became "the way we do business."

The following table lists the cases presented:

Overview of Case Studies

Chapter	Name of Organization	Type/Field	Focus of Intervention	Author, Affiliation
6	Avon Mexico	Corporation/ Cosmetic and other products	Valuing gender diversity	Marge Schiller, Ph.D.
7	British Airways	Corporation/ Commercial airline	Creating a whole-system AI process	Diana Whitney, Corporation for Positive Change
6	DTE Energy Services	Corporation/ Power company's financial services arm	Creating a culture of choice	Marlow Derksen & Tom Osborne, OsborneDerksen
8	Group Health Cooperative	Health care	Performance improvement	Diane Robbins, D.B. Robbins Consulting, & Scott Caldwell, Group Health Cooperative
8	HunterDouglas	Corporation/ Manufacturing	Creating a shared vision	Amanda Trosten-Bloom, Clearview Consultants
4	McDonald's	Corporation/ Food service	Becoming an employer of choice	Jim Ludema, Ludema & Associates
4	MYRADA	Nonprofit organization/ Organization strengthening	Using AI to create and/or strengthen community development organizations in India	Graham Ashford, International Institute for Sustainable Development
5	NASA	Government agency/Space technology	Create a strategic plan; build an inclusive culture	Judy Darling, NASA
7	Star Island Corporation	Nonprofit church-based organization/ Conference center	Strategic planning	David Sanderson, Eagle Point Consulting
5	Syntegra	Corporation/British telecom systems integrator division	Leadership and leadership style transition	Joep de Jong, Syntegra

Acknowledgments

THIS BOOK IS FOR MY MOTHER, who always believed in me. And for my two wonderful children, Gordon Watkins and Laurin Watkins Wittig, who have been my greatest teachers. And for the great people they brought into my life: Susan Keen Watkins, Dean Wittig, and the grandchildren, Wesley and Ben Watkins and Samantha and Alex Wittig. This constellation, plus my terrific siblings, Alice, Anna, Kem, and Neil and their families, and my husband's Mom, Myrtle Childre, and sister, Shirley Kelly, form the remarkable gift of a family that I have come to see as my life's greatest blessing. Then there are those who make up my "chosen" family, several of whom are also colleagues who share my love for this work: Barbara Sloan, Liz and Noel Workman, Marge and Simon Schiller, Janis Goodman, Mette Jacobsgaard, and my African "daughters," Njoke Njehu and Anastasia White.

To David, who gave me the priceless gift of Appreciative Inquiry, and to those others who have also shared AI, thereby increasing my knowledge and practice, I owe a deep debt of gratitude: Cathy Royal who helped me launch the first NTL training in AI; Ada Jo Mann, whose vision of an equitable world led us to a project that has spread AI across the globe; Charles Elliott, dean of Trinity Hall College at Cambridge University, valued friend and colleague, who made it possible for me to spend two wonderful years at Cambridge thinking and studying, an embryo time for this book; friends Vaughn O'Halloran and Alexsandra Stewart, who have shared much of this journey with me; our valued community of AIC colleagues whom Bernard has listed in his acknowledgments; and the many clients who, over the past decade, have been my learning partners.

Kris Quade called me one day and said: "We're editing a new series and we want you to write about your work." Without her call and continuing encouragement, there would be no book. Thank you, Kris! And thank you, Susan Rachmeler, for being such an excellent and patient development editor for us.

Most of all, I acknowledge that my part of this book could not have been written without the unwavering love and support of my remarkable husband and partner, Ralph Kelly, who not only makes life a constant joy, but who has worked so hard on this manuscript that his name ought to be in the author slot! And, of course, Bernard.

> Jane Magruder Watkins
> *Williamsburg, Virginia*
> *Summer 2000*

WRITING A BOOK IS SELDOM A SOLITARY PROCESS, and this was no exception. The web of relationships that sustained me in this effort was naturally centered around my ever-optimistic partner Jane and her nurturing husband Ralph, who have become part of our family in this process.

And then there are my colleagues and friends, fellow travelers—including but not limited to the AIC team—who helped me to pour the foundations for the first large transnational conference in Appreciative Inquiry: Jim Ludema, Ada Jo Mann, Judy Rodgers, Jim Lord, Ravi Pradahn, Joep de Jong, Anne Radford, and David Chandler; plus of course all of the other founding members of Appreciative Inquiry Consulting: Frank Barrett, Steve Cato, David Cooperrider, Marsha George, Mette Jacobsgaard, Jacqueline Kelm, Adrian McLean, Diane Robbins, Marge Schiller, Barbara Sloan, and Diana Whitney; and also my many colleagues and friends in my spiritual home, the STS Roundtable, including but not limited to Don DeGuerre, Merrelyn Emery, Laurie Fitzgerald, Eli Berniker, and Michael Brower.

Most of all, and without hyperbole, I am forever indebted for the support and love from my family, Karen, Alexandra, and Joshua, all of whom endured my many weekend absences and missed suppers with generosity, understanding, and a quality of lovingness that nourished and motivated me in my most difficult times.

To all of you, thank you and may I forever be part of your lives and you of mine.

Bernard Mohr
Summer 2000

Finally, we both want to acknowledge and publicly thank the many colleagues who wrote and generously shared so much of the material that forms the foundation for this book: David and his colleagues and students from Case Western Reserve University; the many people who worked with the GEM project and its predecessor, the OEP; and especially, thanks to Diana Whitney for all of her excellent contributions in the form of working manuals and published articles that have enriched our understanding of AI as well as the contents of this book.

Jane and Bernard

The Case for a New Approach to Change

"Change is not what it used to be. The status quo will no longer be the best way forward . . . we are entering an Age of Unreason, when the future, in so many areas, is there to be shaped, by us and for us; a time when the only prediction that will hold true is that no predictions will hold true; a time, therefore, for bold imaginings in private life as well as public, for thinking the unlikely and doing the unreasonable."

Charles Handy, The Age of Unreason

AS WE ENTER THE 21st CENTURY, there has been a fundamental shift in how we see and experience the world. This phenomena, frequently called a "paradigm shift," calls for new approaches to the theory and practice of organization change. In this chapter, we will briefly describe some of the changes that are observable in the arenas of the natural and social sciences and look at the impact of those changes on organizations and on organization change theories and practice. Finally, we will look at Appreciative Inquiry (AI) as both a theory and practice for organizational transformation.

The Emerging Paradigm

We are living in a time of unprecedented and unpredictable change. The impact of this rapid pace of change on all of our human systems—families, schools, organizations, communities, governments—has become the focus of great interest and concern.

"We've reached a Breakpoint!" George Land and Beth Jarman (1992) write in *Breakpoint and Beyond.* "Breakpoint change abruptly and powerfully breaks the critical links that connect anyone or anything with the past. What we are experiencing today is absolutely unprecedented in all of humanity's recorded history. We have run into change so different from anything preceding it that it totally demolishes normal standards. It has swept us into a massive transformation that will completely reorder all we know about living in this world" (p. 5). What Land and Jarman are describing is a world in the midst of an emerging paradigm, a shift in the way we understand and perceive the world.

In 1970, Thomas Kuhn defined "paradigm" in a book titled *The Structure of Scientific Revolution:*

"Paradigmatic change is change in the way that problems are posed and solved; change in the unconscious beliefs about what is 'real'; change in the basic priorities and choices about what problems to pursue and what social ends to serve; change in those approaches and solutions which display the whole world view as a coherent whole."

Later, Fritjof Capra (1996) defined *social paradigm* as "a constellation of concepts, values, perceptions, and practices shared by a community, which forms a particular vision of reality that is the basis of the way the community organizes itself."

If we are, indeed, in the midst of an emerging paradigm, just what does that mean? Jane recalls, "My grandmother used to tell a story about finding me, a three-year-old, in the center hall of her house holding the earphone and speaking into the mouthpiece of the apparatus that we called a telephone. Our phone number was 339. I was talking to the operator (my Grandmother called her 'Central') trying to arrange to speak to God about coming to take back my newly arrived baby sister. Nearly sixty years later, standing on a hill outside Johannesburg, South Africa, I heard a ring in my purse and reached in to retrieve my cell phone. The call was from a friend in the United States. Under that night sky in that faraway place, I heard the voices of home.

"When Apollo lifted off to take earthlings to walk the face of the moon, my mother, Marjorie Magruder, and her sisters were within sight of the event, looking into the cloudy sky to watch the rocket rise above the earth. My mother was 61 years old in 1969. I asked her why she wanted to attend the launch and she said, 'I remember when I went to school in a wagon drawn by a mule; I remember the first time I heard a radio or saw a telephone or had indoor plumbing. I went to college in my Uncle's Model-A Ford and we had to back up Valley Hill outside Greenwood. If we went up in forward gear, the gas could not get to the engine because of the angle of ascent. I learned to drive in that Model A. I first flew on an airplane in my forties; first owned a TV in the late 1950s. There are still people in my home town who do not believe that we are really sending people to walk on the moon. I wouldn't miss it for the world!' "

In the 1960s, Alvin Toffler wrote a mind-bending book called *Future Shock* in which he talked not just of change, but of the changing rate of change. Those born early in the 20th Century (our parent's generation) have experienced change in both speed and kind unimaginable in all of human history. Toffler and others scanning and predicting the future were like modern prophets, seeing the waves of an emerging paradigm that would call all of what we "know" and "believe" into question.

What happens in a society in which you can now buy a birthday card with a singing message that holds as much computer power as did those first room-sized machines with their punch cards? This unimaginable increase in computer power happened, for all practical purposes, in the last half of the 20th Century. What will be the effect on the human and social systems of the flood of information, accurate and inaccurate, that is available and accessible across the globe? Communication technology is driving our assumptions about how the world really is, about what is true and real, and about what tomorrow will bring. As Jane recalls, "I tried to teach my grandmother to use a dial telephone. My four-year-old granddaughter taught me how to use the drawing function on my computer! My mother was awed by a man going to the moon. Thirty years later, we hardly notice when one of our satellites soars beyond our solar system."

As we embrace the technology that has turned us into a global village and made us space travelers, how do we integrate our beliefs, our values, our sense of who we are into some coherent theory?

There are as many theories and explanations of the phenomena of change as there are theorists and explainers. Appreciative Inquiry is grounded in several of those. Two of particular interest are (1) the impact of the New Sciences (quantum physics; chaos, complexity, and string theory) on human systems and (2) social constructionism (the idea that we create our world by the conversations we have with one another).

Roots and Realities of Our Existing Paradigm

Let's begin in the 15th Century when the dogma of religion and mythic systems that explained the world to our ancestors was giving way to what we call "modern" science and the ascendancy of observation and experimentation. The struggle for intellectual authority was shifting as the emphasis on revelation and reflection, the purviews of the Church, gave way to the theories and experiments of "pure" science, the assertion that truth could be observed, weighed, and measured. After two centuries of ferment, 17th Century classical mechanics emerged, a view of the world that has dominated much of Western thinking since.

Classical (Newtonian) mechanics is the science of how bodies move in our universe. The assumption is that the universe is a vast machine with interacting parts much like a clock. Each part has only a few properties and movements, determined by its mass and the forces acting on it. This view was articulated by the philosophers Descartes and Locke during the time when philosophy and science were the same discipline, and scientifically by Galileo. The key concepts are space, time, mass, forces, and particles. Anything else, such as consciousness, has remained outside the realm of physics altogether.

Newton's work and that of his predecessors led to the scientific paradigm that has dominated our view of what is real for several centuries. Frederick Taylor's early theories of "scientific management" came out of that paradigm, applying the image of a machine to a human system. When studies of the importance of human behavior in organizations began to be developed by social scientists in the 1940s (most notably by Kurt Lewin and his colleagues, Ken Benne, Leland Bradford, and Ron Lippett, who in 1947 founded the National Training Laboratory, now known as the NTL Institute for Applied Behavioral Science), it was often assumed that one could measure human behavior using the methods of the natural sciences. It was assumed that human behavior was governed by the same principles as the material world: cause and effect, natural hierarchy, force exerted to cause movement, and individuals as separate and isolated "parts."

Margaret Wheatley (1994) in her book, *Leadership and the New Science,* describes the impact of this thinking on our behavior and on our organizations.

"Each of us lives and works in organizations designed from Newtonian images of the universe. We manage by separating things into parts; we believe that influence occurs as a direct result of force exerted from one person to another; we engage in complex planning for a world that we keep expecting to be predictable; and, we search continually for better methods of objectively perceiving the world. These assumptions come to us from seventeenth-century physics, from Newtonian mechanics. They are the base from which we design and manage organizations and from which we do research in all of the social sciences. Intentionally or not, we work from a worldview that has been derived from the natural sciences.

"Scientists in many different disciplines are questioning whether we can adequately explain how the world works by using the machine imagery created in the 17th Century. . . . In the machine model, one must understand parts. Things can be taken apart, dissected literally or representationally (as we have done with business functions and academic disciplines), and then put back together without any significant loss. The assumption is that by comprehending the workings of each piece, the whole can be understood. The Newtonian model of the world is characterized by materialism and reductionism—focus on things rather than relationships and a search, in physics, for the basic building blocks of matter." (p. 8)

The New Sciences

In 1927, a group of scientists met in Denmark to discuss revolutionary new discoveries in physics. As technology and new methods of experimentation made possible new discoveries in the realm of sub-atomic particles, all of the orthodoxy of classical physics was being called into question. Albert Einstein and Danish physicist Niels Bohr had been embroiled in a difference of opinion often referred to as the Copenhagen Debates. Bohr had discovered that two particles separated by a vast distance were able to behave coherently as if they were communicating instantaneously. Einstein argued that it wasn't possible because the information between the two would have to travel faster than the speed of light. Bohr argued that such speed would be required only if one assumed that the two particles were separate and independent units. And the paradigm began to shift! What if all things are connected? From the conference in Copenhagen came public statements about these new discoveries that were so confounding the physicists. Since that time, terms such as quantum physics, chaos theory, self-organizing systems, and complexity theory have become common in our vocabulary.

While classical physics focuses on parts, the common denominator of the new sciences is the search for a theory of wholeness. The language of these new sciences has a major impact on how we think about human systems. Certainly the language of quantum physics challenges our most sacred assumptions about the concepts of organization development. Here are a few of the dilemmas:

While classical physics speaks of waves and particles as separate, quantum theory suggests that there is a wave/particle duality (a wavicle) and that these basic building blocks of the universe have the potential to behave as a wave or as a particle, depending on their surroundings. This means that we can never know the momentum (wave) and the position (particle) of these quantum entities at the same time. This turns Newtonian determinism on its head, as the predictability that B will always follow A, as Newton proved, gives way to Heisenberg's uncertainty principle: B *may* follow A and there is a probability that it will do so, but there is no certainty (Marshall, 1997).

Classical physics describes complex things as reducible to a few simple absolute and unchanging components. This is "What is." Quantum physics describes the phenomena of the new properties that come from the combination or relationships of simple things. Possibility is the key. Every quantum in the universe has the potential to be here *and* there, now *and* then. In classical physics things happen as part of a chain of events, of cause and effect. In quantum reality, all things move in harmony as some part of a larger, invisible whole. We might describe this as a quantum shift! From understanding the world as parts, each alone in space and time linked only through force, quantum physics presents us with a universe in which every part is linked to every other part.

This view of the way the world works challenges any assumption about being able to isolate one thing from another, and it goes further to suggest that the observer cannot be separated from that which is observed. It challenges us to reexamine our assumptions about how organizations function as well.

Chaos theory presents another challenge to Newton's clockwork universe with its predictable tides and planetary motion. In chaos theory, very simple patterns become complex and unpredictable, as demonstrated by fractals, weather patterns, and the stock market. No level of accuracy is exact enough for long-term predictions. Such an idea rocks the very foundation of such organizational sacred cows as long-range planning, which in its most linear application requires a belief in a reasonable amount of predictability in the future.

Self-organizing systems behave in the reverse way. A complex and unpredictable situation develops into a larger, more ordered pattern like a whirlpool or a living organism. Although most organizations have, no doubt, experienced the sudden clarity that can come out of seeming chaotic situations, few have learned to embrace chaos, often short-circuiting times and situations that hold the potential for high levels of innovation and creativity.

Complexity theory, the focus of study at the Sante Fe Institute, is most often described as "order at the edge of chaos." It is also the study of complex systems that cannot be reduced to simple parts. Along with quantum and chaos theory, complexity theory focuses on the emergent whole that cannot be reduced to the sum of its parts. It involves unpredictability, nonlinear and discontinuous change—the phenomena that lead to surprising new forms (Marshall & Zohar, 1998).

Wheatley (1994) writes:

"In New Science, the underlying currents are a movement toward holism, toward understanding the system as a system and giving primary value to the relationships that exist among seemingly discrete parts. . . . When we view systems from this perspective we enter an entirely new landscape of connections, of phenomena that cannot be reduced to simple cause and effect, and of the constant flux of dynamic processes." (p. 8)

Table 1.1 illustrates the kinds of shifts that are occurring in response to our broader vision of science. In this post-modern era, the marvel is that all of these things are present and in good order.

These "new sciences" give us radically different ways of making sense of our world. The most exciting ramification for the field of organization change/transformation is the realization that organizations as living systems do not have to look continually for which part is causing a problem or which project is not living up to some set of criteria. The "new" science embraces the magnificent complexity of our world while assuring us that built into the very fabric of the universe are processes and potentials enough to help us and all of our organizations move toward our highest and most desired visions.

Table 1.1. Current and Emerging Paradigms

Current Scientific Paradigm	Emerging Paradigm
Newtonian mechanics; reductionist and dichotomous thinking	Quantum physics and new sciences: self-organizing systems; chaos theory; complexity theory
We search for a model or method of objectively perceiving the world.	We accept the complexity and subjectivity of the world.
We engage in complex planning for a world we expect to be predictable.	Planning is understood to be a process of constant re-evaluation.
We understand language as the descriptor of reality: "I'll believe it when I see it."	We understand language as the creator of reality: "I'll see it when I believe it."
We see information as power.	We see information as a primal creative force.
We believe in reductionism, i.e., things can be best understood when they are broken into parts.	We seek to understand wholeness and the interconnectedness of all things.
We engage in dichotomous thinking.	We search for harmony and the common threads of our dialogue.
We believe that there is only one truth for which we must search.	We understand truth to be dependent on the context and the current reality.
We believe that influence occurs as a direct result of force exerted from one person to another, i.e., cause and effect.	We understand that influence occurs as a natural part of human interaction.
We live in a linear and hierarchical world.	We live in a circular world of relationships and cooperation.

The Dilemma of the Human Brain

Before we leave the world of "hard" science to look at the social sciences (as we will do in Chapter 2), a word about the human brain. Our brains seem to be hard-wired to create order. What we call "reality" is the intersection of our brain's capacity to bring order out of incoming sensory data. This compulsion to order serves us well. The transmission of information and knowledge happens through the orderly use of language, itself a system created by the human mind.

By ordering the world we make sense of our lives and experiences. Although biological studies show that our brains gather data in a neural network—a seemingly chaotic process—the compulsion to make sense of the data is always present. There are those who crave and seem to need an orderly world in all aspects. For others, high levels of ambiguity are fairly comfortable and the need to bring order comes more slowly and more options are tolerated. Whatever our preference, we live in a world that continually reinforces "order" as the preferred state.

And so it is that the Newtonian paradigm fits nicely into the comfort zone for most of us. It is hard, if not impossible, to wrap our brains around such questions as: "Is order essential to the structure of the universe or is it simply a product of human perception?" The challenge is to step out of our dichotomous, simple, and orderly version of the universe and embrace those "wavicles" until we engage with them. Whether we experience wave or particle will depend on what we seek.

And so we come again to "social constructionism" and Appreciative Inquiry. In Chapter 2 we will look at the theoretical basis for AI from a social science point of view, asking: "How is it that we know what we know?" Suffice it to say that in its simplest form, social constructionism suggests that we create the world by the language we use to describe it and we experience the world in line with the images we hold about it. The Appreciative Inquiry process provides human systems with a way of inquiring into the past and present, seeking out those things that are life-giving and affirming as a basis for creating images of a generative and creative future.

Thinking About Problems Using the New Paradigm

So what about all those problems caused by this changing rate of change? Does AI just ignore those? Are we engaging in denial? Doesn't organization development as a method promote the identification and resolution of problems? Indeed, the practice of OD has traditionally highlighted deficits in the belief that the organization can be returned to a healthy state. Appreciative Inquiry would seem to suggest that by *focusing* on the deficit, we simply *create more* images of deficit and potentially overwhelm the system with images of what is "wrong." All too often, the process of assessing deficits includes a search for *who* is to blame. This leads to people being resistant to the change effort and to a large amount of literature in the field describing ways to deal with that resistance.

In Appreciative Inquiry, we take a different perspective. When we define a situation as a "problem" it means that we have an image of how that situation ought to be—how we'd like it to be. Appreciative Inquiry suggests that, by focusing on that image of health and wholeness, the organization's energy moves to make the image real. Indeed, the seeds of the solution are in the images, and therefore it is not unusual to see a system shift directions "at the speed of imagination!"

In the early days of working with Appreciative Inquiry, we compared problem solving and Appreciative Inquiry (See Figure 3.4 in Chapter 3) as if the two were parallel processes, with one being superior to the other. If AI is seen as just one more organization development methodology, it might usefully be compared to traditional problem solving. If, however, we shift into new paradigm thinking, AI becomes not a methodology, but *a way of seeing and being* in the world. In other words, when we are using the AI frame, we do not see problems and solutions as separate, but rather as a coherent whole made up of our wishes for the future and our path toward that future.

The commitment to our current deficit-based paradigm is our "default setting," as it were. That paradigm places high value on the machine metaphor (that we can take things apart, fix what is broken, and return to some ideal state). It takes a great deal of "re-training" of our thought processes to shift our metaphor, our view of the world, to a more organic and holistic image. Margaret Wheatley (1994) writes:

"For months, I have been studying process structures—things that maintain form over time yet have no rigidity of structure. This stream that swirls around my feet is the most beautiful one I've encountered. . . . What is it that streams can teach me about organizations? I am attracted to the diversity I see, to these swirling combinations of mud, silt, grass, water, rocks. This stream has an impressive ability to adapt, to shift the configurations, to let the power balance move, to create new structures. But driving this adapt-ability, making it all happen, I think, is the water's need to flow. Water answers to gravity, to downhill, to the call of the ocean. The forms change, but the mission remains clear. Structures emerge, but only as temporary solu-tions that facilitate rather than interfere. There is none of the rigid reliance on single forms, on true answers, on past practices that I have learned in business. Streams have more than one response to rocks; otherwise, there'd be no Grand Canyon. Or else Grand Canyons everywhere. The Colorado [River] realized that there were ways to get ahead other then by staying broad and expansive." (pp. 15–16)

If we follow the organic metaphor, we begin to value and embrace the unlimited diversity of nature. In such a frame of mind, it becomes easy to believe that finding one truth—or one right way to do anything—is not the goal. Rather, the goal is to engage the organization in dialogue that creates multiple positive possibilities and moves the organization in the direction of the most desired future. It becomes important to create the most generative and effective way to move forward.

Appreciative Inquiry is rooted in the values of the emerging paradigm. In this mode, organizations create and move toward their vision of the desired future in harmony with a world view that sees the interconnection of all parts of a system; that accepts the complexity and subjectivity of the world; that knows planning to be a continuous and iterative process; that embraces the concept of many truths and multiple ways to reach a goal; that understands the relational nature of the world; that believes information to be a primal creative force; and that knows language to be the creator of "reality." In other words, the Newtonian paradigm process of dividing things into parts, believing that there is one best way of doing any action, and assuming that language describes some ultimate truth for which we all search creates a way of solving problems that looks backward to what went "wrong" and tries to "fix" it. Appreciative Inquiry, on the other hand, looks for what is going "right" and moves toward it, understanding that in the forward movement toward the ideal the greatest value comes from embracing what works.

This being said, Chapter 2 provides a definition of Appreciative Inquiry in the context of an approach to organization change that enables OD practitioners to shift not the tools of their practice (team building, strategic planning, organization redesign), but rather to shift the perspective from which they approach these processes.

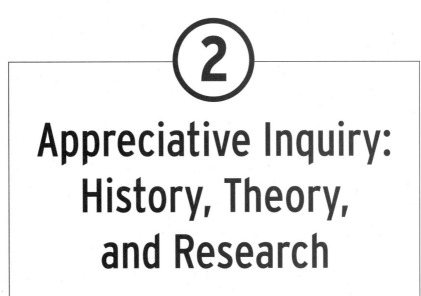

Appreciative Inquiry: History, Theory, and Research

"As I considered the importance of language and how human beings interact with the world, it struck me that in many ways the development of language was like the discovery of fire—it was such an incredible primordial force. I had always thought that we used language to describe the world—now I was seeing that this is not the case. To the contrary, it is through language that we create the world, because it's nothing until we describe it. And when we describe it, we create distinctions that govern our actions. To put it another way, we do not describe the world we see, but we see the world we describe."

Joseph Jaworski, Synchronicity

SUSTAINABLE, **TRANSFORMATIVE CHANGE** in human systems is the Holy Grail of organization development and the focus of this book. Appreciative Inquiry represents a hopeful and radical shift in how human systems, particularly complex organizations, can pursue this goal. Because it is difficult to use language from one paradigm to describe ideas and actions in another, this chapter will provide an operational definition of Appreciative Inquiry and an overview of the theory and research base that underlie AI, that is, social constructionism and the power of image. In this chapter we will also describe what we mean by transformative change in complex organizations and outline the challenges of such change.

In subsequent chapters, we will describe in more detail the phases and processes that are core to an AI-based change process, as well as the practicalities of the early steps.

Appreciative Inquiry Defined

Appreciative Inquiry is a collaborative and highly participative, system-wide approach to seeking, identifying, and enhancing the "life-giving forces" that are present when a system is performing optimally in human, economic, and organizational terms. It is a journey during which profound knowledge of a human system at its moments of wonder is uncovered and used to co-construct the best and highest future of that system.

The term "appreciative" comes from the idea that when something increases in value it "appreciates." Therefore, Appreciative Inquiry focuses on the generative and life-giving forces in the system, the things we want to increase. By "inquiry" we mean the process of seeking to understand through asking questions.

As David Cooperrider (2000) writes in *A Positive Revolution in Change*:

"AI involves, in a central way, the art and practice of asking questions that strengthen a system's capacity to apprehend, anticipate and heighten positive potential. It centrally involves the mobilization of inquiry through the crafting of the 'unconditional positive question' often involving hundreds and sometimes thousands of people.

"In AI the arduous task of intervention gives way to the speed of imagination and innovation. Instead of negation, criticism, and spiraling diagnosis, there is discovery, dream, and design. AI seeks fundamentally to build a constructive union between a whole people and the massive entirety of what people talk about as past and present capacities: achievements, assets, unexplored potentials, innovations, strengths, elevated thoughts, opportunities, benchmarks, high point moments, lived values, traditions, strategic competencies, stories, expressions of wisdom, insights into the deeper corporate spirit or soul – and visions of valued and possible futures."

To give the reader a more informed context in which to consider Appreciative Inquiry, we devote this chapter to the history, theory, and research related to AI.

History of Appreciative Inquiry

The history of Appreciative Inquiry is the history of a major shift in the practice of organization development and transformation. It was an unplanned, unintended shift. Appreciative Inquiry was initiated not as an approach to organization change but as a theory-building process. At its inception, the idea that someday Appreciative Inquiry would become a major approach to change in human systems was far from the minds of its two most central "parents," David Cooperrider and Suresh Srivastva of Case Western Reserve University.

Appreciative Inquiry developed from a theory-building process used primarily by academics into a process for whole system change—but it still has theory building (organization learning) at its core. Appreciative Inquiry enables organizations to build their own generative theory for enabling transformational shifts by learning from their most positively exceptional moments.

Since 1980, David Cooperrider and others have discovered that AI is a powerful way to enable organizations to learn about their systems in ways that result in transformative change. Exhibit 2.1 outlines some of the key developments in the evolution of AI.

Exhibit 2.1. History of Appreciative Inquiry

Date	Event
1980	*Cleveland Clinic Project is initiated.* As a young doctoral student at Case Western Reserve University, David Cooperrider does a conventional diagnosis and organizational analysis for the Cleveland Clinic, asking, "What's wrong with the human side of the organization?" In gathering his data from staff members at the clinic, he is amazed by the level of positive cooperation, innovation, and egalitarian governance in the organization. Suresh Srivastva, Cooperrider's advisor, notices his excitement and suggests making that excitement the focus of his research. Influenced by earlier writings by Schweitzer on the "reverence for life," Cooperrider obtains permission from the clinic's chairman, Dr. William Kiser, to focus totally on an analysis of the factors contributing to the highly effective functioning of the clinic. The Cleveland Clinic thus becomes the basis for an organizational analysis with AI. The term "Appreciative Inquiry" is first used in an analytic footnote in the

Exhibit 2.1. History of Appreciative Inquiry, Cont'd

Date	Event

feedback report of "emergent themes" prepared by Cooperrider and Srivastva for the Board of Governors of the Cleveland Clinic. The report creates such a powerful and positive stir that the Board calls for ways to use this method with the whole group practice. The momentum set the stage for Cooperrider's seminal dissertation, the first and one of the best articulations of the theory and practice of Appreciative Inquiry.

1982 *Ken Gergen publishes* Toward Transformation of Social Knowledge, *which has a major impact on Cooperrider's thinking.* It offers a powerful critique of conventional scientific meta-theory, pointing to a whole new way of thinking. Gergen calls this new method "generative theory," described by Cooperrider as "anticipatory theory that has the capacity to challenge the guiding assumptions of the culture, to raise fundamental questions regarding contemporary life, to foster reconsideration of that which is taken for granted, and thereby furnish new alternatives for social action" (AI listserv, 1999).

1984 *NTL Institute for Applied Behavioral Science holds an international conference in Tampa, Florida.* The conference is focused on innovation in the theory and practice of applied behavioral science in the field of organization development. John Carter presents a case study of the work that he and Cooperrider did with a major accounting firm using an Appreciative Inquiry approach.

1984 *AI at the Academy of Management.* Cooperrider makes the first public presentation of his still-evolving ideas about AI and organizations as "miracles" of human interaction, dialogue, and infinite imagination to the Academy, where, he reports, his ideas are met with skepticism and even laughter.

1986 *Cooperrider completes his doctoral dissertation "Appreciative Inquiry: Toward a Methodology for Understanding and Enhancing Organizational Innovation."* What began as a study of the development of generative theory had evolved into a strategy for organization change. This paradigm-shifting work laid out the principles and logic of Appreciative Inquiry, the phases of AI: affirmative topic choice, discovery, developing provocative propositions, and so forth, and provided a social constructionist meta-theory arguing the need to go beyond a deficit or problem focus.

1986 *Srivastva and Cooperrider publish "The Emergence of the Egalitarian Organization."* This case history presented their work at the Cleveland Clinic from 1980 through 1985, which had started out as an organizational diagnosis of pathologies and problems and had become instead the first major large-scale AI project.

1987 *Cooperrider and Srivastva publish "Appreciative Inquiry in Organizational Life."* This marked the first time that the term Appreciative Inquiry appears in a professional publication. For many, the article is considered the classic

Exhibit 2.1. History of Appreciative Inquiry, Cont'd

Date   **Event**

statement on AI, calling for a shift in the field from its deficit-based theory of change to a positive life-centric theory. The authors argued that organizations are not "problems to be solved," but centers of infinite human capacity—ultimately unpredictable and unknowable. They offered the hypothesis that human systems grow in the direction of what people study; therefore, the search is for the true, the good, the better, and the possible in human systems. The article is noteworthy not only because it made public the term Appreciative Inquiry but because it represented the beginning of the transition from thinking of AI as just a theory-building approach to seeing its potential as a full-blown intervention framework.

1987   *The first public workshop on AI.* Promoted by two MBA students, the workshop was held in San Francisco with David Cooperrider as the key presenter.

1987   *The Roundtable Project.* Held at a Canadian accounting firm with John Carter as the external lead, this was the first large-scale change effort in which AI was seen as a comprehensive intervention framework from data gathering to implementation. After four years of searching for the right organization-wide intervention, Carter offers Appreciative Inquiry as a framework for change and brings in David Cooperrider to explain AI. Within three months and without any coaching from Carter, the client selects AI. Over a one-year period, Carter, Cooperrider, and the client system plan and implement a twelve-step process, starting by establishing a philosophically congruent project structure that incorporates a customized AI protocol, including widespread interviews. The interviews led to the development of provocative propositions (PPs), followed in turn by widespread consensual validation of the PPs and an organic, rather than mechanistic, implementation process. Some four hundred partners came together in a "roundtable" to help create a plan for the future. A major innovation in the use of AI—having members of the organization interview each other—was piloted and has become a major part of AI methods. Although this project was highly collaborative, the data analysis was still in the hands of the external consultants.

1988   *The Appreciative Research Carnival.* An innovation that resulted from Tojo Joseph Thatchenkery's dissertation research, this marked the first time that clients took over the "meaning making" (analysis) of the data. As part of his dissertation research at Case, Thatchenkery began a major three-year, AI-based, data-gathering process with the U.S. branch of the Institute for Cultural Affairs (ICA). Much to his surprise, members of the client system took control of the data analysis and the process of developing future plans. The original purpose (gathering the data to build more grounded theory about how organizations develop) led to the actual development of plans. Thatchenkery named the process "The Appreciative Research Carnival." The following year

Exhibit 2.1. History of Appreciative Inquiry, Cont'd

Date	Event

Thatchenkery experienced the same phenomenon again. ICA inadvertently became the most "fully blown" collaborative use of Appreciative Inquiry to date.

1988   *The "generative metaphor intervention."* This intervention was conceptualized and carried out by Frank Barrett and David Cooperrider in the mid-1980s, as a way of working with a hotel management team locked in seemingly intractable conflict. The paper that Barrett and Cooperrider wrote on this use of AI won the Best Paper of the Year award in 1988 at the National Academy of Management in the OD Division.

1989   *SIGMA Center for Global Change.* This organization was founded by The Weatherhead School of Management at Case as a center for research and education dedicated to the study and development of worldwide organizations and leaders capable of addressing the most complex and pressing global issues of our time. Committed to the premise that there are no limits to cooperation, the center mandate asserts that virtually every item on the global agenda for change can be dealt with, given the appropriate forms of effective management and organization. SIGMA is focused on innovative organizations that are pioneers in building a healthy and vibrant world future using AI.

1989   *The Social Innovations in Global Management Conference, held at Case Western in November.* The conference highlighted studies of five global social change organizations. Articles from these studies, along with papers on the subject of social innovations in management in the global arena, were subsequently published in *Research in Organizational Change and Development, Volume 5,* (Pasmore & Woodman, 1989) and in a special series of articles in *Human Relations.* This marked the first major activity of SIGMA and laid the groundwork for what later developed into a role for SIGMA in the Global Excellence in Management Initiative.

1990   *AI in Romania.* Suresh Srivastva, Ron Fry, and David Cooperrider teamed up in SIGMA to work with Romania's health care system and to create a model to describe Appreciative Inquiry. This model described the cycle of AI as "Discovery, Dream, and Destiny."

1990   *Suresh Srivastva and David Cooperrider publish* Appreciative Management and Leadership: The Power of Positive Thought and Action in Organizations. This book contained Cooperrider's much-quoted article entitled "Positive Image; Positive Action."

1990   *The Taos Institute.* Founded by Diana Whitney, Ken and Mary Gergen, Sheila McNamee, Harlene Anderson, David Cooperrider, and Suresh Srivastva, the Institute became a center for the advancement of social constructionist thinking and practice. It brought together organization consultants, family therapists, and educators with a focus on dialogue, learning, and co-creating

Exhibit 2.1. History of Appreciative Inquiry, Cont'd

Date	Event

relational approaches to human and social change. It has become a world-recognized center for training in Appreciative Inquiry.

1990   *The Organizational Excellence Program (OEP).* A pilot project to create ways for the U.S. Agency for International Development (USAID) to offer innovative management and leadership training to private voluntary organizations in the United States, the program was founded under the leadership of Ada Jo Mann. Case Western Reserve was chosen as the university partner for the pilot. At the end of the pilot phase, the OEP became the *Global Excellence in Management Initiative (GEM)* operating under a USAID grant. GEM's goals are (1) to promote organizational excellence in development organizations in the U.S. and abroad, (2) to create new forms of global cooperation, and (3) to sustain excellence and develop capacity to continually learn, adjust, and innovate over time. The OEP and the GEM Initiative have fostered major innovative ways to use AI in the international development field, creating strong AI groups in Asia, Africa, and Latin America. This work was the laboratory for creating approaches and models that are being used in all type of organizations today. It was during GEM's work with the Save the Children organization that the 3-Ds were transformed and elaborated into the "4-D" cycle.

1992   *Imagine Chicago, a major community development effort based heavily on AI principles and practice, was created.* Bliss Browne, who created and implemented the project, introduced the idea of having children do hundreds of AI interviews with adults and elders throughout the city. This project, more than any other AI initiative, spawned "Imagine" clones from Western Australia to South Carolina.

1993   *Diversity Study.* NTL Institute for Applied Behavioral Science conducted an internal AI-based diversity project to discover and promulgate the innovative and effective lessons that NTL had learned. Cathy Royal was the lead consultant for the project. In preparation, Jane Watkins, Cathy Royal, David Cooperrider, and John Carter offered a three-day AI lab for NTL members who would work on the project.

1994   *NTL's Professional Development Workshop in Appreciative Inquiry was offered for the first time.* Subsequently, Jane Watkins, Cathy Royal, Bernard Mohr, and Barbara Sloan staffed annual workshops in basic AI and an AI practicum workshop.

1995   *An international conference, "Crossing Boundaries: Building Creative Partnerships," was held in Cambridge, England.* This conference brought together people from corporations, foundations, NGOs, government, and development organizations from Europe, the United States, and Africa to use AI as a way of building partnerships.

1995   *Cooperrider was elected president of the Academy of Management (OD Division).*

Exhibit 2.1. History of Appreciative Inquiry, Cont'd

Date	Event
1996	*AI and Gender—The Avon Project.* Schiller and Associates sent Marge Schiller, David Cooperrider, Jane Watkins, and Rusty Rennick to work in Mexico on a project focused on gender equity. The sustainability of the continuous changes in the direction of equity was recognized in 1997 when Avon Mexico won the Catalyst Award, given by the Catalyst Foundation of New York to the company that has done the most to promote equity for women.
1996	*The* Organization Development Practitioner *published an issue devoted completely to AI.*
1996	*The* Thin Book of Appreciative Inquiry *by Sue Annis Hammond was published.* The book provided the first widely available, basic introduction to AI as a philosophy and methodology of change.
1996	*AI and Diversity.* Cathy Royal and Alexsandra Stewart led the first Citizen's Summit and Public Dialogue on Building Communities that Work, a project of the state of South Carolina. Called "Imagine South Carolina," the project was subsequently recognized in two publications, *Interracial Dialogue Groups Across America* and *Racial Divide,* as one of the nation's most effective programs on improving racial dialogue.
1996	*United Religions Initiative.* Under the leadership of Bishop William Swing, a movement was started to unite the world's religions in support of peace. Appreciative Inquiry was selected as the process for their work. David Cooperrider, Diana Whitney, Guradev Kalsa, and many Case graduate students worked with the URI in the creation of an organization charter that was signed in the summer of 2000. This was the first global initiative to use AI in all aspects of the planning and implementation.
1997	*The AI listserv was established by Jack Brittain at the University of Texas, Dallas.* It now serves as a forum for practitioners at all levels to share and learn from one another.
1998	*GTE received the ASTD award for "Best Organization Change Program."* The award was based on work done over two years in the U.S. with AI, guided by David Cooperrider and Diana Whitney.
1998	Lessons from the Field *was published.* Edited by Sue Hammond and Cathy Royal, this was the first widely available book of case histories of organization development projects done from an Appreciative Inquiry perspective.
1998	*The electronic* AI Newsletter *was established by Anne Radford in London.*
1999	Appreciative Inquiry: Toward a Positive Theory of Human Organization and Change, *edited by David Cooperrider, Peter Sorenson, Diana Whitney, and Therese Yeager, was published.*

Exhibit 2.1. History of Appreciative Inquiry, Cont'd

Date	Event
1999	Locating the Energy for Change: An Introduction to Appreciative Inquiry, *written by Dr. Charles Elliott, dean of Trinity Hall at Cambridge, was published.*
1999	*Work with the Dalai Lama.* David Cooperrider was asked to facilitate and to bring Appreciative Inquiry into a program started by His Holiness the Dalai Lama in an effort to have religious leaders create new levels of cooperation and peace. This effort highlighted the essence of AI practice—the crafting of "the unconditional positive question." An article about the project was written called "The Surprise of Friendship."
1999	*Academy of Management symposium.* Ed Schein and Richard Beckhard invited David Cooperrider to join them at the symposium for a session titled "The Past, Present, and Future of Organization Development." This was Beckhard's last major talk at the Academy before his death. Beckhard said this of AI: "Appreciative Inquiry is creating a powerful and enduring change in the way OD will be conceptualized and practiced now and in the future. . . . It is changing the way we think about change itself."
2000	The OD Practitioner *devoted its millennium special issue to AI.* Peter Sorenson of Benedictine University, the editor, argued that AI is more than a method; it is a paradigm change uniquely created for the opportunities of the 21st Century, while at the same time extending the deepest and most important early values of the field.
2000	*European AI network was launched.* David Cooperrider and Diana Whitney met and worked with over seventy European consultants at a training session in Italy, launching the European AI network.

AI and Organization Development

Describing Appreciative Inquiry as yet another OD tool, technique, or intervention would be only partially accurate and a disservice to those who seek to facilitate the co-creation of quantum shifts in the capability of an organization to meet the needs of its customers, members, and other key stakeholders. Rather, we invite the reader to think of Appreciative Inquiry as a *philosophy and orientation to change* that can fundamentally reshape the practice of organizational learning, design, and development in much the same way that process consultation reshaped the field of management consulting forty years ago.

In the early days of management consulting, the consultant was the outside expert who came to study an organization, decide what needed to be done to "fix" it, and propose a course of action. Long reports were written and, more often than not, sat on shelves gathering dust. Consultants became discouraged, employees resisted, and clients became cynical. With the advent of organization development (OD) as a discipline, the behavioral scientists, who were experts not in the work of the organization but in the behavior of people, introduced the idea that the people of an organization were the ones best equipped to identify what had to be changed and to formulate ways to make those changes. Instead of prescribing solutions, consultants began to help members of the organization to formulate their own solutions to problems that they had identified.

Called "process consultation," this new philosophy of consulting was used sometimes in the form of a tool, technique, or method. For example, a consultant might sit with a team and comment on the members' interpersonal and group-level processes. But it was when "process consultation" was used in the macro sense—for example, providing a client system with processes for co-creation of its future—that the value of process consultation as a philosophy, an orientation to all that a management consultant does, really emerged. The paradigmatic shift was from consultants bringing in solutions to the problem to consultants providing models and processes to help organizations study themselves and formulate their own unique solutions.

What is happening with Appreciative Inquiry is very similar. Like process consultation, AI can be and is sometimes applied effectively as a micro tool. For example, in team building, a team could engage in a process of inquiry to strengthen its capability to function effectively. We often hear people say, "We did AI in our team and it really energized us." (A team-building session would generally use positive questions, follow-up visioning, and some form of planning.) But, as with process consultation, the real power and impact of AI is seen when it is used as a comprehensive orientation to change in complex systems. By comprehensive change we mean change in orientation—strategic shifts in the relationship of the enterprise with its environment, changes in the way the work of the organization is done, and/or changes in how the organization approaches problems of leadership, performance, conflict, power, and equity. Appreciative Inquiry is one way to approach strategic planning, organization design, diversity, evaluation, and so on, rather than an alternative to these interventions.

Appreciative Inquiry as a theory and a process continues to expand, develop, and change as we learn about its power and how to integrate that perspective into all the work done under the umbrella of organization change. It has already evolved substantially since David Cooperrider introduced the term in 1986. If those of us using AI remain true to its principles and theoretical base, it will undoubtedly look different in every setting and in subsequent years. Any attempt at a simple, static definition is challenged by the rapidly evolving nature of AI theory and practice, as well as by the subtle and dramatic implications of the paradigm shift.

The evolution of Appreciative Inquiry from an academic interest in grounded theory building to AI as a new orientation and philosophical base for organization development is documented in the history of AI. We will next examine how AI can be used in the process of complex change in today's organizations.

The Use of AI for Complex, Transformational Change

Although Appreciative Inquiry is a useful approach to change in any human system of any scale, our focus in this book is toward the use of AI in the more complex levels of human systems. We will describe a process that can be used in organizations that are multi-functional and multi-level with multiple stakeholder systems operating in unstable environments. In such complex organizations the socio-technical architecture, the organizational culture, and the interactions of individuals are highly interconnected.

Change in the essence of such complex organizations may begin with any of the following seven areas (Beckhard & Pritchard, 1992):

1. Change in the kind of work done within the organization and how it is done in the pursuit of producing the organization's service or product;

2. Change in the roles people hold and the relationships they have with one another;

3. Change in the identity of the organization in the marketplace;

4. Change in the relationship of the organization to customers and the outside world;

5. Change in the mission of the organization;

6. Change in the culture of the organization; and

7. Change in the organization's processes for adapting to continuous shifts in the organizational environment.

AI and the Challenge of Organization Transformation

Complex change of this sort is no small challenge, whether it is in the context of a small not-for-profit or a major public corporation. In fact, the Holy Grail of organization change has long been to create sustainable, transformative change in an organization. Transformative change enables quantum leaps forward in an organization's capability to deliver needed products and services, while at the same time enriching the quality of life for all those connected with the organization. It embeds in the organization the capability for continuous, ongoing development.

Pursuit of rapid, sustainable, and transformative change has spawned a collective effort of almost biblical proportions, considering the time, dollars, and energy that organizations have spent on the multitude of initiatives—retraining, re-forming, re-culturing, reprogramming, restructuring, re-engineering, redesign, and so on. But attainment of OD's Holy Grail has been elusive. Short-term gains appear in one area of performance indicators such as productivity, customer satisfaction, employee engagement, or market penetration, often at the expense of other indicators. Sometimes the inherent slowness of traditional change processes makes organizations vulnerable to yet another shift in the environment or in leadership before the change effort can demonstrate results.

Traditional complex system change efforts all too often leave behind a legacy of cynicism that, together with the accompanying loss of energy, make the next effort at change or transformation even more challenging. Yet there is a geometrically increasing demand for people in organizations to shift direction, make more effective use of new technologies, and respond to crises in shorter and shorter time frames with fewer and fewer resources. At both the personal and organizational levels, an increasing number of people are floundering, with consequences that we are just beginning to understand at the societal, community, and family levels. Within this context, and in response to these challenges, AI has emerged. It provides consultants and their clients with a new framework or a new paradigm for the co-creation of quantum change at both individual and system levels, as one must change to change the other.

Complex Change and the Two Gifts of Appreciative Inquiry

Because it can be used to face the challenge of transformative change in complex systems from the perspective of an emerging paradigm, AI has the potential to flourish in arenas in which many only moderately successful techniques have been applied previously. Appreciative Inquiry's potential comes from the integration of (1) a *practical change process* and (2) *a new paradigm view of how we shape our future.* The integration of these two valuable gifts makes AI a powerful shift from the current practice of OD.

The *practical change process* of AI can be described using the well-known Four-D Model that was developed from the work of the GEM Initiative (see Exhibit 2.1).

Our model uses an additional D (definition) that is roughly analogous to the contracting stage of OD consulting. The five D's follow:

1. A *Definition* Phase during which the goals, including the framing of the question and the inquiry protocol, the participation strategy, and the project management structure are developed.

2. A *Discovery* Phase during which members from the system develop an in-depth understanding of (a) the life-giving properties that are present in those exceptional moments when the organization is performing optimally in human, economic, and organizational terms, and (b) the structures, dynamics, and other associated conditions that allow those life-giving properties to flourish.

3. A *Dream* Phase during which system members create shared images of what their organization would look, be, feel, and function like if those exceptional moments and the life-giving properties in the system became the norm rather than the exception.

4. A *Design* Phase during which system members agree on the principles that should guide changes in the organization's sociotechnical architecture and develop the details of whatever changes are thought to be needed, based on the previously articulated guiding principles.

5. A *Destiny* Phase, sometimes called the *Delivery* Phase, during which the organization evolves into the preferred future image created during the Dream Phase using the work done in the Design Phase.

Although this Five-D process can be reduced to a linear model, the system change begins with the first questions asked in the Definition Phase. We recently had a client, struggling with a design process, exclaim in frustration that it was hard to make a plan when people were already working to bring about ideas that were articulated in the Discovery and Dream Phases. This is almost inevitably the case. The change begins with the articulation of the image, not at the end of a linear planning process.

The second "gift" of AI combines the notion of AI as a philosophy of knowledge and AI as an intervention theory that articulates an *alternative view* of how we shape our future. Grounded in social constructionism and the research on the power of image, this alternative view of OD interventions emphasizes the role of language, dialogue, and ordinary organizational conversations—particularly as they influence the crucial choice of how the topic or issue for inquiry is framed—and the subsequent development of the inevitable inquiry protocol that accompanies almost all change efforts as the organization seeks to understand what Beckhard described as "the present state." Because this alternative view is a total reframing of our current theory of practice, it leverages all that we do in organization development, design, and change consulting.

The Theoretical Base for AI
Social Constructionism

Appreciative Inquiry is grounded in the theory of social constructionism. An understanding of social constructionism can give us a basis for the scientific research (much of it done in the current paradigm's pure science method) that points to the power of images and the way we use them to create our own realities and our own futures. Only through a solid grounding in these concepts will practitioners be able to co-create the organization change processes congruent with the needs of a particular client.

Social constructionism answers the age-old question: How do we know what we know? It calls all of our traditional answers into question. Ken Gergen, whose work on social constructionism has had a major formative impact on AI, describes the idea of language as creator of reality:

> "Social constructionist dialogues—of cutting edge significance within the social sciences and humanities—concern the processes by which humans generate meaning together. Our focus is on how social groups create and sustain beliefs in the real, the rational, and the good. We recognize that as people create meaning together, so do they sow the seeds of action. Meaning and action are entwined. As we generate meaning together we create the future."
> (The Taos Institute website)

This statement captures the core of Appreciative Inquiry. As the people of an organization create meaning through their dialogue together, they sow the seeds of the organization's future.

We talked in Chapter 1 about the shifting paradigm that is moving our understanding of the world from Newtonian linearity to quantum relational theories. This shift in how we see and experience the world has been at the heart of academic debate.

To recap, the "modernist" era (usually from the mid-18th Century until recently) brought with it the ascendancy of "pure" science typified by Newtonian thinking. People began to make judgments based on what was conceived to be "objective, scientific evidence" about what was real and what was true. The search for truth led to the belief that there were underlying rules and structures that defined the "right" way of doing things. The assumption was that the "right" way could be discovered. This thinking had an impact on the arts and architecture, literature, the social sciences—indeed on every sector of human endeavor.

Post-modernism, on the other hand, rejects the idea of an underlying structure and of an underlying truth. Post-modern thought embraces the idea of multiple and contextually determined realities. Social constructionism is a formative theory of the post-modern era.

Let's begin with an overview of social constructionism, about which Vivian Burr (1995) writes: "There is no single description which would be adequate for all the different kinds of writers whom I shall refer to as social constructionist. This is because, although different writers may share some characteristics with others, there is not really anything that they all have in common. What links them all together is a kin or 'family resemblance.' . . . There is no one feature which could be said to identify a social constructionist position."

Summing up the writings of several constructionist thinkers, major among them being Ken Gergen, Burr articulates four key assumptions of "things you would absolutely have to believe in order to be a social constructionist." They are listed below.

1. A critical stance toward assumed knowledge:

    - Social constructionism challenges traditional positivist/empiricist ideas that the world, ourselves included, can be known as it is through objective, unbiased observation—that what we perceive is what is real.

    - Social constructionism cautions us "to be ever-suspicious of our assumptions about how the world appears to be"—a radical agnosticism.

    - The categories with which we "know" the world don't necessarily reflect real divisions.

2. Historical and cultural specificity:

    - The ideas and categories we commonly use are rooted in the specifics of our own history and culture.

    - *All* ideas and categories for understanding the world are products of their own histories and cultures and are best seen as cultural artifacts.

    - Our ways of understanding are not necessarily closer to the truth than are other ways.

3. Knowledge sustained by social processes:

   - Our currently accepted ways of understanding the world arise not from the world as it really is, but from our own *shared constructions* of the world.

   - Our daily social interactions and relationships are the source of what is true for us.

   - For social constructionism, language is the essential tool for creating the world as we know it, and we construct it between us together.

4. Knowledge and social action go together:

   - There are many possible social constructions of the world, and each one invites or impels a different kind of human action. Descriptions or constructions of the world therefore sustain some patterns of social action and exclude others.

   - Social constructionism is frequently interested in the patterns and arrangements of power in human life and in how language reflects, sustains, and/or works against them.

Social constructionism suggests that the social realities of our world (how people behave, the design or sociotechnical architecture of our organizations, the corporate culture, etc.) are neither fixed by iron laws of human behavior nor are they solely a function of past experiences and history. Neither are the social realities exclusively the result of contextual and environmental factors. Rather, social constructionists argue that our world is shaped by the many dialogues and discourses that we have with one another—conversations in which we both selectively make sense of our past and present experience and history and create shared images of what we anticipate in the future. Appreciative Inquiry takes this one step further into an intervention process based on the power of dialogue generated by inquiry itself, that is, the power of the questions we ask. As Cooperrider (1995) said:

> "The most important thing we do as consultants is inquiry. We try to read situations, we do . . . organizational analysis and diagnosis. It all starts with inquiry. The key point is that the way we know is fateful. The questions we ask, the things that we choose to focus on, the topics that we choose determine what we find. What we find becomes the data and the story out of which we dialogue about and envision the future. And so, the seeds of change are implicit in the very first questions we ask."

At the crux of AI is the choice we make by the first question we ask. For example, traditionally an organization wanting to heal the wounds of racism will inquire into instances of racism in the workplace with the idea that once a system is really clear on what racism looks and feels like and what causes it, it can be eliminated. Alternatively, using AI the organization can choose to inquire into stories of exceptionally good cross-race working relationships, discover the conditions present at those times, and create images of desirable relationships. AI acts on the theory that the very act of inquiry shifts the system in the direction of the inquiry by evoking anticipatory images created in the dialogue, positive inquiry leading to positive images.

The Power of Image

Cooperrider turned to research in a wide range of social sciences to understand more fully the impact of positive images in the creation of the future. And he began to tie what he found into his thinking about the impact that these new theories could have on organization change theory and practice. When we interviewed him in 1999, he said:

> "I decided to refocus my dissertation to Appreciative Inquiry. Then, of course, we had to explain the 'why' of this phenomenon. We did this by bringing together a multidisciplinary group in a conference at Case. The purpose was to explore the relationship of image to action; to understand where the positive images come from and how they are developed. That conference provided the basic material for my chapter 'Positive Image: Positive Action' in the book Suresh and I edited called *Appreciative Management and Leadership.*"

Taking research from widely diverse fields such as medicine, sports, behavioral science, and anthropology, Cooperrider thoroughly documented the phenomena of the relationship between our images and our behavior; between what we believe to be true and what we create as truth. This research formed the basis for his dissertation.

For example, since the mid-1950s, Western medical science has become increasingly aware of the power of the mind to heal the body. This concept has always been the basis of healing in Eastern cultures. The split between mind and body that began with the Greeks, was reinforced by the Newtonian paradigm, and remains dominant in Western thought and behavior today, is giving way to a greater understanding of the connection between mind and body. The belief in the holistic nature of the "self" is becoming mainstream, from studies in major scientific research institutions to the daily press.

Appreciative Inquiry is, in part, the art of helping systems create images of their most desired future. Based on the belief that a human system will show a heliotropic tendency to move toward positive images, AI is focused on the generative and creative images that can be held up, valued, and used as a basis for moving toward the future. The research described briefly below is well-documented. Our intention is to familiarize practitioners with the roots of AI and to provide citations for those who want to explore these ideas in greater depth.

The Placebo Effect: The Power of Our Own Images of Ourselves

Perhaps the best-known studies of the impact of our minds on our bodies are the widely documented placebo experiments that began in the mid-1950s. Although the placebo phenomenon has been controversial, most of the medical profession now accepts the fact that anywhere from one-third to two-thirds of all patients will show marked physiological and emotional improvement in symptoms simply by believing that they are being given an effective treatment. Further, the effect is even more powerful if the doctor prescribing the medicine or treatment also believes that it will help (Beecher, 1955; White, Tursky, & Schwartz, 1985).

Norman Cousins popularized the notion that a person's mental state impacts his or her health. In his book, *Human Options,* he writes of the therapeutic value of hope, faith, love, will to live, cheerfulness, humor, creativity, playfulness, confidence, and great expectations, all of which contribute to the body's healing system. A landmark experiment was undertaken by the Simontons (1981), who documented an unusually high rate of recovery from terminal cancer by patients who worked to resolve their psychological issues and practiced positive imagery. Bill Moyers created a whole series for the Public Broadcasting System on the power of the mind to heal the body. Almost daily, new books and articles document studies or propose theories about this connection between our mental processes and our mental and physical well-being.

The Pygmalion Studies: The Impact of Another's Image of Us

The Pygmalion studies, carried out in classrooms with schoolchildren, demonstrate the power that another person's image of us can have in shaping our performance. Teachers were told that some of the students were not very intelligent, tended to do poorly, and were often not well-behaved in the classroom, while other students were bright, hard-working, and successful. The teacher believed these categorizations to be true, although the students had actually been divided into the two groups randomly. Within a very short time, however, almost without exception, those labeled low potential were performing poorly and those labeled high potential were excelling (Jessum, 1986; Rosenthal & Rubin, 1978).

Researchers discovered that the teachers responded to students in line with what they believed about a student's potential and ability. If the teacher thought that a student was smart and competent, body language was encouraging, verbal exchanges were supportive, and the teacher made allowances for the student when he or she did not perform well. On the other hand, the teacher's interactions with those thought to be less capable were much more terse, perfunctory, and dismissive.

Long-term follow-up showed that this image affected the students far into the future. (By inference, the same can be anticipated with images held by parents, bosses, and other authority figures.) Furthermore, it was proven that the image that the teacher held of the student was a more powerful predictor of a child's performance than were IQ scores, home environment, or past performance. So damaging were these experiments to the students labeled "poor" performers that the scientific community discontinued them.

Positive Thinking

In another set of studies, behavioral scientists looked at the ratio of positive as opposed to negative thought patterns in people facing major heart surgery. The studies demonstrated that those who approached the operation with a feeling that their doctor was the best available, the medical techniques used were proven and safe, and their chances of being well again were excellent recovered at a much greater rate than those who approached the operation with feelings dominated by fear and concern. In these studies, it was concluded that the desired ratio of positive thoughts to negative thoughts is approximately 2 to 1 (Cooperrider & Srivastva, 1990, p. 109). With a 2:1 ratio, a marked difference can be predicted in the level of well-being that a person experiences.

Meta-Cognition: Using Our Internal Dialogue for Positive Impact

Evidence suggests, especially in the arena of sports, that we can learn how to create positive images for ourselves that will impact our performance, our health, our sense of well-being, and even our relationships with others.

Books such as Jack Nicklaus' *Golf My Way* argue that positive affirmations ("I'm going to hit it down the middle of the fairway," rather than "Don't hit it into the woods.") cause the whole body to respond to what the mind imagines is possible. Paradoxically, most of us believe that elimination of failures and negative self-monitoring ("No, not the woods!") will improve performance, when exactly the opposite appears to be true.

With this kind of scientific evidence emerging, it makes sense to rethink our approach to organization development. It is not hard to make the connection between the research and people's lives in an organizational setting. For example, the Pygmalion studies suggest that performance appraisals that focus on people's shortcomings, particularly if the appraisals come from one who has power over the person being appraised, are likely to assure that the employee will not perform well in the future. The placebo studies document ways that the power of our minds can keep our bodies healthy. It is not an unreasonable connection to make that employees who hold self-images of competence and success are much more likely to be high-performing. And the power of our inner dialogue to impact out behavior suggests that the cynicism so prevalent in Western culture is quite likely to be a self-fulfilling prophecy.

Taken to the organizational level, if we accept that there is at least a possibility that we socially construct our world and a reasonable amount of evidence that we have the power to create what we imagine, it follows that a process for facilitating organization change would consciously focus on empowering employees to believe that they *can* make a difference; rewarding leaders who know how to empower others; and directing the energy of the system toward the positive, generative, and creative forces that give life and vitality to the work.

Social Constructionism + the Power of Image = AI in Organization Change

As we know from research (Cooperrider, 1990), human beings are strongly impacted by anticipatory images of the future. In myriad ways ranging from physiological responses at the individual level to the creation of new strategies and organization architectures, we collectively create the very future that we anticipate.

This *view of how we shape our future* gives us a whole new way of understanding the process of change in an organization. Rather than being limited to the traditional view of change as an event that has a beginning, middle, and end (for example, Kurt Lewin's model of Unfreezing-Changing-Refreezing), we now see change as a continuous process, ongoing in every conversation we have, in every inquiry we make, in every action we take to "know" or understand something about our organization and/or about the world. Hence the notion of AI as a philosophy of knowledge.

Within the social constructionist perspective, taking into account the research cited above, we realize that some very significant doors open for us as we pursue transformative change in our organizations. Specifically, because all change processes begin with framing an issue and collecting data, we become aware that in the very act of doing these preliminary activities, we are socially constructing our future through the choices we make and the dialogue we use. For example, we can choose to frame an issue as, "What's keeping us from being able to get our innovations into production faster?" or we can choose to frame the issue as, "In those exceptional periods, when our new product development process is moving at the 'speed of light,' what conditions, factors, or contributing dynamics are present?" Our choice is fateful, as either framework will start a snowball of inquiries, dialogues, and the resultant anticipatory images of the future.

Thus, an alternative theory of organizational intervention would suggest that a fundamental pre-condition for all organization change work—whether focused on process innovation, stakeholder relationships, business strategy, organizational culture, diversity, the capability to adapt and improve, or team effectiveness—is to shift the flow of "issue framing dialogues" in the direction of health rather than pathology in order to shift the flow of dialogue from an analysis of malfunction to a holistic understanding of moments of optimal performance. The choice to focus on moments of optimal performance and our conscious use of inquiry are powerful interventions in and of themselves.

Now that we've laid the groundwork for AI, we will present its practical application.

Appreciative Inquiry
As a Process

"Modern management thought was born proclaiming that organizations are the triumph of the imagination. As 'made and imagined,' organizations are products of human interaction and social construction rather than some anonymous expression of an underlying natural order. Deceptively simple yet so entirely radical in implication, this insight is still shattering many conventions—one of which is the long-standing conviction that bureaucracy, oligarchy, and other forms of hierarchical domination are inevitable. Today we know this simply is not true.

"Recognizing the symbolic and relationally constructed nature of the organizational universe, we now find a mounting wave of socio-cultural and constructionist research, all of which is converging around one essential and empowering thesis: that there is little about collective action or organization development that is pre-programmed, unilaterally determined, or stimulus bound in any direct physical, economic, material, or deep-structured sociological way. Everywhere we look, seemingly immutable ideas about people and organizations are being directly challenged and transformed on an unprecedented scale. The world, quite simply, seems to change as we talk in it." (page 91)

David Cooperrider, Frank J. Barrett, and Suresh Srivastva

WE BEGIN THIS CHAPTER WITH A DISCUSSION of the "DNA" of Appreciative Inquiry and then explain the five core principles and the five generic processes (phases) that differentiate AI from other approaches to organization change. Finally, we outline a description of the skills needed by those (internal or external, staff or line) who seek to lead and/or consult to an AI-based change process.

The DNA of AI

As with any approach to organization change, old or new, the question can be asked of AI: "What are the essential components of this approach?" In other words, "What is the DNA of AI?" The essential ingredients of AI are, first, the beliefs and values that are reflected in five core *principles* (constructionist, simultaneity, anticipatory, poetic, and positive) and second, five core *processes* (focus on the positive as a core value; inquire into stories of life-giving forces; locate themes that appear in the stories and select topics from the themes for further inquiry; create shared images for a preferred future; and find innovative ways to create that preferred future). These principles and processes will be covered in detail below.

Taken in tandem, these two building blocks—five principles and five generic processes— form the DNA of any process that calls itself AI. Absent the translation of these two building blocks into practice, the change process could not be considered an AI process.

Like everything in Appreciative Inquiry—even these basic building blocks are continuously being transformed, redefined, and used in creative ways.

It is also essential to have a sense of the theoretical and research foundations underlying AI—the soil out of which the five core principles and five core generic processes emerge. These are:

1. Social constructionism;

2. The "new" sciences (quantum physics, chaos theory, complexity theory, and self-organizing systems); and

3. Research on the power of image.

Figure 3.1 shows how the practice of AI rests on these foundations. Each is explained in detail in the following paragraphs.

Figure 3.1. The Structure of AI

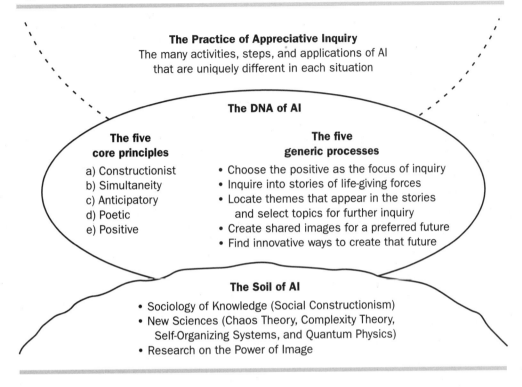

With a thorough understanding of the five core principles and the five generic processes, AI practitioners can adapt and/or create appropriate steps and activities for virtually any situation in which human beings play a key role. Without such an understanding, AI becomes just another tool or technique, severely limiting its power.

The Five Core Principles of AI

The five core principles shown in Figure 3.1 are the essential beliefs and views that make up, along with the five generic processes, the DNA of AI.

The Constructionist Principle. This principle states that knowledge about an organization and the destiny of that organization are interwoven. To be effective leaders in any situation, we must be skilled in the art of understanding, reading, and analyzing organizations as living, human constructions. What we believe to be true about an organization will affect the way we act and the way that we approach change in that system. The first task of any organization change process is *discovery*—learning and making sense of what is believed and said about that system. Thus, the *way* we know *is* fateful.

The Principle of Simultaneity. This principle recognizes that inquiry and change are not separate, but are simultaneous. Inquiry is intervention. The seeds of change—the things people think and talk about, discover and learn, and that inform dialogue and inspire images of the future—are implicit in the very first questions we ask. One of *the* most impactful things a change agent does is to articulate questions. These questions set the stage for what we "discover," and what we discover creates the stories that lead to conversations about how the organization will construct its future.

The Anticipatory Principle. This principle says that the most important resources we have for generating constructive organization change or improvement are our collective imagination and our discourse about the future. The image of the future in fact guides the current behavior of any person or organization. Much like a movie projecting on a screen, human systems are forever projecting a horizon of expectation that brings the future powerfully into the present. Organizations exist, in the final analysis, because people who govern and maintain them share some sort of shared discourse or projection about what the organization is, how it will function, and what it is likely to become.

The Poetic Principle. This principle acknowledges that human organizations are open books. An organization's story is continually being co-authored by the people within the organization as well as by those outside who interact with it. The organization's past, present, and future are endless sources of learning, inspiration, or interpretation, just as a good poem is open to endless interpretations. The important point is that we can study *any* topic related to human experience in *any* human system. We can inquire into the nature of alienation or the nature of joy. We can study moments of creativity and innovation or moments of debilitating stress. We have a choice!

The Positive Principle. This principle has grown out of years of experience with Appreciative Inquiry. Momentum for change requires large amounts of both *positive affect* and *social bonding*—things like hope, inspiration, and sheer joy in creating with one another. Appreciative Inquiry demonstrates that the more positive the questions used to guide a group process or organization change effort, the more long-lasting and effective the change effort (Bushe & Coetzer, 1995). Human beings and organizations move in the direction of what they inquire about. Thus, inquiry into "empowerment" or into "being the best organization in the field" will have a completely different long-term, sustainable impact for positive action than will a study into "low morale" or into "process breakdowns" done with the idea that those conditions can be "cured."

The Five Generic Processes for AI

The other half of the DNA of AI are the five generic processes for applying it as a framework for organization change, shown in Figure 3.1. We use the term "generic processes" as a way of drawing attention to the essence of what AI is about while emphasizing the flexibility of these processes. The five generic processes are:

1. Choose the positive as the focus of inquiry;

2. Inquire into stories of life-giving forces;

3. Locate themes that appear in the stories and select topics for further inquiry;

4. Create shared images for a preferred future; and

5. Find innovative ways to create that future.

The limitations of the written word impose certain constraints on our description of the generic processes. For ease of comprehension, we have listed them above in sequence. But in the world of client work the generic processes don't begin and end neatly. They overlap and repeat themselves without predictability, which is another reason that you must be grounded in the theory, research, and principles of AI as you begin translating these generic processes into practice. A somewhat more descriptive view of the five generic AI processes is shown in Figure 3.2. As can be seen, each process is part of a larger whole and each overlaps with other processes. Chapters 4 through 8 describe these processes in detail.

Figure 3.2. The Five Core Processes of AI

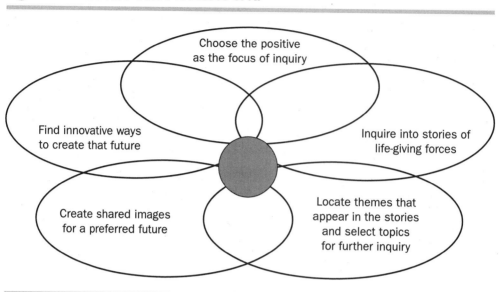

Multiple Models of the Five Generic Processes

Although our five generic processes for applying Appreciative Inquiry can be presented as a systematic approach to organization change, variations on, or even alternatives to, this approach will inevitably emerge as each system makes the AI approach its own. In this section we will look at three other models: The original Cooperrider/Srivastva model; the GEM Initiative Four-D Model; and the Mohr/Jacobsgaard Four-I Model.

By reviewing and comparing these models, we can see both the evolution of Appreciative Inquiry and its adaptation to many circumstances.

After describing each of these models, we provide a graphic summary (Figure 3.7) of how they relate to one another, demonstrating that they are variations of the five generic processes, each created to emphasize a certain point.

The Original Cooperrider/Srivastva Model

When first introduced (Cooperrider & Srivastva, 1987), this model was part of the transition from thinking about AI as purely an approach to the building of generative theory to thinking about AI more directly as a process for intervening in and changing organizations. In this model (see Figure 3.3), Cooperrider and Srivastva suggest four aspects of AI that make it unusually robust as a theory of management. The model shows how AI is simultaneously scientific/theoretical (leading to an awareness of the "best of what is"), metaphysical (establishing ideals of "what might be"), normative (creating consensus on "what should be"), and pragmatic (leading to an experience of "what can be").

The term "vision logic" in the second column refers to the fact that powerful images "inform qualitatively distinct modes of inquiry that then shape our awareness" (Cooperrider & Srivastva, 1987, p. 184).

Figure 3.3. Dimensions of Appreciative Inquiry

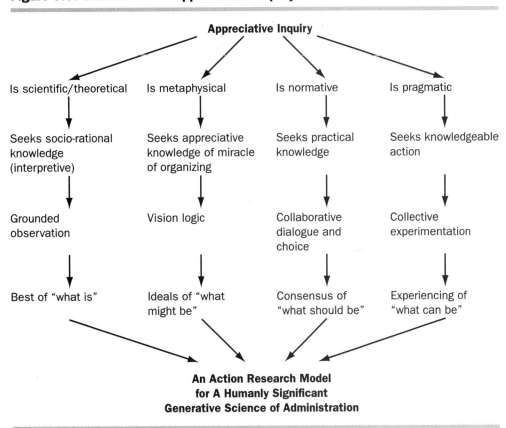

Cooperrider & Srivasta, 1987.

This same model was later depicted more explicitly in a way that also served to contrast what Cooperrider and Srivastva called Paradigm 1 action research versus their Paradigm 2 model. In Paradigm 1, the root metaphor is "the organization as a problem to be solved." In Paradigm 2, the root metaphor is "the organization as a mystery to be embraced." The two are shown in Figure 3.4.

Figure 3.4. Two Different Processes for Organization Change

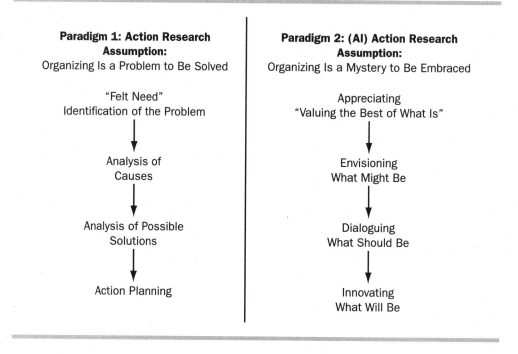

Paradigm 1: Action Research	Paradigm 2: (AI) Action Research
Assumption:	**Assumption:**
Organizing Is a Problem to Be Solved	Organizing Is a Mystery to Be Embraced
"Felt Need" Identification of the Problem	Appreciating "Valuing the Best of What Is"
↓	↓
Analysis of Causes	Envisioning What Might Be
↓	↓
Analysis of Possible Solutions	Dialoguing What Should Be
↓	↓
Action Planning	Innovating What Will Be

The GEM Initiative Four-D Model

The Four-D model (discover, dream, design, deliver) was developed by members of the GEM Initiative in Harare, Zimbabwe, as part of a joint program with Save the Children to develop partnerships among northern and southern NGOs. Ada Jo Mann (1997) writes in "An Appreciative Inquiry Model for Building Partnerships":

> "Having successfully used Appreciative Inquiry in other GEM programs focusing on the factors that give life to 'organizations,' GEM staff believed that a similar model—but one inquiring into what gives life in 'partnerships'—would uncover new learnings in this domain. To this end, a process previously used in GEM's Organizational Excellence Program was adapted for use in partnerships and became the 4-D model."

Figure 3.5. The GEM Initiative's Four-D Model

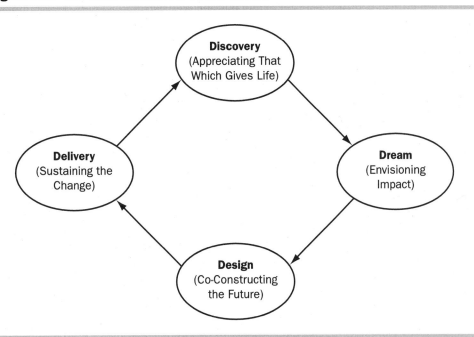

The Four-D model is widely used, and it contains all of the five core generic processes. Detailed descriptions of the tasks are provided below.

Discover (Appreciating That Which Gives Life). The core task of the *discover* phase in this model is to appreciate the best of "what is" by focusing on times of organizational excellence—when people have experienced the organization as most alive and effective. In order to understand the unique factors that made the high points in an organization possible, people deliberately let go of analysis of deficits and carefully inquire into and learn from even the smallest examples of high performance, success, and satisfaction. They tell stories about all aspects of their organization: inspired leadership; generative relationships and partnerships; technologies that make work go more smoothly or facilitate better service; structures that support innovation and creativity; planning that encompasses new ideas and diverse people; opportunities to learn; and so on.

In the discover phase, people share stories of exceptional accomplishments, discuss the core life-giving factors of their organizations, and deliberate on the aspects of their organization's history that they most value and want to bring to the future.

Members come to know their organization's *history as positive possibility,* rather than as a static, problematic, eulogized, romanticized, or forgotten set of events.

Dream (Envisioning Impact). The *dream* phase involves challenging the status quo by envisioning a preferred future and describing that future in a "macro" provocative proposition. The organization's stakeholders engage in possibility conversations about the organization's position, its potential, its calling, and the unique contribution it can make to global well-being. For many, this is the first time they have been invited to think great thoughts and create great possibilities for their organization. As the various stories of the organization's history are shared and illuminated, a new historical narrative emerges, one that engages those involved in re-creating the organization's positive history, which, in turn, gives life to its positive future. Thus, the dream phase is both *practical,* in that it is grounded in the organization's history, and *generative,* in that it seeks to expand the organization's potential.

Design (Co-Constructing the Future). The *design* phase includes the creation of the *social architecture* of the organization and the generation of *micro provocative propositions* that articulate the organization's dreams for each of the ongoing activities. These two processes ensure that everything about the organization reflects and is responsive to the shared vision of the future created in the dream phase and articulated in the macro provocative proposition.

As stakeholders create the organization's social architecture, they are defining the basic infrastructure. This step requires careful consideration and widespread dialogue about what the structure and the processes of the organization will be. Possibilities for the organization are raised by the kinds of questions asked: What is the best kind of leadership structure for the organization and what is the preferred behavior of the leaders as they do their work? What is the organization's strategy and how is it formulated and carried out? What are all of the structural elements needed?

After there is agreement on the myriad possibilities for structuring the organization and an image of how the many elements of the organization's sociotechnical architecture will function in relationship to each other and to the organization as a whole, the task of the group is to articulate those decisions in "micro" provocative propositions. These make explicit the desired qualities and behaviors that will enable each part of the organization to function in a way that moves it toward the higher visions articulated in the "macro" provocative proposition written in the dream phase.

Both the dream and the design phases involve the collective construction of positive images of the future. In practice the two often happen in conjunction with each other.

Deliver (Sustaining the Change). The final phase creates ways to *deliver* on the new images of the future—both the overall visions of the dream phase and the more specific provocative propositions of the design phase. It is a time of continuous learning, adjustment, and improvisation. The momentum and potential for innovation is extremely high by this stage of inquiry. Because of the shared positive images, everyone is included in co-creating the future.

The deliver phase is ongoing. In the best case, it is full of continuing dialogue; revisited and updated discussions and provocative propositions; additional interviewing sessions, especially with new members of the organization; and a high level of innovation and continued learning about what it means to create an organization that is socially constructed through poetic processes in a positive frame that makes full use of people's anticipatory images.

The Mohr/Jacobsgaard Four-I Model

As with the development of the Four-D Model, the need to create something in the field that would fit a certain situation led to the development of the Four-I Model (*initiate, inquire, imagine, innovate*). During an advanced NTL Institute AI workshop, Bernard Mohr and Mette Jacobsgaard asked two questions:

1. "How can we graphically highlight the critical phase of foundation building—educating the client system so that members can make an informed choice about proceeding with AI, put into place the necessary management structures to support the change process, and also, of course, choose the focus and topics of the inquiry?"

2. "How can we graphically spotlight the terribly important phase of moving from the dreams and provocative propositions to reconnecting and modifying the sociotechnical architecture of the organization to bring the dream and propositions to life?"

Mohr and Jacobsgaard were also concerned with the clients' need to have a model that spoke to their experience of "initiating" something and the need of the program participants to have a model that covered all key processes of an AI-based change effort. The model they created is shown in Figure 3.6.

Figure 3.6. The Mohr/Jacobsgaard Four-I Model

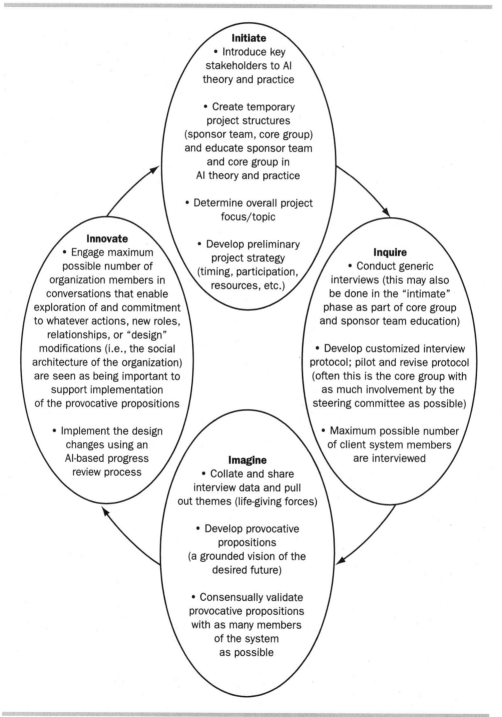

Initiate
- Introduce key stakeholders to AI theory and practice
- Create temporary project structures (sponsor team, core group) and educate sponsor team and core group in AI theory and practice
- Determine overall project focus/topic
- Develop preliminary project strategy (timing, participation, resources, etc.)

Inquire
- Conduct generic interviews (this may also be done in the "intimate" phase as part of core group and sponsor team education)
- Develop customized interview protocol; pilot and revise protocol (often this is the core group with as much involvement by the steering committee as possible)
- Maximum possible number of client system members are interviewed

Imagine
- Collate and share interview data and pull out themes (life-giving forces)
- Develop provocative propositions (a grounded vision of the desired future)
- Consensually validate provocative propositions with as many members of the system as possible

Innovate
- Engage maximum possible number of organization members in conversations that enable exploration of and commitment to whatever actions, new roles, relationships, or "design" modifications (i.e., the social architecture of the organization) are seen as being important to support implementation of the provocative propositions
- Implement the design changes using an AI-based progress review process

Connecting the Models

All the models we have described have within them the core processes of AI. Each emphasizes something a bit different, depending on the context in which it was created. Figure 3.7 connects the five generic processes to all the models.

Figure 3.7. Connecting the Models

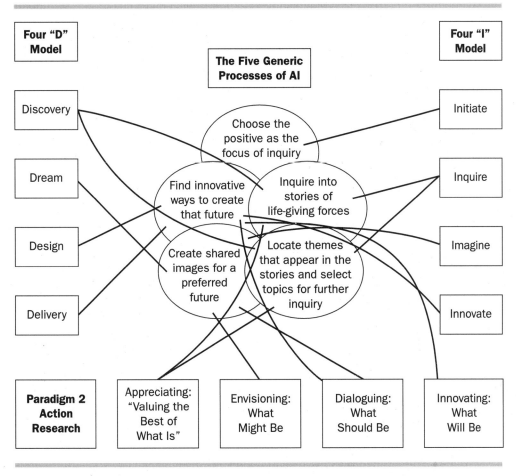

Skills and Knowledge Necessary to Lead an AI Process

After practitioners grasp the idea that AI is not a "method" in the traditional OD sense, they realize their need for solid skills in experiential educational methods and in organization development theory and practice, as well as a need for in-depth knowledge of behavioral science and experience with group process. These skills and knowledge are critical for those who want to use AI in their practice because a major characteristic of an AI intervention is that it is co-created with the client. There is no AI "cookbook"!

We do not mean to imply that AI can be used only by long-time, highly skilled practitioners. Indeed, one of the wonders of AI is that people can begin to experiment with its use after only a small amount of exposure to the theory and practice. However, those with a broad range of consulting skills and long experience with OD practice will be more able to undertake large-scale change projects using AI.

We might usefully differentiate between professional development at three levels. These we have named:

- AI Facilitators,
- AI Practitioners, and
- AI Meta-Practitioners/Trainers.

In response to participants in our workshops, we created the following chart, intended to provide useful guidelines for the professional development of those wishing to work as facilitators and practitioners in Appreciative Inquiry. We see these guidelines as a "work in progress" as we all gain more experience with this evolving practice.

Role Definition: AI Facilitator

AI facilitators are internal staff or line people whose training in AI could come from internal two-to-five-day workshops conducted by AI practitioners. They work collaboratively under the guidance of an internal or external AI practitioner or meta-practitioner.

Competencies for the Role

AI facilitators should be comfortable:
- Co-facilitating the development of customized protocols;
- Conducting interviews;
- Co-facilitating the writing of provocative propositions; and
- Co-facilitating a variety of large-group processes for systemic/structural changes

Role Definition: AI Practitioner

AI practitioners are consultants (internal or external, in staff or line management roles) who are competent at guiding client systems through the whole appreciative inquiry process, including:

- Advising the client on how/where to get started;
- Conducting training of internal facilitators/interviewers;
- Working with internal teams in topic selection and protocol development; and
- Co-designing with the client a variety of processes for consensual validation and for redesigning the systems and structures of the organization to support the propositions.

Competencies for the Role

AI practitioners function best when they are comfortable in the following:

1. Theory and research, including:
   - Social constructionism;
   - Image-action connection;
   - Role of language and inquiry in image creation;
   - People and organizations as mysteries to be embraced;
   - The emerging paradigm as context for AI; and
   - A wide range of AI applications (e.g., strategic planning, organization and business process design, quality improvement, career counseling, mergers and acquisitions, team building, diversity initiatives, evaluation)

2. Coaching clients in the following:
   - Identifying topics (life-giving forces) from generic interviews;
   - Crafting customized protocol AI questions;
   - Conducting interviews;
   - Identifying themes from the customized protocol interviews;
   - Writing provocative propositions (PPs);
   - Consensual validation and possibilities for expanding appreciative conversations throughout the system;
   - Innovating the sociotechnical architecture of the organization

(the structures, roles, processes, and systems) to support and help bring to life the provocative propositions; and

- Helping the system to build ongoing internal capability.

3. Collaborative/AI Consulting Skills:
   - Experiential education
   - Model appropriate behavior and language that is consistent with AI theory
   - Contracting/client relations/ project management
   - Integration of AI with large group/interactive methods (e.g., Open Space, Future Search, Whole-System Design)

Role Definition: Meta-Practitioner

Meta practitioners/trainers of practitioners can run extended in-depth professional development events (such as those offered by Taos and NTL) for AI practitioners.

Competencies for the Role

In addition to the proficiency in the same areas as a practitioner, a meta-practitioner would typically:

- Have extensive experience in a variety of AI applications and settings;
- Be actively participating in an ongoing forum for peer consultation and development;
- Have a firm grasp of AI theory, research, and models of practice and be aware of what is going on worldwide in this field; and
- Have experience in developing and delivering workshops to train organization change agents.

As we continue to participate in the spread of AI theory and practice, we share the challenge of making this thinking accessible to many without either trivializing it or overcomplicating it. Over the next five chapters, we will examine the five processes that are core to the understanding and use of AI.

Choose the Positive
As the Focus of Inquiry

"The simpler way summons forth what is best about us. It asks us to understand human nature differently, more optimistically. It identifies us as creative. It acknowledges that we seek after meaning. It asks us to be less serious, yet more purposeful, about our work and our lives. It does not separate play from the nature of being."

M.J. Wheatley and M. Kellner-Rogers, A Simpler Way

EACH OF THE NEXT FIVE CHAPTERS IS FOCUSED on one of the generic processes of Appreciative Inquiry. We present a detailed explanation of each process followed by generic and case-specific intervention designs, handouts, sample tasks, and hints to help you work with a group using AI.

Choose the Positive

Significant organization change is usually catalyzed by some form of external pressure or opportunity (for example, decreasing customer satisfaction, emerging technologies, new government regulations, shifting competition, unforeseen market opportunities, changing stakeholder expectations, etc.). As an organization begins to contemplate systematic and deliberate change in response to these pressures or opportunities, one of the first activities is generally to undertake a situation analysis. In other words, faced with some impetus for change, the first conscious step undertaken by human systems is to study the situation and to generate "data," that is, information about the situation. This critical first decision—to search for data/information—starts a chain of events that is fateful. Ways to change the organization's relationship to the identified "issue X" are defined.

The AI perspective suggests that, before the first question is asked, the client organization is faced with the most important choice of the whole change process. Appreciative Inquiry *begins* when the organization consciously chooses to *focus on the positive as the focus of inquiry.* As a result, the first choice point is not *whether* to collect data about "issue X," but rather what the focus of the data-collection process will be. In our experience, most organizations make this choice without even knowing that there are alternatives open to them.

If clients follows the *traditional* approach, they will focus on the obstacles they face, the problems they have, the malfunctions that have caused them to be in their current situation, and so on. The AI approach is to seek out the positive history of "issue X," to generate knowledge by exploring moments in the organization's present or past when "issue X" has given life to their organization. For example, if "issue X" is "increasing customer dissatisfaction," the choice is between the traditional questions ("What are we doing wrong that is causing customer dissatisfaction? What do we need to do to decrease customer dissatisfaction?") and the AI questions ("When have our customers been really happy and satisfied with our company? What were we doing then that we can learn from and build on? What images and ideas come from these success stories that lead us to new ways to increase customer satisfaction?").

Raising the Choice Point

The following examples of opening dialogue with client systems make clear the first generic process of AI—choose the positive as the focus of inquiry. Although it is simple enough to suggest that organization interventions for solving problems can be approached from a positive rather than a deficit frame, it is quite another matter to convince clients or your own organization that this positive frame will work. Remember that, from the point of view of our current paradigm, we are taught in all of our cultural institutions that analysis of deficits will lead to future success. So your first conversations with the organization are critically important, and the choice of focus will determine how the whole process will unfold. However, you are not selling AI as an intervention. Rather, you are proposing to facilitate whatever intervention the client requests by approaching it from an AI perspective. The following two examples, a gender project and an evaluation project, demonstrate how the opening dialogue might go.

Example 1: Increasing Gender Equity

The international division of a large corporation was facing regulatory, outside stakeholder, and employee pressure to deal with an organizational culture that limited the contributions women could make to the health and vitality of the corporation and levels in the company's management structure to which they could aspire. The "problem" was defined as a male-dominated culture in the company, the history, tradition, and beliefs that defined the behavior of men and proscribed the role of women. The company decided to move globally toward gender equity in all parts of the corporation. In the international division described in this example, managers were ready to address the "problem." Their first thought, and the advice of some consultants who regularly worked with the company, was to collect information about the breadth and depth of the "problem." They called in a consulting team known for its work on gender issues and outlined for the consultants the "problem" and their readiness to address it by finding out what was wrong and figuring out how to fix it. The response of the consulting team went something like this: "We all agree that the first step is to understand more about what's really going on. We have a big choice to make. We can search for evidence of sexism and incidents of discrimination in order to see how widespread this problem really is. And when we find them we can analyze the factors and dynamics that allow this sort of behavior to flourish." The division managers nodded their heads in recognition of this traditional approach. The next statement from the consultants, however, raised some eyebrows and led to some doubts and skepticism, as well as many questions: "Or," the consultants continued, "we can search for examples of exceptional cross-gender relationships. We can search out stories and examples of moments when both parties in the relationship felt fully valued and very productive together, and we can use that data to determine what conditions and factors were present in those instances that supported such a good relationship. Our choice is whether to focus on moments of breakdown in cross-gender relations in this company or to focus on and learn from moments of excellence, no matter how rare they may be."

Example 2: Evaluation Becomes Valuation

We received a call from the OD/HR department of a transnational pharmaceutical company. The company had just spent a large amount of money and a lot of corporate "goodwill" on putting their top four hundred research managers and scientists through an intensive workshop using a computer simulation to give participants experience with the company's portfolio and process management model. The question to us as consultants was whether we could provide an outside evaluation of the degree to which the workshop had been a good investment of corporate resources, both human and financial. The HR representative indicated that, depending on what we found, a decision would be made to continue or to cancel the training program. After some reflection on the request we said, "We know you want to collect information from within your organization about the impact of the workshop and we know that you need to decide whether and how to proceed. You could do this in one of two ways. The traditional 'scientific' way would be to determine through external judgment whether or not your program had any impact on behavior at all and just how much the participants in the program actually understood. From this traditional perspective we could help you focus on the gaps and how to bridge those gaps in future program design. Or we could study together the assumption that participants had some degree of learning and that they have, to some degree, translated that learning into changed behavior in the workplace. In other words, you could choose to search for, understand, and then find ways to enhance examples of times when participants successfully learned the company's approach to portfolio and process management. Or you could find moments of high transfer of learning from the classroom to the workplace and determine what conditions contributed to that success. You could then find ways of creating those supporting conditions more frequently."

The two examples are the beginnings of the first generic process in AI—*choose the positive as the focus of inquiry.* Because clients, like the rest of us, have been educated in a deficit-oriented, problem-solving approach that emphasizes looking for the obstacles, the gaps, or the dysfunctions in a situation, they are often taken aback by any suggestion that solving their problems could be done more effectively by focusing on the positive as a core value.

Explaining and Demonstrating AI

Whether you are an external consultant, internal staff person, or line manager responsible for a particular operating group, one of the very first challenges in beginning an AI-based change process is to introduce the concepts and research underlying AI. Of course it is also desirable to connect this first introduction of AI with some sort of participative decision making as to the applicability of AI and next steps for the system. Key questions to ask are listed below:

- Is this approach right for you and this situation?

- If this approach feels right to you, what will the topic of the inquiry be? And how shall we phrase the topic in a manner congruent with a choice to focus on the positive as a core value?

- If we proceed with this approach, what are the essential elements that must be present for the change to be successful?

- If we proceed with this approach, who should be involved in developing the customized protocol and in designing the overall inquiry architecture. Should there be a core team of people to do this design work and, if so, what group in the organization will guide and support the work of the core team?

In all of our work with client systems, we request a core team made up of a diverse cross-section of the organization. In most cases we have been successful and the members of this group become the co-creators of the AI process for the organization. We often have found that they are also the people who embed AI in the organization so that it thrives long after we are gone. We have come to believe that, just as the first questions we ask are fateful, this first group—its composition, enthusiasm for the project, and commitment to the organization—can be "fateful." A really first-rate core team has a powerful positive effect on the success of the AI process in the organization. We will talk more about the role of this team in subsequent chapters. Suffice it to say that the earlier you can have the organization identify such a group and the more they are involved from the very beginning, the more you will be able to co-create an AI process that will be unique and appropriate to that organization.

In any case, clarifying and agreeing on this first core AI process typically calls for many dialogues between the AI practitioner and the representatives of the organization. Sometimes these dialogues happen over the phone or in conjunction with face-to-face meetings and the decision is made through those conversations.

In some cases, the potential client may ask for a brief, formal presentation by the consultant to some decision-making group. An outline for a forty-five-minute presentation is given below. Forty-five minutes is the very minimum amount of time necessary to introduce the AI concept. Clearly, it is too short a time to expect that all the questions about AI will be answered. However, the introduction is presented here for you to use because of its utility in building a base for longer sessions.

▶ SAMPLE 45-MINUTE INTRODUCTION TO AI

The goal of this outline is to introduce the concepts and research underlying AI in a way that is both energizing enough for people to want more and sufficiently comprehensive so that people get a sense of AI's full potential, rather than seeing it as just the process of asking a few questions or looking at the world with an appreciative eye.

What Is Appreciative Inquiry?

- Appreciative Inquiry is a *practical philosophy* of being in the world at a day-to-day level, and it is also a highly flexible process for *engaging* people to build the kinds of organizations and world that they *want to live in.*

- As a practical philosophy, AI invites us to choose consciously to seek out and inquire into that which is generative and life-enriching, both in our own lives and in the lives of others, and to explore our hopes and dreams for the future.

- As a process for *engaging* people in building the kinds of organizations and a world that they want to live in, AI involves collaborative, inclusive discovery of what gives a system "life" when it is most effective and capable in economic, ecological, and human terms. It weaves that new knowledge into the fabric of the organization's formal and informal infrastructure.

- Appreciative Inquiry is not another OD intervention; rather, it is a *new approach* to existing OD interventions, such as strategic planning, business process redesign, team building, organization restructuring, individual and project evaluation, coaching, diversity work, and so on.

What Is the AI Process Like?

Choose a model from Chapter 3. Re-create the model on flip-chart paper or on an overhead transparency and use it to give a brief explanation of the overall AI process, making it clear that there is no set formula for using AI, but guiding principles and some models created by practitioners who have tested and adapted them.

An AI Mini Experience

After you have presented your introductory comments, tell participants that they will now take part in a brief inquiry experience. Ask the participants to form pairs. (A threesome works fine if you do not have an equal number of participants.) Tell them that one partner will interview the other for five minutes and that then the partners will switch roles for another five minutes.

Tell the *interviewers* that their goal is to encourage a vivid description of events and to help the interviewees tell very descriptive and detailed stories. Encourage expansion of the stories' richness by using comments such as, "Tell me more about. . . ."

Post the following two interview questions on a flip chart and tell the participants to begin.

1. Think about a time when you were really engaged in and excited about your work. Tell me a story about that time. What was happening? What were you feeling? What made it a great moment? What were others doing that contributed to this being a great moment for you? What did you contribute to creating this moment?

2. If you had three wishes for your organization, what would they be?

After the interviews are complete, debrief the interview process by asking participants, "What was that experience like for you?"

Two Intertwined Ideas Undergirding AI

Next, use the following notes to give a brief lecture about two ideas that have had a significant impact on AI—the power of positive images and social constructionism.

The Image/Action Connection

What happens when:

· You tell a three-year-old: "Don't go near the pool"?

· Just before she swings the club, you tell your golfing partner: "Be really careful not to hit your ball into those trees on the right!"

· You are on your way to meet with someone who always makes you feel very good about yourself, someone with whom you find yourself laughing frequently and behaving in an unguarded spontaneous manner?

Using your own knowledge and the information on positive images and action presented in Chapter 2, explain to participants the connection between positive and negative images and human behavior. If you have time, ask the audience for examples from their own lives.

Social Constructionism:
The Role of Conversations in Creating Social Reality

The traditional view of "reality," particularly as it applies to human behavior, is that:

· Reality only exists external to us;

· The eye is a neutral mirror of the reality that is out there; and

· The function of language is *to describe* that reality.

The social constructionist perspective holds that, through language and social discourse, we are constantly evolving and creating new realities:

· The images of things that we anticipate (such as the anticipation of seeing someone who makes you feel really good about yourself) are a powerful reality in and of themselves.

· These images lead to actions/behaviors.

· Conversations (particularly inquiry) continuously create new images that in turn lead to new actions, which in turn create new realities.

Because we can decide what to focus on in our conversations, we have a choice. If we are focused on "improving" an organization, a team, a family, or a relationship, we can choose to focus on what is broken, what is a problem, and what is frustrating us. Or we can choose to focus on that which is life-giving, energizing, and valuable to us. The choice is fateful!

In Summary

Appreciative Inquiry is an approach to the development of human systems that recognizes that we can choose the view that either (1) Human systems are primarily constellations of problems/obstacles to be analyzed and overcome, or (2) Human systems contain mysterious life-giving forces to be understood and embraced.

Appreciative Inquiry recognizes that, whichever assumption we make about the nature of reality, the choice will lead us to a certain focus in our conversations. And those conversations will lead to certain images being dominant in our minds, and those images will in turn lead to action at both the conscious and unconscious levels.

Appreciative Inquiry uses the power of inquiry to engage our imagination, which in turn influences our actions. By focusing through inquiry on that which is life-giving, that which is energizing, that which is joyful and fun, and by amplifying those qualities by involving the "whole system" in co-construction and co-innovation based on the findings of the inquiry, AI enables systems to transform themselves. ◀

If there is time left, people generally have a lot of questions!

Identifying the Focus for Inquiry

In the process of choosing to focus on the positive, the early dialogues must also lead to a topic choice (the primary area of focus described in Chapter 5). The topic choices are guided by the overall purpose of the project, such as gender equity and evaluation, as in our previous examples.

These discussions about the focus of the work and the resulting topics to be explored are governed by the *Principle of Simultaneity:* As we seek to understand a situation by gathering data, the first question we ask is fateful. The organization will turn its energy in the direction of that first question, whether positive or negative. The seeds of change are embedded in that first question. Careful, thoughtful, and informed choice of topic(s) is important, as it defines the scope of the inquiry, providing the framework for subsequent interviews and data collection.

Because AI begins and ends with valuing that which *gives life* to organizations, during their preparation work inquirers choose affirmative topics based on bold hunches about what gives life to their organization and formulate questions to explore those topics. They also write questions that encourage conversations about the desired future of the organization. The topics and questions focus the organization members on what they most want to see grow and flourish.

Unless the client system makes the choice to focus on the positive as a core value, it is not possible to proceed with an AI process. The client has to understand that choosing to focus on the positive does not mean excluding any reference to difficulties or obstacles. In fact, truth telling in Appreciative Inquiry is just as valued as it is in the traditional, deficit-based, problem-solving approach. And it is a great deal easier to tell the truth about positive experiences! The way that difficult situations will be resolved lies in both the choice of the primary focus for inquiry (positive or deficit-based) and in whether difficulties are seen as immovable obstacles or as sources of insight into strategies for effective forward movement. Appreciative Inquiry is at its most powerful when it is used to seek out the ray of light in what seems to be a totally dark and dismal situation!

As in all things with Appreciative Inquiry, there are multiple ways to proceed. Topics are sometimes chosen by the client who brought you into the organization or, if you are an internal consultant or manager, by you from your own understanding of a situation. In time-limited and subject-focused processes (team building, conflict resolution, etc.), the topic is clear. Often your task in those situations is simply to help create AI questions about that topic: "Tell me a story about the very best team you ever worked or played with," and so on. However, in complex system change (the major focus of this book), the second step in embedding the positive core value is to facilitate a group—ideally a core group assigned to you— to identify key topics that are affirmative. For example, an AI topic to study might be "excellent customer service," rather then "improving customer service." This process of topic selection goes from the simple naming of the topic to identifying topics that are most important to people in the system. The following is a description of an actual four-hour workshop that led to topic choices.

Design to Initiate an AI-Based Process

The design presented in Table 4.1 was used at the initial meeting of an eight-person leadership team at a school recently formed through the merger of three schools. The response to the merger ranged from hostility to confusion, apathy, and a sense of loss to moderate support for the merger. The hoped-for change was the creation of a new culture that would contain the best of the past cultures.

The meeting included the school principal, who was our primary client, and his leadership team, which included representatives of all sections of the school. Prior to this four-hour meeting, the principal, an internal evaluation specialist, and one of us had met for two hours to explore the possibility of working together using AI as a framework. During that two-hour meeting, the principal explained the following:

- The school of about six hundred students and around fifty staff (including faculty administrators and teachers' assistants) was a "new" school in the sense that about 30 percent of the faculty had moved there from other schools.

- The principal was also new to the school and in his first year as principal there.

- Both the faculty who had come from other schools and the original faculty felt as if they had lost something. In the case of the original faculty, they felt a sense of loss of the "old family," including a much-liked previous principal; in the case of the new faculty, they were missing the schools they had left behind.

- The time available for the involvement of school faculty in the determination of the school's future educational environment/culture and their roles within it was very limited, only six hours in two-hour increments over a period of six weeks.

By the end of the two-hour meeting, the author, the principal, and the evaluation specialist had concluded that an appropriate next step was to gather the existing leadership team at the school for four hours:

- To obtain support for proceeding with this process by introducing Appreciative Inquiry as a process for positive change;

- To describe the phases of the process and the choices available, the role of this group in supporting and guiding the process, and the role of an interviewer group;

- To agree on an overall project focus and scope;

- To agree on preliminary project strategy, including the timing of various phases/steps, who was to be involved in which phases/activities, and how to involve them;

- To brainstorm the resources available to draw on throughout the process and what other activities are underway to which the process could be linked; and

- To clarify next steps and individual responsibilities.

Table 4.1 presents the design of the actual meeting, along with key notes.

Table 4.1. Sample Four-Hour Design

Time	Activity	Lecturette Notes
8:00–8:15	Introductions; goals and participants' hopes for this session	• How we got to this point • Principal's hopes for this process and the school's future • Agenda for today
8:15–8:25	Micro Overview of Appreciative Inquiry	"Over the last thirty years of working in both the public and private sectors, my experience has been that people are usually willing to talk about what's wrong, but as they talk about it, there seems to be a downward spiral of despair. Instead of being energized, people became de-energized. David Cooperrider reviewed research on the connection of image and action, research from medicine, education, and psychology, and developed Appreciative Inquiry—the idea that there is a connection between the images we hold of what is possible and the questions we ask about our past and present. The AI approach to change can be applied to your family, your team, your school. The approach is like a journey that engages people in creating the sort of school or team or family or community that they want to live in. It focuses people on what happens when things are at their best. The rationale is twofold: (1) When you focus on the positive, it becomes a springboard (energizer) for the future and (2) It also generates exceptionally useful information about what to enhance and build on as you move into the future together.

Table 4.1. Sample Four-Hour Design, Cont'd

Time	Activity	Lecturette Notes
		"Very briefly, the phases of an AI-based change process are *initiate* (this meeting); *inquire* (find out what contributes to moments of greatness so we can expand this in the future; we want to articulate profound knowledge of a system when it is operating at its best); *imagine* (collectively imagine what could be, how it would be if the moments of greatness are the norm, rather than the exception); and *innovate* (What changes do we want to make so that what we imagine can happen?)"
8:25–9:15	Paired "exceptional moment" interviews	Form the participants into pairs (if the number is uneven, form one group of three). Ask the pairs to take turns interviewing each other using the following questions. Each interview should last twenty minutes.

1. What first attracted you to your work, to your profession? What were your initial impressions? What excited you?
2. In each of our lives there are special times when we just know that we have made the right career choice, moments when we feel really good about the work we are doing and what we are contributing to others. As you think back over the last four or five years, can you *tell me a story* about one of those special moments when you felt most alive, involved, and excited about your work and when you were affirmed in your commitment to being part of the teaching/learning?
   - Who were the significant others and what made them significant?
   - What was happening at that time in
   - your life?
   - What made it a peak experience?
   - What factors in the school (in your environment) made it a peak experience?

Table 4.1. Sample Four-Hour Design, Cont'd

Time	Activity	Lecturette Notes
		3. Without being humble, tell me what you value deeply • About yourself? • When you feel best about your work? 4. What is the single most important thing your work has contributed to your life? 5. What is the *core factor* that gives vitality and life to this school—the one thing without which this place would just not be the same? 6. If you had three wishes to spend on creating a participative change process that would lead to the best possible learning and working environment, an environment that would be a significant expansion of the best that you have experienced in your past, what would you wish for?
9:15–9:20	Debrief of the interview process	What was the process like for you?
9:20–9:30	BREAK	
9:30–10:30	Exploration of interview content	• Sharing of interview high points; identification of what gives life to this school. What stood out for you in the interview with your partner? What sparked your imagination? What made your heart sing? • Pairs draw pictures of what the "new" school would be like and share. • Identification of criteria for a good participative change process at this school.
10:30–11:30	Description of and dialogue about the proposed journey/AI process and the choice points, plus. . .	• Initial thoughts on how widespread the participation in this process should be • Decision on whether they want to be the interview team or whether they think a fifty-person paired interview process in a large-group setting is better • If we have time, what do you have enough curiosity about so that we should include it in the final customized protocol?

Table 4.1. Sample Four-Hour Design, Cont'd

Time	Activity	Lecturette Notes
11:30–11:45	Clarify next steps	Create an action plan for: • Developing a customized protocol • Communication of the decisions from this meeting • Designing/planning the large-group meeting (if that is the choice)
11:45–12:00	Appreciative debrief of today's meeting and meeting closure	• Which part of today's meeting most intrigued or engaged you? • What part of today's meeting should we try to build on as we meet with others in the future? • What wishes do you have for the next time we meet?

In larger, more complex organizations, this topic selection process is often embedded in a longer workshop that leads to the second generic process of AI (inquire into stories of life-giving forces). We offer clients an exploratory workshop (see the two-day preparation workshop in Chapter 5) for a decision-making group in the organization. The workshop clarifies the difference between the AI approach and more traditional approaches to change. It includes an introduction to Appreciative Inquiry, a discussion of the shifting paradigm, and an examination of the theory of change that underlies this approach. It often includes identifying topics and writing questions for the Appreciative Inquiry protocol used in the *inquiry* phase, the second generic AI process. The outcome of this exploratory workshop can be a go/no go decision. Alternatively, this can be the kickoff event to an already agreed-on AI change process. In this case, the workshop includes creation of a customized interview protocol and decisions on inquiry architecture. We will describe both of these in more detail in the next chapter.

Overall, the first generic AI process can be considered complete when: (1) The client system makes an informed choice to focus on the positive as a core value and (2) the choice of topics for the AI process are congruent with the decision to focus on the positive.

▶ CASE STUDY: MYRADA

BY GRAHAM ASHFORD

Focus of the Appreciative Inquiry

Create and strengthen community development organizations.

The purpose of this project is to build capacity within a network of eleven Southern India nongovernmental development organizations (NGOs) in the use of Appreciative Inquiry.

Client Organization

MYRADA is a 450-person nongovernmental organization working in the areas of micro-credit, forest and natural resource management, micro-watershed development, poverty alleviation, empowerment of women, and community development. It works directly with 75,000 families and several thousand other village-level institutions in three Southern Indian states. MYRADA's staff collaborates directly with state and national level government agencies, institutions, banks, other NGOs, and international aid agencies. MYRADA is recognized as a leader in participatory community empowerment methodologies and arid eco-zone development strategies.

Client Objectives

All of the partners in the project are interested in exploring approaches to community development that are participatory and empowering and that lead to sustained local involvement in project activities. MYRADA is particularly interested in developing a process that it can use to help village-level institutions establish group visions that will guide the projects and partnerships that they initiate.

What Is Being Done

Through fieldwork in two Southern Indian states, Andhra Pradesh and Karnataka, the project will test the effectiveness of Appreciative Inquiry as a methodology for helping community groups design and implement projects that contribute to sustainable development and secure livelihoods. The International Institute for Sustainable Development (IISD), MYRADA, and a network of NGOs and community groups will work together and use Appreciative Inquiry to plan and implement village-level projects that emphasize the satisfaction of basic human needs, the promotion of gender equity, the diversification of income-generating opportunities, and the improvement of local environmental conditions. By working in three regions, each facing distinct challenges, the aim of the project is to identify and document the most effective methods of applying Appreciative Inquiry at the community level. It will then communicate these methods to a larger international audience through progress reports, the production of a video and field guide, and the establishment of an Internet site.

Outcomes to Date

At the time of writing (February 2000), the project is still in its early stages. Four training courses have been completed with many of MYRADA's senior training and project officers participating. Initial fieldwork has been conducted as part of the training program and, although preliminary, the results of using Appreciative Inquiry at the village level are encouraging. The appreciative process appears to be quite transformative, with both MYRADA staff and the villagers redefining themselves in the context of their achievements and aspirations.

In one story that came out during the fieldwork, a woman described how, with the support of the other self-help group members, she had been able to expose her husband's covert gambling and drinking activities and convince him to lead a better family life. The self-help group later developed a vision and action plan around ending drinking and gambling in the village. This type of outcome does not often occur when Participatory Rural Assessment (PRA) exercises alone are used, and although it was a locally identified priority, it is not the kind of project that most development agencies would initiate.

Because project ideas are growing from local priorities, there is a high level of participation in their planning. Moreover, there seems to be an undercurrent of optimism in the groups that has led to several smaller and more spontaneous projects being initiated by one or two people. Determining how to sustain these effects during the implementation of these projects will be a major focus during the remainder of the fieldwork.

Contact

Graham Ashford

International Institute for Sustainable Development

161 Portage Avenue East

Winnipeg, Manitoba

Canada R3B 0Y4

e-mail: gashford@iisd.ca ◀

▶ CASE STUDY: MCDONALD'S

BY CHERYL RICHARDSON and JIM LUDEMA

Focus of the Appreciative Inquiry

Becoming the best employer in each community around the world

Client Organization

Human Resources Group of McDonald's Midwest Division.

Client Objectives

As it moves into the 21st Century, McDonald's is turning its attention worldwide to "People First." Its plan is to focus on attracting, educating, and retaining the very best employees; setting the industry standard for progressive employment practices and opportunities; and becoming an admired member of the local and global communities in which it works. Its goal is to "Be the best employer in each community around the world."

To make this happen, in 1999, McDonald's CEO Jack Greenberg called on his Human Resources professionals to shift from a traditional role of hiring, compensation, and benefits into the role of strategic business partner. Its new task would be to build the intellectual and social capital of the organization and its people, to prepare the organization for the future, and to enter into catalytic partnerships with company-owned and owner/operator restaurants around the globe to enhance image and expand service excellence. This shift represented a major, yet crucial, culture change for the organization.

What Was Done

To speed the change, McDonald's Midwest Division, under the leadership of then Division Vice President John Charlesworth, Senior Director of Human Resources Juan Marcos, and Director of Human Resources Cheryl Richardson, launched a division-wide Appreciative Inquiry into "Becoming the World's Best Business Partner for the New Millennium."

The inquiry began by having HR managers in the Midwest Division interview their most important stakeholders (restaurant managers, operations managers, regional managers, owner/operators, field service managers) using three core appreciative questions:

1. What makes us successful when we are at our best as a strategic business partner (principles to preserve)?

2. Imagine McDonald's three years from now as *the* best employer in each community around the world in the quick service food industry. What does it look like? What are we doing more of . . . less of . . . completely new (image of the future)?

3. If you could develop or transform the HR function in any way to advance fully the People First agenda, what three wishes, in order of priority, would you make to contribute to its excellence (growth opportunities)?

The second and third phases of the Appreciative Inquiry were carried out in the context of an Appreciative Organizational Summit meeting. All of the division's HR managers, supervisors, recruiters, assistants, coordinators, and some of their stakeholders gathered at the Midwest Division's annual HR business meeting. The purpose of the summit was to identify "principles to preserve" by exploring examples of peak performance in the past. Principles to preserve are values, structures, strategies, practices, and ways of doing things that the team values so strongly that they must be sustained and nurtured, no matter what else changes as the organization moves into the future. The principles identified by the group included integrity, trust, valuing diversity, confidentiality, collaboration, and expertise.

The participants then worked together to develop a positive guiding image of their future by identifying the most important hopes or wishes they had for the future and by creating an "opportunity map" of the key strategic initiatives they wanted collectively to pursue in the next three to five years.

Outcomes

On the final day of the summit, participants created and launched a series of "design initiatives" intended to translate their opportunities into action. They formed teams around the different initiatives, created plans for implementation, and then shared the plans with the larger group to obtain buy-in and commitments for resources. Specific initiatives included:

- Building the business knowledge skills of the HR team;
- Training in organization development and change for the HR team;
- Restructuring the HR Department into a Development Department;
- Launching a global Appreciative Inquiry into staffing and recruitment;
- Influencing the organization to increase market share; and
- Identifying and developing strategies for issues that have the highest return on investment (ROI).

The Appreciative Inquiry process continues. In addition to the above design initiatives, the HR function of the Midwest Division sponsored a global symposium on becoming the best employer in each community around the world in the quick service food industry. Appreciative Inquiry was used to collect and share best practices and to spark innovations in staffing and retention around the world.

Learnings

The McDonald's Appreciative Inquiry had a dramatic impact for a couple of reasons. First, it boosted positive energy for change when HR managers discovered anew the common aspirations they held with each other and with their most important stakeholders (restaurant managers, operations managers, regional managers, owner/operators, field service managers). Second, the Appreciative Inquiry Summit spurred innovation because it brought all the key stakeholders together "in one room" to envision, design, and implement the change. In any organization, important knowledge and information is widely distributed, and the people closest to the customer often have the information most critical to organizational success. The AI summit, by involving a broad spectrum of people, harnessed a wide range of ideas and information that enriched organizational learning and sparked innovation throughout the system.

Contact

Cheryl Richardson
McDonald's Corporation
3075 Highland Parkway, Ste. 700
Downers Grove, IL 60515
(630) 623-6991
e-mail: cheryl.richardson@mcd.com ◄

James D. Ludema, Ph.D.
Benedictine University
520 Willow Lane
Geneva, IL 60134
(630) 208-6507
e-mail: jludema@compuserve.com ◄

Inquire into Stories of Life-Giving Forces

"The universe is made of stories, not of atoms."

Muriel Rukeyser, American poet & writer

"Those who do not have power over the stories that dominate their lives, power to retell them, rethink them, deconstruct them, joke about them, and change them as times change, truly are powerless because they cannot think new thoughts."

Salman Rushdie, One Thousand Days in a Balloon

THE PRIMARY WORK IN THE SECOND GENERIC AI PROCESS is conducting the interviews that constitute the research into the topics that have been identified in the first generic process. The Appreciative Inquiry interview is a tool for exploring the "life-giving" forces of an organization. It is a process of discovery. The data collected will help you locate, illuminate, and understand the distinctive strengths that give your organization life and vitality when it is functioning at its best.

This interview—in no way a traditional interview—is a mutual learning process. Both the interviewer and the interviewee learn as they explore one another's peak experiences and values and their wishes for the organization.

In preparation for this process, the client system, usually with help from an experienced AI practitioner, must do the following:

- Understand and support the rationale for collecting data in the form of stories rather than using more traditional quantitative, analytic, and reductionist methods;

- Develop a customized interview protocol based on the primary topic chosen for inquiry; and

- Agree on who is be interviewed, by whom, when, how, where; how the data will be synthesized; and how it will be used to make decisions about the future of the organization.

In this chapter we will explore each of these points in more detail. At the end of the chapter we will also deal with the question of training for interviewers.

Rationale for the Use of Stories

We assume that all initiatives that people undertake to alter, develop, or in some way shift their world have, in their beginning stages, some form of "data gathering" about the current status or functioning of the system that we are seeking to alter, develop, or change in some way. In AI, we refer to this data gathering as "inquiry." The "data" is gathered in the form of stories from people in the system because we hold the dual assumptions that (1) people in the system are able to provide the richest responses to our questions and (2) the very act of asking and answering the questions begins to shift the system in the direction of the questions asked.

In traditional action research or organization development, data is collected as if it reflects an objective reality. It is assumed that the data stands apart from the people and process used to gather it.

In contrast, the AI interview serves as the starting point for the positive dialogue that is core to Appreciative Inquiry. The interview explores and brings to life the positive stories of the organization. Further, the interview initiates dialogue that generates and catalyzes the thinking about positive possibilities for the future. This collective surfacing of memories makes possible multiple forms of organizational innovation that could not be achieved though the linear extension of memories recollected within a reductionist, deficit-based paradigm. In addition, this kind of data collecting stimulates participants' excitement and delight as they share their values, experience, and history with the organization and their wishes for the organization's future.

The use of the story as the primary format for conducting an Appreciative Inquiry is not an inconsequential choice. Stories have a depth and breadth that allows meaning to be conveyed much more effectively than would a list of key points or other more analytical reports. Stories engage the imagination in ways that analytic discussions cannot. In the words of American author and storyteller, Laura Simms (personal correspondence 1999):

> "Storytelling is acultural. As an art form, storytelling is not a solo performance of one person telling a story and someone else hearing their words. It is a very subtle transformative event that always takes place in the present and is reciprocal. Image is not something one speaks and the other hears. It is a very complex set of responses based on the listener's previous experience, openness, own well of imagery and association, and the speaker's own unspoken biases and capacities which comes from presence, intention, voice, understanding and openness to communication which is reciprocal.

> "Storytelling has the capacity to directly engage the heart and imagination in such a way that a deeper level of listening is activated, which opens the eyes of perception. The greatest value that arises from a story does not arise from the content of the story text. That is the apparent value. The deepest learning happens in the unspoken story that is generated by the mind mixing of images called forth during the telling. And, the space of timeless sacredness experienced in the process. The thinking mind is kept entranced by the content, while the images dip down and uncover and awaken the dreaming imagination and intuitive intelligence of the listener."

Using a Preparation Workshop

In actual client work, both (1) the development of a customized protocol and (2) decisions about inquiry architecture are often done during a two- to three-day "preparation workshop." This typically takes place after the client system has decided that AI is the right approach. The attendees are, ideally, a microcosm of the larger organization, reflecting as many of the different voices and constituencies as possible, including but not overemphasizing senior management. This group, often called the "core group," will have been identified and selected as part of the con-cluding work of the first generic AI process. Whether this core group reports to and is supported by some senior steering group is a function of what was determined in the first generic AI process when the question was asked: "What are the essential elements and conditions that must be present for this change process to succeed?" Although AI is an energizing and exciting process, in larger organizations we have found it helpful to have some formal linkage between the core group and the exist-ing senior management group, if only to ensure that the core team has the resources and support needed.

Typical goals of the preparation workshop include the following:

- To clarify the difference between the AI approach and the more traditional change processes that focus on individual skill building and/or deficit-based problem solving;

- To help participants create their own AI interview guidelines (customized protocol) for gathering data; and

- To develop a plan (inquiry architecture) for collecting data and for working with it after it has been collected, including:

Who should be interviewed and how?

Who should conduct the interviews, and what training should they receive?

Who should be involved with the data after the interviews?

Who should be involved in developing the image of the preferred future?

Who should be involved in creating the "design" of the new organization?

Because the work that is done in the preparation workshop sets the foundation for the rest of the change process, selection of members of the core group is a critical task.

Developing a Customized Interview Protocol and Inquiry Architecture

Step 1   Set up a Project Management Structure

Step 2   Orient Participants to Their Roles and the Goals of the Preparation Workshop

Step 3   Give Participants an Experience with AI (Introduce the Four Generic Questions)

Step 4   Debrief the Interview Experience

Step 5	Share Highlights of the Interviews and Select Topics for Further Inquiry
Step 6	Create Questions to Be Added to the Four Generic Questions
Step 7	Develop the Inquiry Architecture

Greater detail about each of these steps as well as ideas, sample designs, handouts, and task sheets is given in the following sections.

Step 1: Set up a Project Management Structure

There is no set way to proceed once you have been hired to facilitate an AI process. However, in almost every case we set up a planning team to work with us on the planning and management of the project. For large and complex projects, the planning team is usually composed of you, your client, perhaps one or more internal consultants, and one to a dozen people who have a high stake in the project or who can provide various kinds of linkages that are needed to ensure its success. This planning team will work together throughout the process to provide links to the organization and to co-create the steps in AI. (If the group is large, a subgroup can do actual planning and share with the larger group.) Other structures may be created to fit the situation in your client organization.

The planning team (also variously referred to as a sponsor team or steering team) may be small and informal (the consultant and the internal OD/HR person and/or the primary client) or it may be more formal (a steering team with as many as twelve people). In either case, the role of the planning team is to set overall direction and focus. For example, a planning team may decide that the general focus of the AI process should be "cross-gender relations" or "customer service" or "high-performance teamwork." This group also makes the initial decisions about which parts of the organization should be involved in the inquiry, for example, the sales and marketing division, the customer service division, and so on. Based on these initial parameters, the planning team often selects a core group, a microcosm of the target areas in the organization. The core group typically helps to develop the customized protocol and to evolve the inquiry architecture. Because AI is so different in each case, even these generalizations do not always hold true.

The planning team and the core group should be selected whenever possible from representatives of each part of the organization and each staff level. A "diagonal" slice of the organization works well. At the beginning of an Appreciative Inquiry process, it is very important to talk about the inclusive and democratic nature of the work. Encourage the client to involve, as quickly as possible, people from all parts of the organization. The more diversity you have at every stage, the more you will be working in the spirit of AI.

Step 2: Orient Participants to Their Roles and the Goals of the Preparation Workshop

Once you have decided on the group to guide the project, the next step is to ask the group to attend a meeting that will launch the Appreciative Inquiry process. The meeting can be held in one day; however, if you are working with multiple languages or a complex system, two to three days is much better.

Begin the preparation workshop by explaining the purpose, the agenda, and the norms for working together, then conduct an introductory exercise. Discuss any logistical issues. Allow time for questions. Using information from the section titled "Topic Choice: A Fateful Act," explain to the group the importance of the work they will be doing in this step of an Appreciative Inquiry. (*Note:* The material can be found on page 89 in Chapter 6.) The actual goals and agenda for a two-day preparation workshop are listed below.

Example of Goals and Agenda for a Preparation Workshop. This example is drawn from our work with a transnational pharmaceutical company that had asked us to "evaluate" the impact of a major intervention—a computer-based, interactive simulation of the company's research process—that had been conducted by their internal HR/OD division. In attendance at this workshop were members of their staff (both internal OD staff and scientists) who had designed the OD intervention we were evaluating.

The five goals of this two-day preparation workshop were:

1. To clarify the difference between the AI approach to valuation and traditional (e)valuation approaches.
   - Introduce Appreciative Inquiry;
   - Discuss the shifting paradigm;
   - Examine the theory of change that underlies this approach; and
   - Present Appreciative Inquiry principles and practices.

2. To agree on desired outcomes and critical success factors for this process— and how we will get there.
   - Discuss the desired outcomes and critical success factors; and
   - Discuss the major phases of the AI valuation approach.

3. To jointly develop a customized draft interview protocol for gathering data using this approach and to practice it.

   - Decide how we capture data and what data to record;
   - Create a draft customized interview protocol; and
   - Practice AI interviewing skills.

4. To jointly create a plan for collecting and analyzing the valuation data.

   - Identify stakeholders;
   - Outline the key steps in data collection; and
   - Determine how the data will be collected, organized, and compiled.

5. To agree on next steps (actions, responsibilities, and dates).

The design of the preparation workshop is shown in Table 5.1.

Table 5.1. Design for Two-Day Preparation Workshop

Time	Day One	Time	Day Two
8:00	Gather for coffee	8:00	Gather for coffee
8:30	*Opening Session* · Welcome · Overall purpose of this evaluation process · Goals of this two-day preparation workshop · Agenda for this workshop · Norm setting · Appreciative introductions: Who we are and what we bring	8:30	*Check-in and Questions* Note: Past workshop participants have found this unstructured time to be among the most valuable components of the workshop, as it allows participants to focus on whatever their unique learning needs are at that moment
9:30	*The AI Evaluation Process* Context, assumptions, approach, desired outcomes of the evaluation process, steps, roles, and critical success factors for this process	9:00	*Step 3b: Test Protocol Draft 1* Test Interview 1: Members of the simulation design group or simulation participants are interviewed by our workshop participants one-on-one
10:30	BREAK	10:00	BREAK

Table 5.1. Design for Two-Day Preparation Workshop, Cont'd

Time	Day One	Time	Day Two
10:45	*Create Customized Protocol and Data-Collection Strategy* *Step 1: Conduct Generic Interviews* Workshop participants interview each other using the four generic AI questions	10:30	*Test Interview 2:* Members of the simulation design group or simulation participants are interviewed by our workshop participants one-on-one
11:45	*What Is Appreciative Inquiry?* Overview of theory, research, & principles	11:30	*Interview Debriefing* Questions, comments
12:30	LUNCH	12:15	LUNCH
1:15	*Step 2: Identify Themes/Topics* From the generic interviews, identify key themes/topics and language to be used in developing the customized protocol	2:00	*Step 3c: Create Draft 2 of Customized Interview Protocol* Revise the protocol based on results of test interviews
2:00	*Step 3a: Create First Draft of Customized Interview Protocol* Combine themes emerging from the generic interviews with research questions into a first draft	3:00	*Step 4: Develop Plan for Data Collection and Analysis* • Identify key stakeholder groups • Plan the interview process • Create a preliminary plan for data compilation, analysis, and presentation
3:30	BREAK	3:45	BREAK
4:00	*AI Interviewing Skills* • Interview tips • Practice introducing AI • Practice conducting interviews • Documentation/note-taking guidelines	4:00	*Plan Next Steps* • Conduct pilot interviews • Final protocol revision • Company-wide AI-based evaluation interviews • Steps beyond interviews
5:30	*Review of the Day* Questions; preview of Day Two; interview assignments for Day Two	5:30	*Debriefing* Workshop debriefing and closure
6:00	ADJOURN	6:00	ADJOURN

Example of a Process for Establishing Workshop Norms or Ground Rules. Norms or ground rules are the agreed-on behaviors that the group will use to guide its work. It is a good idea to share a few examples like those below and then let the group members make their own list.

- Listen to each other.

- One person speaks at a time.

- Respect everyone's contribution.

- Begin and end on time.

Example of a Process for Introductions Using a Mini AI Interview. Give the participants the following instructions: "Choose a partner whom you do not know or you want to know better. Ask the following questions of each other. You'll have five minutes each for the interview:

- Tell me a story about a time in your life when you have felt particularly joyful, creative, successful—a real high point. Make yourself the hero/heroine of the story. Give me the details about what happened, who was there, what you did, and so forth.

- Without being humble, tell me what it is that you value most about yourself.

After everyone has finished this mini interview, be prepared to introduce your partner to the group by sharing a high point in his or her life and one thing that he or she values about himself or herself that you learned from your interview."

Step 3: Give Participants an Experience with AI: Introduce the Generic Interview

Introduce the four generic questions by giving a simple explanation of AI as a different approach to understanding organizations (five minutes). These four generic questions form a useful preliminary protocol that exemplifies the spirit of AI, while also being easily modified to fit whatever topic the organization has chosen to focus on. Assign the interview task and review with the group the Tips on How to Conduct an Appreciative Interview on pages 85–88.

Examples of the Four Generic Questions. The development of the customized interview protocol is frequently done by having core team members interview each other using a slightly modified version of the four generic questions below:

1. *Best Experience:* Tell me about the best times that you have had with your organization. Looking at your entire experience, recall a time when you felt

most alive, most involved, or most excited about your involvement. What made it an exciting experience? Who was involved? Describe the event in detail.

2. *Values:* What are the things you value deeply; specifically, the things you value about yourself, your work, and your organization:

    • *Yourself:* Without being humble, what do you value most about yourself as a human being, a friend, a parent, a citizen, and so on?

    • *Your Work:* When you are feeling best about your work, what do you value about it?

    • *Your Organization:* What about your organization do you value? What is the single most important thing that your organization has contributed to your life?

3. *Core Life-Giving Factor or Value:* What do you think is the core life-giving factor or value of your organization? What is it that, if it did not exist, would make your organization totally different than it currently is?

4. *Three Wishes:* If you had three wishes for this organization, what would they be?

An example of the use of the generic question is shown in the four-hour workshop presented in Chapter 4. In that example, the questions were modified for an academic setting. The people involved in that workshop, having interviewed one another using the generic questions, went on to work with the data from their own responses: (1) to design an overall inquiry architecture that engaged students, parents, school faculty and staff, school board members, and senior administration within this school system and (2) to develop three customized interview protocols, one for faculty and staff, one for students, and one for other key stakeholders, such as parents, senior administration, and school board members.

Example of Language for Introducing the Generic Interview. "Appreciative interviews differ from traditional interviews in that the questions are simply guidelines that lead the interviewee to delve into the most creative, exciting, life-giving experiences that they have had in their life and work. It is not as important to answer every question as it is to tell a complete story, evoking the situation—complete with details of what happened and the feelings involved. The goal is to help the person doing the interviewing experience as much as possible the situation being described. The interviewer's role is to *listen*, occasionally prompting the interviewee to be more descriptive or to enlarge the story. *This part of the process is a monologue by the person being interviewed."*

Sample Task Statement for the Paired Interview Assignment Using the Four Generic Questions. *Note:* Prior to giving this explanation, you should give each participant a printed copy of the four generic questions (or put the questions on flip-chart paper at the front of the room).

"Select a partner whom you do not know well or someone you'd like to know better. Participant 1 will interview Participant 2 for thirty minutes (or up to an hour, depending on the time available) using the questions shown on the flip chart. The interviewer's role is to ask the questions, to encourage the interviewee to be very descriptive, and to expand his or her story. The person being interviewed is encouraged to tell the story in language that evokes the feelings and the experience so that the interviewer can feel that he or she really understands the event. After the allotted time, the partners change roles and Participant 2 conducts the same interview with Participant 1.

Everything we do from here on will depend on the data from these interviews, so please listen intently and make note of words, phrases, and ideas that are present when the person being interviewed is telling an exciting story of a creative and successful experience."

Tips on How to Conduct an Appreciative Interview

Explain Appreciative Inquiry. Like anything new, appreciative interviewing may seem awkward at the beginning. It may be equally awkward for the person you are interviewing. The interviewee, too, may be caught up in looking at the organization as a problem to be solved and may not understand the rationale for the new approach. Try saying something like this:

"Before we start, I would like to explain a little bit about what we are going to do. It may be a little different from what you are used to. This is going to be an 'appreciative interview.' I am going to ask you questions about times when you see things working at their *best*. Many times, we try to ask questions about things that aren't working well so that we can fix them. In this case, we try to find out about things at their best so that we can find ways to infuse more of what works into the organization's performance. It is also like what we do with children or athletes when we affirm their smallest successes and triumphs so that they will hold a positive image of themselves and then envision even greater possibility. The end result of the interview will help us understand those 'life-giving forces' that provide vitality and distinctive competence to your organization. Do you have any questions?"

Start with Specific Stories. Appreciative Inquiry seeks the "whole" of an image or idea rather than an opinion about or analysis of a situation. This is best done with stories that describe in detail what happened, who was there, how people felt, and the part the person being interviewed played. Say to the person: "Tell me a story about a time when you. . . " or "Tell me a story about a time when you experienced (the topic) at its best." Probe deeply and intently, like an interested friend hanging on every detail. Ask, "Who did what when? What were you thinking? Then what did you do?" You are trying to get what they *did* (behavior) and what they *thought* or *felt* while they were doing it.

Generalize About Life-Giving Forces. After you have heard the story, try to get the interviewee to generalize. "What is it about this organization—its structure, systems, processes, policies, staff, leaders, or strategy—that creates conditions under which cooperation [for example] can flourish?" As a metaphor, think of your topic (i.e., cooperation) as a plant. You are trying to find out about the kind of organizational soil, water, and sunlight conditions that nourish it. Sometimes people don't know what you mean by organizational conditions, factors, or forces. Give examples: "Are jobs designed a certain way, for example, to foster cooperation? How does the culture or climate of the organization foster cooperation?" And so on. Get them to think a bit abstractly about what is present in the organization that really allowed them to have that peak experience.

What to Do with Negatives. Sometimes, people work in places they don't like. Using the preceding explanations, you can generally get them to identify things at their best. But people *should not* feel that they do not have permission to talk about things that need fixing. You can use each of the following techniques for dealing with negativity, either individually or in combination:

- *Postponing:* Say that you would like to make a note of what the person has said and come back to it later. When you get to the question about what he or she would wish for the organization in the future, this is the time to discuss this "negative" data.

- *Listening:* If the person has some real intensity about problems, let him or her express it. If it is the major focus of the person's energy, you are not going to get any appreciative data until he or she gets it out. This may mean muddling through quite a bit of organizational negativity, and the biggest threat is that you will take it in and lose your capacity to be appreciative. Keep a caring and affirmative spirit.

- *Redirecting:* If the person is not adamant about dealing with the negative, or if you have listened sufficiently to understand the negative issues being raised, find a way to guide the person back to the positive: "I think I understand a little bit about some of the problems you see [paraphrase a few of the ones you've heard], and now I would like to guide us back to looking at what is happening when things are working at their best. Can you think of a time, even the smallest moment, when you saw innovation [for example] at its best?" If the person says it never happened where he or she works, find out if the person has had the experience of something working well in any organization or work context.

- *Using Negative Data:* Everything that people find wrong with an organization represents an absence of something that they hold in their minds as an ideal. For example, if the interviewee says something like, "The communication in this organization is terrible," say to them, "When you say that the communication is terrible, it means that you have some image in your mind about what good communication would look like. Can you describe that for me?" In fact, one could argue that there is no such thing as negative data. Every utterance is conditioned by affirmative images. If the interviewee cannot reframe his or her statement into a positive image, use the negative information and reframe it yourself into a wish or vision statement and then confirm that statement with the interviewee.

- *Watch Your Time:* If the interview is planned to be an hour, you make sure, as you are probing with fascination into what the person is saying, that you are also aware of the time. If you decide that you are learning so much that it is okay if you run over an hour, check it out with the person also. It is best to pace your questions appropriately to the time you scheduled.

- *Be Yourself and Have Fun:* Approach the interviewee as if he or she is a very special person. Be humble. No matter how sophisticated you might be about the world of management, for this hour the interviewee is your teacher. Be yourself. Don't try to ask every question in the interview protocol exactly right. The protocol is a guide, not a questionnaire. This is a conversation to be enjoyed. Almost everyone likes to share knowledge and wisdom with people who genuinely want to learn. If you have an affirmative spirit going in, mistakes in wording will not stop you from getting great data. As you hear fascinating and interesting stories, jot down a note or two as reminders. This is not data that will be "aggregated," so it is not necessary to write down every detail. It is more important to note key phrases and ideas.

- *A Word About Anonymity:* Tell the interviewees you will keep the information they provide and the conversation anonymous. You will use the data, but it will be combined with other interview data and compiled into themes. No names will be associated with the overall summary or report. Stories and quotes from interviews may be used without a name associated with them.

Step 4: Debrief the Interview Experience

After the paired generic interviews are completed, bring the group together and conduct a short discussion about how the process felt. Make your own comments about what you noticed—the high energy level, the buzz of excitement in the room, the way people were interacting with one another. Give the group a presentation on "What is Appreciative Inquiry" using the material from Chapter 4, pages 58–61 (although you can skip the mini inquiry experience). Answer any questions the group has.

Debriefing the Paired Generic Interview Experience. Ask the group: "What was that experience like for you?" It's very important to keep the group focused on debriefing the "process" of the experience rather than getting into the "content." They will have plenty of time to do that later. It's also useful to write the short one- to three-word responses on a newsprint chart. This honors all the responses, even those that are not overly positive. Don't worry if you hear a few responses that say the interview was difficult. Remember that this sort of interviewing is counter-cultural for most people and generates a level of closeness between interviewer and interviewee that not everyone immediately feels comfortable with.

Be patient and highlight the affirmative responses while acknowledging that this is a different sort of interview process and that they will have a chance to modify it later.

Step 5: Share Highlights of the Interviews and Select Topics for Further Inquiry

Have the group members share the highlights from the stories they heard and select a list of three to five topics that they want to know more about.

Sample Handout: "Topic Choice—A Fateful Act." Topic selection is the next step in the Appreciative Inquiry process. Careful, thoughtful, and informed choice of topics defines the scope of the inquiry, providing the framework for subsequent interviews and data collection. Topic choice is a fateful act. Your organization will move in the direction of the topics it inquires about.

In choosing topics, be imaginative and creative. Select topics that are positive affirmations of the strengths of your organization and the powerful entity it seeks to become. Remember the following:

- Topic choice is a fateful act; organizations move in the direction of inquiry;
- Involve those who have an important stake in the future in choosing the topics;
- Two days or more may be required to identify the additional topics;
- Everyone should be an active participant;
- Diversity is essential;
- Vocabulary is not "just semantics"; words create worlds; and
- People commit to topics they have helped develop.

Other General Guidelines

- Encourage participants to choose a reasonable number of topics so there will be a manageable number of questions in the customized protocol.
- Topics are phrased in affirmative terms.
- Topics are driven by curiosity and a spirit of discovery.
- Topics are genuinely desired and people want to see them "grow."

Example of a Task Statement for Topic Identification. Give the following instructions: "For each question, each person will share what he or she has heard—the best story, things that were the most meaningful, good ideas, etc.—as descriptively as possible. (Be careful not to share stories that were told to you confidentially. Ask you partner's permission if you are unsure.)

"As you listen to the stories, make notes of important topics that seem to be present when people's actions and their values are aligned. Using your notes, create a list of the topics that have emerged from all the interviews.

"Next, we will decide on several topics that the whole group thinks are very important and make a list of those. A recorder will capture the topics on a flip chart and we will have a group discussion about this list.

"At the end, we will determine those topics that are the core factors that have given life and vitality to the organization and its work in the world. These will be the topics that you will be asking questions about in the interview guide that you will create for your organization."

Note: If the group has eight or fewer members, do this exercise together. If it is larger, break the group into small groups of two to four interview partners—four to eight people per group. In a small group, these decisions can be made through dialogue and synergy. If there are several small groups doing the same task, you can have each group's work posted on a wall and create a scattergram. To do this, you will need either stickers, such as dots, or colored markers. Ask the participants to study all of the lists, decide on their three most important topics, and put a sticker or a mark on each of those three. This will give you a visual image of which topics are most important. Then the group can discuss and decide on the final three to five topics from those that have the most marks. (Occasionally in these discussions the energy of the group will shift around a topic and they will choose to include one with few marks or exclude one with many marks. This is fine! The point is not to "vote," but rather to have dialogue that discerns the real wishes of the group.)

Examples of Topics from a Variety of Organizations

From an African NGO

- Spiritual Values

- Commitment to Grassroots

- Development of Human Potential

- Teamwork

From a Financial Institution

- Being the Best

- Shared Ownership

- Cooperation Across Boundaries
- Integrity in Customer Service
- Empowering People

From a Health Delivery Organization

- Winning Organization
- Excellent Service and Quality
- Sense of Ownership

Step 6: Create Questions to Be Added to the Four Generic Questions

Using the selected topics that the group wants to know more about, write interview questions about those topics. Use those questions, plus the four generic interview questions, to construct an Interview Guide for your organization.

Example of a Task Statement for Creating Additional Interview Questions. Give participants the following instructions: "Using the topics chosen in the last step, create additional questions for an Interview Guide. Make the questions appreciative and affirmative, focused on stories, details, feelings, and words that evoke the situation as the person actually experienced it in all of its excitement and creativity.

"Put a complete interview protocol document together as you want to use it in your data gathering. The questions formulated for each topic will be added to the four generic questions to form a complete Interview Guide that will be used to interview stakeholders in your organization. You may want to write some introductory material to explain the project and the purpose of the interview."

Sample Handout: "Creating the Customized Protocol" (Interview Guide). Creating the interview guide is an exciting task: What we ask determines what we find. What we find determines how we talk. How we talk determines how we imagine together. How we imagine together determines what we achieve. There are typically three parts to the interview guide, as follows:

- Stage-setting questions: A *best experience question* focused on the general area of inquiry, e.g., best learning environment, best cross-gender relationships, best team experience, etc.; and a *values question* focused on what people value most about themselves, their work, and their organization;

- Additional questions using topics identified in the topic selection process; and

- Concluding questions: Somewhat more open, externally focused, and offering a place in the interview for identifying things the person wants to change, for example:

  What are the core factors that give life to this organization?

  Looking toward the future, what are we being called to become?

  What three wishes do you have for changing the organization?

Sample Handout: "Key Considerations in Crafting Good Appreciative Inquiry Questions"

Good Questions

- Are stated in the affirmative. They describe what is wanted rather than what is not wanted.

- Build on the assumption that "the glass is half full." Because Appreciative Inquiry is based on the belief that positive affect is as contagious as negative affect, AI questions are intentionally in search of the generative, the creative, the moments of achievement and of joy. Therefore, questions are often preceded by an explanation of the positive intent of the question.

- Give a broad definition to the topic. It is desirable for people to make their own meaning of the questions.

- Are presented as an invitation to tell stories, rather than as an inquisition about "facts" or opinions.

- Value "what is." They spark the appreciative imagination by helping the person locate experiences that are worth valuing.

- Convey unconditional positive regard of the person and his or her involvement.

- Evoke essential values, aspirations, and inspirations.

Sample Questions. Following are some examples of questions written with "half-full" assumptions. Appreciative Inquiry questions are based on the assumption that we are looking for the positive—the "half-full" view of the glass.

Leadership: People in this organization have described leadership as the act of facilitating people to come together to accomplish the things they want to do. By assuming leadership, a person or organization helps the people focus and realize their desires and goals that reflect their highest values for achieving the common good. We like the following quotations:

> "The best leader is the one that when the job is done the people say, 'We did it ourselves.'"—Lao Tsu

> "Here are my people going; let me follow them because I am the leader."—Gandhi

Describe a time or occasion when you experienced this kind of leadership. Tell us a story about it. Be very descriptive. What happened? Who was involved?

Shared Vision and Ownership: Based on actual experiences in this company, members of our core group have concluded that organizations work best when everyone thinks, acts, and feels like an owner of the business. That sense of ownership is highest when there is a shared vision for where the business is heading in the future, when people are involved in major decisions that are relevant to them and their work, when appropriate information about the business is shared openly, when people know the whole picture in terms of others' tasks or jobs, and when people feel they are at the center of things, rather than on the outside.

Describe a time when you felt most involved in the "big picture" of the organization, a time when you felt most like a partner or even an owner of the business. What was it about that experience that gave you this sense of ownership?

Example of a Complete Customized Protocol. The following is an example of a customized interview protocol package that includes not only the questions but also guidelines for those who will be conducting the interviews. This example comes from the valuation project with the transnational pharmaceutical company mentioned earlier.

Opening Statement

"Thank you for giving time to participate in this evaluation study. We are coming to the end of the rollout of the research process simulation in its current form. The purpose of this evaluation study is to gather information on:

- How people have made connections from the simulation experience to their everyday work;

- How we might follow up and further leverage the simulation in the company; and

- How we might enhance our use of simulations within the company in the future.

"Before we start. I would like to explain a little bit about what we are going to do because it may be different from what you are used to. This is going to be an 'appreciative interview.' I am going to ask you questions about times when you have seen things working at their *best*. Many times interviews such as this ask questions about things that aren't working well so that we can fix them. In this case, we're trying to find out about things at their best so that we can find out what works and do more of the things that work.

"I'm interested in identifying and understanding those areas and situations where your participation in the research process simulation has helped you in your work. I'm interested in you, in your work, and in understanding more about those times when you feel you are excelling and any connections that you might make between that and the simulation.

"All the information provided will be treated as from anonymous sources and will be used to ensure that the company is capitalizing on its investment in the simulation. My interest today is in learning from you and your experiences. I will be summarizing the information I capture today with data from other interviews. No names (unless permitted) will be associated with the overall summary or report. Please let me know whether you are interested in receiving the summary and we will make sure to send it to you. The probable time frame is two to three months from now.

"I'm confident that it is through these collected comments, experiences, and suggestions that we will find what enlivens the organization and how the simulation contributes to making it a better place to work. The interview takes approximately one hour. Do you have any questions?"

Interview Protocol

1. Before we get to the questions about the simulation, I'd like to know a bit about your experience here at the company and I'd like to do it in the style of Appreciative Inquiry. Could you tell me a story about a time at this company when you felt particularly excited, creative, or productive? What happened? Who was involved? What part did you play?

2. Now I'd like to ask you about your participation in the simulation. Can you tell me a story about a high point when you felt excited and engaged in the

course? Looking back at that experience, what made it exciting? Who was involved? Describe the event in detail. Are there other high points? What did you learn that you valued?

3. One of the purposes of the simulation is to provide opportunities for you to learn about both the research process and about your style of working with a team. The desired outcome is for you to feel that the things you experienced during the workshop are useful in your work in the organization and in your life in general.

    a. In that context, can you tell me some examples (stories) of ways that the things you experienced during the simulation workshop have had a positive impact on your work and/or the quality of your life *at work?* Tell me a story about that. What happened? Can you tell me another story (example)?

    b. (Give a copy of the list below to the person you are interviewing.) As you look at this list are there any stories that come to mind on any of these areas?

    Your leadership style and skills

    Your interaction with other departments

    Your membership on a project team

    Your ability to champion your research effort

    Ability to manage projects

    Planning/strategy of your existing research effort

    Willingness to take risk

    Decision making

    Managing in the context of the discovery portfolio

    c. If you had three wishes for how we leverage our investment in the simulation program, what would they be? (Future simulations? Things that would be helpful to you on your job in the future? Ideas for further use of this simulation?)

4. Now I'd like to ask you a few questions about the organization itself:

    a. What is it that *you* value most about the organization?

    b. In your opinion, what is the core value (driving force, essence, underlying principle, life-giving force) of the organization? What is it that, if it did not exist, would make the organization totally different than it is now?

c. The future of an organization is greatly impacted by the images we hold. Our images are often expressed in our desires and hopes for the future. In that context, if you had three wishes for the future of the organization, what would they be?

Two additional examples of customized interview protocols follow.

Fairview School Customized Protocol and Opening Statement: "Creating a Positive Future for Fairview School by Building on the Best of the Past." This approach to creating your future is based on learning from the best of your past. Every human system (families, schools, companies) has moments of exceptional performance—times when it is doing something really well. By involving as many members of the Fairview School system as possible in learning what was happening at those moments, what ingredients were present, what dynamics were operating—and then finding ways of replicating those conditions—we can create a more positive future faster than by focusing only on that which is broken, sick, or failing.

Appreciative Inquiry is a *journey* during which *profound* knowledge of a human system at its *moments of optimal performance* is used to construct the *best and highest future* of that system.

The process for creating a positive future at Fairview School has four phases. The "Initiate" phase was completed on February 10 when the Fairview Leadership Team agreed that this would be a good process for the school and that they would serve as the sponsor team for this process. The second phase of this process, the "Inquire" phase, begins today.

The Fairview School Protocol for Staff (separate protocols were used for children and for outside stakeholders) follows:

1. In each of our lives there are special times when we just know that we have made the right career choice—moments when we feel really good about the work we are doing and what we are contributing to others. As you think back over your last four or five years at Fairview (or another school), can you *tell me a story* about one of those special moments when you felt that your teaching was really alive and meaningful for your students—a time when you felt particularly excited about your involvement in your field, when you were affirmed in your commitment to being part of the teaching/learning

field? *(Use the questions below to probe more deeply, to help your interviewee expand his or her story.)*

What made it a peak experience? What was happening at that time in your life?

What were the students doing?

How were you interacting with them?

What was it about the learning climate and task that sparked their engagement?

2. Without being humble, tell me what you value deeply about yourself as an individual? As an educator?

3. In planning this process, the sponsor team has said that one of the things that enables great teaching/learning is when people in the school "feel connected," when they feel "part of a family." Thinking back over the last few years, can you *tell me a story* about a time when you felt that sense of connectedness, that sense of family? *(Use the questions below to probe more deeply, to help your interviewee expand his or her story.)*

What role did you play?

What did others contribute?

What other factors in the situation, in the environment, contributed to this connectedness?

4. With the hectic pace of today's world and the need to juggle lots of different balls at once, feeling valued and supported by the people around you can make a big difference. Would you *tell me a story* about a specific time, an experience when as a professional, *you* felt genuinely supported and or valued by students? By your peers? By the administration?

5. In your view, what are the community and societal expectations of Fairview School for the future?

6. What is the *core factor* that gives vitality and life to the Fairview School—the one thing that is important for us to retain, to bring with us as we move into the future?

7. What three wishes do you have for this school—things that would enable it to become even more vibrant and truly the sort of place in which great learning and teaching take place on a daily basis?

Optimal Margin Protocol with a Transportation Company. A major North American transportation company invited David Cooperrider to talk with organization representatives about Appreciative Inquiry. The senior managers in attendance wanted to know whether AI could address solid business issues or whether its usefulness was limited to human relations topics. Cooperrider explained that AI can be used to inquire into and move forward any issue, business or otherwise. In response to the managers' identification of "optimal margin," Cooperrider created the following protocol, which served as the basis for an initial inquiry and was then expanded to all the levels of the organization and became even broader in focus.

1. *What results do you want?* With revenues, tonnage, and sales at record levels, one of the most important opportunities we face is to engage everyone in increasing positive margins now. To do so will call on discovery of new strengths, build on old strengths, and carry us to higher levels financially.

   As you look at this company from the perspective of your capabilities, and as you think about the business context and opportunities, how do you define "optimal margin"? What is the positive margin you want and believe you have the capability to create? Right now? In the moderate time frame? Longer term?

   What results do you want from this meeting? What would make this day a good one for you?

2. *Insights from your work.* We all pride ourselves on the things we do that add the most value in terms of creating margin. Some of our work activities add lots of value, while others do not. Likewise, there are some aspects of our leadership—our style, our approaches to managing people—that engage everyone else in increasing margins. Let's reflect on some of the essential things you do that you feel add the most value.

   When you think of your precious time and how you spend it, what are the things you do that, in your view, add the most value in terms of creating margin? Any examples?

   In the ideal, if you were able to re-craft what you do, what parts of your work (from the perspective of creating margin) would you want to keep doing? Let go of (things that are not really needed)? Do differently?

   As you reflect on *your* leadership here at this company—times when you have mobilized or helped develop others—there have been high points and low points, successful moments, etc. Please describe one situation or change initiative that you are proud about—an achievement that you feel had an impact in realizing better margins. What happened? What were the challenges? What was it about you or your leadership style? Lessons learned?

Let's think about other leaders or successful stories of change—situations you have heard about or seen here at this company and how they relate to engaging people to achieve good margins. Is there a story or example that stands out for you, something that exemplifies the kind of leadership approaches we should aim for more often? Can you describe the leadership?

3. *Continuity search.* Good organizations know how to "preserve the core" of what they do best and are able to "work out" or let go of things that have built up or are no longer needed. Preserving the right things is key. Letting go of other things is the next step.

   In relationship to building optimal margins, what are the things we do best organizationally? For example, measurement systems, leadership systems, ways of developing others, accountability systems, ways of delegating and building trust, technologies, etc. What are the things that should be preserved even as we change in the future?

   Assuming that things do build up, there is a need to "work out" and streamline. There is a need to let go of things that, given precious time constraints, are not needed. Assuming that very few things are sacred, what things (small or large) do you feel we should consider letting go of?

4. *Novelty.* Let's imagine new possibilities for optimal margins.

   If anything were possible, if there were no constraints whatsoever, what would the ideal organization look like if we were to move rapidly into the stage of delivering optimal margins? Describe, as if you had a magic wand, what we would be doing new, better, or differently.

5. *Transition.* How do we get from A to B?

   What is the smallest step (an action, a decision, an initiative) we could take that would have the largest impact?

   What is one thing we have not even thought of yet—something that could have a real payoff?

Step 7: Develop the Inquiry Architecture

Create a stakeholder scan, a list of individuals or groups that you know have a stake in the outcomes of the change process. Decide whether you want to have core group members conduct multiple interviews or whether you want to bring large groups of people together in an AI summit meeting to interview one another in pairs, or some combination of both. Create a plan for how the data will be synthesized and who will be involved in the development of the image of the preferred future and the design phase of the AI process.

Stakeholder Scan. Successful data collection/narrative exploration requires the identification of key stakeholders in your organization, those who have a vested interest in or strong impact on the organization's growth and future and who can supply you with valuable insights into your selected topic area(s). After identifying the stakeholders, make arrangements for preparing your interview questionnaire, collecting the data, recording the information, and collating or distributing the data. The data you collect at this stage will serve as the basis for the next stage: creating the organizational dream.

Sample Handout: "The Stakeholder Scan." Stakeholders are those who have a stake in the organization's future. They may be inside or outside the formal boundaries of your organization. Categories of stakeholders might include:

- Employees (various segments & levels)
- Board of Directors
- Funders
- Regulatory agencies
- Neighbors of the organization
- Unions
- Vendors/suppliers
- Alliances/partner organizations
- Clients/customers
- Family members
- Competitors

The following three-step process will help you conduct a stakeholder scan.

1. After you have finished writing the Interview Guide, brainstorm about the people who might possibly be interviewed. It is fun to make a large chart of this and to write names in different areas or colors according to their connection to the organization. Once you have all the possible names, you will need to decide how many interviews each person on your team can reasonably do and to identify those people on the list who are the most important to be interviewed. Remember that the same guidelines apply to those interviewed as to the team itself—maximum diversity!

2. To maintain a good record of the interview process, create an assignment sheet that lists the following information:

   - Person to be interviewed;

   - Phone or contact;

   - Address;

   - Time and place; and

   - Comments.

3. Finally, create a report sheet for the interviewers to fill out after each interview. An example of such a sheet follows. However, there are many ways to organize the information from the interviews, and it is important that the members of the organization be clear on what they want to capture and how.

Sample Interview Summary/Report Sheet: Pharmaceutical Company Valuation Project. *Note*: Interviewers should fill this sheet out *immediately* after the interview.

Interviewee name:

Department:

Years' experience in this company:

Current roles in the company:

Past roles in the company:

Date/location of simulation attended:

Interviewer name:

Date of this interview:

Stories

- What were the most compelling stories that came out of this interview about the simulation workshop?

- What were the most compelling stories that came out about how the learning was applied?

Learnings

- What were other learnings/applications reported in this interview?

Wishes

- What were the three wishes for the simulation?

- What were the three wishes for the organization?

Values

- What were the individual values?

- What was the core value for the organization?

Quotes

- What were the most quotable quotes that came out of the interview? (What questions do these relate to?)

Implications

- What did you learn through this interview that will make a difference in how you and the company plan and manage other training designs?

Other

- List any other interesting things you heard during this interview.

There are many ways to use the information from the interviews at this point. The important thing is to make it available to the whole community, and especially to that part of the community that will be working on the dream and design phases. Of course, it is always preferable to have as much of the organization as possible involved at every phase. Work with the people who are available, and always build into any planning some ideas for ways to get consensual validation from the whole organization.

If you create a summary sheet for each interview, it is possible to compile all of that information by category. Another possibility is to create a story book that captures the most compelling stories and quotes. Another way is to have continuing dialogue about the data in many different places with a wide cross section of the organization.

The important thing at this point is to understand that the information gathered and compiled is the raw material for the organization's dreams and visions that people in the organization create based on the best of what is as told in the stories (*continuity*) to inspire the articulation of the best of what will be (*novelty*). The design and deliver stages are the *transition* processes for creating a desired future.

The final work to be done in this core process is the generation of an agreement on the inquiry architecture. The core team typically does this work during the preparation workshop after the rationale for the use of stories is understood and the customized protocol has been developed. In the event that the core team reports to a steering group, it is obviously advisable to have ongoing connections between the core team and that group as the core team works out its plan to move the AI process forward.

The role of the consultant here is to co-create with the client system in a manner that continues to ensure that the change process is "owned" by members of the client system and not by the consultant. This may mean helping the client system (in this case the core team and others) to explore the various choices and scenarios for each of the five questions relating to the development of an inquiry architecture. It may also require the consultant/AI practitioner to help client system members apply the five core principles of AI to their discussion of the inquiry architecture. For example, the traditional guideline for determining how many people to interview revolves around the concept of "representative sampling," getting the minimal number of people to create an accurate picture of the situation. The five AI principles, however, suggest an interviewing strategy that is as inclusive as possible. By including as many people as possible, the AI process creates a highly unusual but positive form of energy—a critical mass moving in the direction of the inquiry questions.

For example, the *Constructionist Principle* reminds us that it is through dialogue that we learn about and make sense of our world. The *Principle of Simultaneity* reminds us that through our act of asking questions we can shift the focus of the dialogues. The *Anticipatory Principle* reminds us that we are drawn toward images we have created in our dialogues, particularly when they are attractive images of the future. We also know from the *Poetic Principle* that when people are involved in the storytelling approach to inquiry, they will be involved not only at the level of their heads but also at the level of their hearts. And we know from the *Positive Principle* that as people start to talk about life-giving forces during the interviews, the positive affect that is created will be highly contagious.

Interviewer Training

There is a paradoxical relationship between the high importance we attach to the interview and the relatively minimal quantity of training that the "interviewer" receives during many AI-based processes. Within traditional approaches to organization change, interviewers are engaged in extensive practice and feedback sessions on how to interview. This traditional approach to interviewer preparation is grounded in the notion of the interview as an attempt to uncover some guarded "truth" that the interviewee is reluctant to share. By contrast, the AI interview, partly because of its storytelling format and partly because of the positive nature of its questions, quickly leads to an interpersonal rapport between the interviewer and the interviewee. Consequently, it has been our experience that clarity about the goal of the interview, the role of the interviewer, and a few interview tips is all that interviewers need in most cases. This is particularly true when the interviews are done within a large group meeting wherein each person functions both as interviewer and interviewee. The guidelines we provide (in the form of a task sheet) in such group situations are as follows:

Guidelines for Interviewing

- Choose someone whom you do not know or would like to know better.
- Use the interview guide as your script, to interview each other for forty-five minutes each. Chose a location where you both feel comfortable.
- Capture key words/phrases.
- Introduce and ask the questions as they are written.
- If necessary, use additional questions to encourage the interviewee.
- Let the interviewee tell his or her story. Try to refrain from giving yours. You will be next.
- Listen attentively. Be curious about the experience, the feelings, and the thoughts. Allow for silence. If your partner does not want to or cannot answer a question, it is okay.

- Have fun.
- At the end of the two interviews, take some time to talk to your partner about what the interview was like for each of you.

In the case of an organization choosing to have all interviews conducted by a small group of people (such as the core group), we often spend time going over the following information, prepared in a handout.

Key Characteristics of an Appreciative Interview

- The interview is based on an assumption of health and vitality. You are seeking incidents and examples of things at their best.
- The connection between the interviewer and the person being interviewed is through empathy. Questions are answered in a way that evokes feelings in the listener.
- Personal excitement, commitment, and care are qualities that are present when the interviewer and the person being interviewed are sharing stories of their personal peak experiences.
- Intense focus by the person listening to the stories leads to the experience of being fully heard and understood—a desirable effect from the close sharing that takes place.
- Generative questioning, cueing, and guiding make up the role of the interviewer. The skill is to encourage and question without interrupting the storyteller.
- Belief, rather than doubt, is the proper stance. This is not a time for skepticism or for questions that imply a need for "proof." The trust that develops from simply listening with interest and acceptance is a major positive effect of this process.
- Remember that these are stories being shared, not a reporting of facts. Detail is always useful, as is allowing for the person's unique individual expression of his or her world.

One final note: We find that when a small group undertakes to conduct multiple interviews per interviewer, it is very helpful to build in an early meeting for the interviewer group. The purpose of this meeting is to discuss "what we are learning about how to conduct great interviews." Of course, a mini Appreciative Inquiry interview is the basis for this meeting.

This second core process of AI can be considered to be complete when the client system has:

- Understood and accepted the rationale for collecting data in the form of stories;

- Developed a customized protocol that is based on the selection of the primary topic chosen for inquiry;

- Agreed on an inquiry architecture, that is, who will be interviewed, by whom, when, how, and where, and how the data will be synthesized and used to make decisions about the future of the organization; and

- Completed the actual interviews.

In the next chapter, we will discuss the process of working with the data from the interviews in ways that are consistent with the holistic approach of Appreciative Inquiry.

▶ CASE STUDY: NASA

BY JERI DARLING

Focus of the Appreciative Inquiry

Strategic planning, cultural change

Client Organization

In 1996, NASA created its Strategies for the 21st Century, which then flowed out to the individual NASA centers and then to the various offices to create strategic plans that aligned with the overall NASA vision. The Office of Human Resources (OHR) is a seventy-five-person organization that supports more than two thousand members of the Goddard Space Flight Center of NASA. We began work with them in April of 1998, using Appreciative Inquiry as a primary orientation in guiding a strategic planning process for the OHR.

In addition to strategic planning, the OHR had also experienced a recent change in leadership (including leadership style), as well as a significant downsizing. Many staff members felt extremely overworked, and the mood was quite beleaguered and skeptical.

Client Objectives

The project goals were to create a strategic plan for OHR that aligned with larger NASA vision and values and, concurrently, to work to build a more inclusive, participative culture in the organization. It should be noted that most employees had never attended a meeting that included the full staff.

What Was Done

Over a nine-month period, we went through the 4-D cycle, beginning with paired interviews and a two-day retreat with the management team (fourteen members), and then conducting paired interviews throughout the organization that were shared at a full-day meeting with the entire staff. Provocative propositions were generated, which ultimately were transformed into the organization's goals in the strategic plan. Action teams were organized to work through how these propositions could be implemented. The plans were shared at a second full-day, offsite meeting three months later, at which the teams were highly energetic and creative.

The final phase of the project involved action teams integrating the feedback from this offsite meeting, followed by team representatives working together to create an operations plan that was shared and edited with the management team. The written plan was shared at a final staff meeting three months later and was well-supported. From there, the organization began work on implementation (coined "Race for Change") that has been self-managed during the past nine months.

Outcomes

There were many positive benefits to this process. Members of the organization described a stronger sense of unity and increased familiarity and trust. They demonstrated a new capacity for mutual understanding and creativity and increased trust and confidence in the new organizational leader. As a community, they were able to work through their real priorities.

The self-reported impact of the process thus far is primarily in four areas. First, the internal organizational culture continues to become increasingly open, honest, collegial, and inclusive. (However, employees are still somewhat slow to assume responsibility for decision making.) Second, the organization has developed a stronger customer focus, recently responding to feedback from the employee community with two clear commitments: (1) All phone calls will be returned within one day, and (2) All commitments made by OHR members will be met!

Strategically, the organization's focus has begun to shift in a meaningful way toward greater employee advocacy. In addition, three clear areas of priority have emerged and are being addressed: the staffing process, workforce planning, and identification and delivery of training. Finally, the leadership team has restructured, from fourteen members to seven, and has adopted a primary focus on supporting the change process. It has also changed its way of working together and its decision-making process. The organizational leader has articulated an open invitation for initiative and ownership in the organization.

Learnings

As consultants, we would have wished for more time in the early phase of the project in order for the interviewing and storytelling process to have had maximum impact and to fully work its magic. There were also some historical issues and events that required more space and processing time. Finally, the choice of topics, leading to provocative propositions (and later to strategic goals), were very significant in terms of their strategic impact. Deeper exploration of the interview data might have led to greater clarity and shared commitment to the goals that emerged.

Contact

Jeri Darling
e-mail: Darlingjsd@aol.com ◄

► CASE STUDY: SYNTEGRA

By Joep De Jong

Focus of the Appreciative Inquiry

Leadership and leadership style transition

Client Organization

Syntegra Netherlands, a daughter company of British Telecom, which employs around thirteen hundred people. The case covers a division employing around one hundred people.

In July 1998 this division of Syntegra (a unit with its own profit-and-loss responsibility) was facing a serious situation due to the fact that its former director had left the company, the unit was focused on delivering one single type of product, and it was rapidly losing its competitive edge in that area.

The management style used up to that moment could be described as very directive in the sense that the former director made all key decisions and delegation had been poor. Performance up to May/June 1998 was okay, although from an organizational point of view tension was high and performance was falling.

In July a new director was appointed and a management team of five people was formed.

Client Objective

Team building in a division of a large company. Developing market approaches.

What Was Done

In July 1998 the newly appointed manager of training (MT) decided to brainstorm the themes that needed to be addressed in order to assure that the division would meet budget requirements and to change the organization to a model in which the input of each individual would be valued. Themes that emerged were working in teams, trust within the division, communications between the various groups within the division, and reward and recognition.

In September an interview protocol on these four themes was developed with the help of two external consultants. These external consultants, working with two internal experts on AI and one administrative person, planned a full day offsite meeting for October. It was decided that, in order to cover all four themes, the group of approximately ninety people would be split into four smaller groups, each covering a theme.

In October at an offsite location, a full day AI intervention was organized and the full 4-D AI cycle was covered. At this meeting, it was remarkable that very few stories were told from within the organization. Most of the stories were experiences that people recalled from former jobs. Another fact was the ease with which people engaged in the storytelling, even though there were so few stories from within the organization. Special attention was paid to the issue of how to ensure that the results of the day would be sustained. Among other concrete actions, the provocative propositions that were developed at the meeting were placed in frames, together with photographs of the groups. These four frames are still displayed in the main corridor in the main building of the division, so most employees see them daily. Other actions included things like producing a little booklet with names, addresses, and other personal information that people wanted to share. Also, *The Thin Book of Appreciative Inquiry* by Sue Hammond was distributed to all employees a few weeks after the event. A serious attempt was made to implement an action item each month. Two of the very much appreciated actions were and still are (1) the fact that management pays attention to each employee's birthday and (2) the system of signals that was in place to correct things that had gone wrong was adapted to also reward people when clients or colleagues expressed their appreciation.

In June 1999 it was decided that a follow-up event would be useful. Together with some employees, the MT decided on the themes to be addressed this time. It appeared that there were two major themes that needed to be addressed: (1) teams/team building and (2) service, both internally and to outside clients. This time only one external consultant was used. During the preparation, special attention was paid once again to the issue of how to retain as much as possible of the spirit that an AI intervention brings. The organizing committee came across a company called Arts in Rhythm, an organization that helps to set organizational issues to music. It was decided that they would be involved in the session, both at the beginning, as an opening, as well as at the end during the sharing of the provocative propositions.

In July 1999 the second AI day was organized. Around one hundred employees were present. The day was opened by the people of Arts in Rhythm, who split the group into six smaller groups, each equipped with its own simple rhythm instrument. Within forty-five minutes, they had the whole group performing as an orchestra, actually capable of producing a harmonic piece of music, including variations in tempo, volume, and loudness. The people of Arts in Rhythm made the comparison to a dynamic organization. This definitely had a positive influence on the AI process that followed, as it clearly demonstrated what people are capable of doing and set a positive stage for telling the life-giving stories that each person had to tell. After this session, the group was split into four smaller groups, each working in the normal way on the 4-D cycle. Each group of around twenty-five people had its own facilitator. A striking difference from the first AI intervention for the whole group was the fact that this time almost all of the stories were from within the organization. An attempt was made to use the instruments that people had learned to play during the introductory session in the retelling of the stories. People within each group were asked to express their feelings during the retelling by using the instrument they had learned to play. This appeared not to be very successful. As was later explained by the participants, this was mainly due to their relative inexperience in the use of the instrument and the fact that the listening during the retelling required so much energy that it was not possible to use the instruments properly. The combination of words, music, and dance proved to be extremely successful during the presentation of the provocative propositions to the other groups. Each of the groups had produced one or more provocative propositions on the themes. The assignment was to put these propositions not only to words, but also to music and dance. The main reason for this request was the belief that this would increase the sustainability of the provocative propositions. The whole group was gathered in a stage-like setting, and each of the four groups presented its propositions in a complete act with words, dance, and music. After these presentations, each of the groups split up again and produced a list of concrete action items that would contribute to the realization of the statements produced. The day was concluded with a social event (a barbecue) in which everyone took part.

The follow-up consisted of framing the statements, together with some of the photographs made by a professional photographer who was present, and placing them next to the statements produced during the first AI intervention nine months earlier. In the month of August 1999, six individuals volunteered to ensure that the AI process was continued within the unit. Two of the group will be participating in an AI workshop in order to get a more in-depth knowledge of the process.

Outcomes

1. The division appears to have successfully mastered a dramatic change in both leadership/follower style as well as in organizational structure. Within a fourteen-month time frame, the people came up with a totally different view on how the market should be approached, as well as a realization that their views and personal responsibilities made the difference.

2. The division is currently on a growth track of 40 percent, compared with a local market growth of 10 percent.

3. The turnover of staff in the division has fallen from more than 35 percent to less than 15 percent.

4. A dramatic change in market approach has taken place in the whole unit, which has resulted in a much more customer-friendly approach by each of the departments in the division.

5. A platform has been created (the group of six volunteers) to ensure the continuation of the process. This is regarded as a key element in meeting the challenge of sustaining the AI process in a rapidly changing environment.

Contact

Joep C. de Jong
Syntegra Knowledge Transfer
P.O. Box 30
3920 DA Elst (U)
The Netherlands
31 (0) 79–368 2089
e-mail: joep.dejong@syntegra.nl ◀

Locate Themes that Appear in the Stories

"Implied in . . . scholarly research . . . is the intriguing suggestion that human systems are largely *heliotropic* in character, meaning that they exhibit an observable and largely automatic tendency to evolve in the direction of positive anticipatory images of the future. What I will argue is that just as plants of many varieties exhibit a tendency to grow in the direction of sunlight, there is an analogous process going on in all human systems."

David Cooperrider

AFTER THE INTERVIEWS ARE COMPLETE, the third core process, *locating the themes that appear in the stories,* encompasses the work of "mining" the data by looking for themes of life-giving forces in the interview data and expanding the positive dialogue about these themes to people throughout the organization.

This process, heliotropic in nature, encourages the organization to turn toward images of its most life-giving forces and, through continuing dialogue, to assure that the future will be built on those themes and images.

Of course, because many people will have conducted the interviews—anywhere from two to two thousand, in our experience—it is necessary to create a mechanism by which all that data can be absorbed and digested by people in the organization. (Notice that we do *not* say "analyze" the data.) The search here is not for the norm, the most mentioned idea, even the best idea. The process of absorbing and digesting data is one that allows people to take it all in and to react to the messages and meaning in ways that move the organization in the direction of the combined positive energy of the members. It is more about creating synergy than about consensus.

The group working with the interview data can also range from two to two thousand or more! Remembering the theory that we get more of what we focus on, it follows that the more people involved in sharing the stories, "mining" the data, and identifying the themes of life-giving forces, the more the organization will move in the direction of those themes.

There are many ways of sharing and working with the data, just as there are many choices in the earlier processes about who does the interviewing, who "collates" the data (if that is the decision), and who works with the data to pull out the themes/life-giving forces. Before we get into identifying the choices in data collation and data synthesis (that is, making meaning of the data), let's focus on the idea of themes and life-giving forces, as well as on ways to identify the themes and life-giving forces in the data.

In describing the second core process of AI (*Inquire into Stories of Life-Giving Forces*), we stressed that the very action of asking people to reflect on and tell stories about exceptional moments in the present or past of their organization and to identify how they hope things will be different in the future (the wish question) is a powerful intervention that begins to move the system in directions that are positive and life-giving. We argued that it is the combination of positively focused inquiry, positively focused dialogue, and the resultant influence on the collective imagination that propels forward movement. In this third core process of AI, we want to keep those conversations and that dynamic alive and extend them for the same reasons we asked the questions in the first place. However, it's not just a question of talking about good things. Rather, we must work with the data in a way that continues the inherent value of conversations focused on life-giving forces, while also developing the ground from which we can later build shared images, dreams, and visions of a preferred future.

Identifying Themes

Themes of life-giving forces can be found in the information gathered in the generic interviews, as well as in the customized protocol interviews. In fact, one never knows where a life-giving force will come to the light of day!

Themes are important threads from the inquiry data. They are short answers to the question: "What do we hear people describing in the interviews as the life-giving forces in this organization?" Identifying the themes and life-giving forces not only continues the reality-creating conversations, but also provides a link between the inquiry we have conducted into the past and the image of the preferred future we will create in the fourth core process. The themes become the basis for *collectively imagining what the organization would be like if the exceptional moments that we have uncovered in the interviews became the norm* in the organization.

Example of Themes

The following example of themes comes from our work with an international pharmaceutical company. To put the themes in context, this example shows the preceding processes of topic choice, question formulation, and interviewing, as well as the next step after theme selection, which is articulating the dream, a process often referred to as writing "provocative propositions." More will be said about that step in the next chapter.

Topic. Transfer of learning from the workshop to the workplace (*Note:* In this example, the topic had been identified by the HR group that wrote the original request for proposal for an evaluation of the simulation training process that had been delivered to nearly five hundred people in a major division of their organization.)

Question. One of the purposes of the research simulation is to provide opportunities for you to learn both about the research process and about your style of working with a team. The desired outcome is for you to feel that the things you experienced during the workshop are useful in your work in the organization and in your life in general.

In that context, can you tell me some examples (stories) of ways that the *things you experienced* during the simulation workshop have had a *positive impact* on your work and/or the quality of your life at work? Tell me a story about that. What happened? Can you tell me another story? (*Note:* During the start-up session, the consultants worked with the internal team—the core group—that guided the whole valuation process. We began with an AI training session during which the core group learned about AI theory and experienced the process by doing the generic interviews, agreeing on the topics, and formulating questions that became the official interview protocol for the AI process.)

Themes. The major themes that emerged from the examples interviewees gave of applications back in the workplace were as follows:

- Participants overwhelmingly reported a clearer and more detailed understanding of the research system as a whole and of the roles and phases within the research process; application of this knowledge has enabled them to be more efficient and effective in their jobs.

- Many participants reported that they now place a greater value on their personal expertise and are more proactive in making contributions and taking initiatives.

- As a result of the experience of teamwork on the program, participants are now using their collective expertise more effectively to make decisions and to progress their research efforts.

- Participants are continuing the process of networking that began on the research simulation and are using their new and broader links within the organization to assist in developing and working on new ideas more quickly and effectively.

- Many participants have taken the opportunity to examine and further develop their leadership styles; some have also identified and addressed additional development needs for their staff.

- Participants also reported being more purposeful and rigorous in planning their research efforts, more effective in requesting and allocating resources, and more timely and effective in their decision making.

These themes were identified and compiled by the core group and the consultants. First, the answers from the more than one hundred interviews were collated into one document so that all of the answers to the above question were simply listed together under that question. Taking that list, the core group and consultants gleaned the themes listed above. They also compiled the answers to the "wish" questions that applied to the transfer of learning as listed below.

Wish Question. Ideas for how transfer of learnings could be promoted further and for follow-up activities were as follows:

- Build into the program more help with how to apply the learning back on the job; involve managers in preparing participants for the program and in helping them to apply their learnings afterward;

- Make a desktop tool available;

- Provide other educational forums and follow-up workshops on specific topics; and

- Use the model for scenario modeling/challenging assumptions.

The following provocative proposition (an activity that is part of the next core process, *create shared images for a preferred future*) was formulated from these themes and used to guide the next stage of work for the HR team.

Provocative Proposition (Topic I: Transfer of Learnings). When the simulation program is most effective, the workshop experiences are directly translated to the workplace. With an increased understanding of the research process and the roles of the complementary disciplines, scientists plan more effective research efforts and become more proactive in their interactions with other departments. More timely decisions are made and resources are more focused on critical activities.

Through effective teamwork, scientists leverage the skills and expertise of others to plan and implement research efforts more efficiently. With greater confidence in their own abilities to impact drug research, they more actively contribute to scientific discussions and initiate new research activities. Leadership is displayed through proactively developing staff and enabling them to participate in cross-functional initiatives.

Outcome. The HR team used this guidance for designing the next simulation training.

Additional Examples

Below are some additional examples of the kinds of themes (life-giving forces) that people identify from the interviews done in their organizations:

- Themes from interviews with a group of professional sociotechnical systems consultants on the interview query: "Tell me about a time when you felt most alive as a practitioner?"

  Working with people's core values;

  Putting integrity into practice;

  Recognizing the "footprints" of our work long after the steps have been taken;

  Being real and authentic; and

  Designing organizations that create more humanity than they consume.

- Themes from interviews with a group of line managers in a social service agency telling stories about their working lives:

  Doing things collectively;

  Removing barriers to unity and collaboration, for example, our current individually focused performance appraisal process;

  Ownership, support, commitment to common good;

  Commitment to appreciating each other;

  Getting together, sharing information, and socializing; and

  Transitioning from prosperity to austerity can lead to innovation and creativity.

- Themes from interviews with a group of line managers in a national bank:

  Being the best;

  Shared ownership;

  Cooperation;

  Integrity; and

  Empowering people.

There is no prescription for a theme. It is entirely up to the group to decide on the life-giving forces of its own system. Often a discussion of themes found in the interview data will lead to conversations that uncover other themes that the group believes are equally important. The challenge for the AI facilitator is to let the group go where it needs to go with as little constraining structure as it is possible to have and still maintain enough order to get the work done. There are no right or wrong answers here, only answers that have meaning to the group itself.

The Theme Identification Process

Now that we have provided some possible themes, we will share an exercise that you can use to help a group identify its own themes. The material is meant to be informational, not instructive, because there are as many ways to do this process as there are organizations and consultants working with them.

In a complex system intervention, the work preceding this step has likely been (1) to identify a core group from the organization; (2) to conduct an AI workshop that includes the theory of AI, the generic interview process, and the identification of topics for further study from the interview data; and (3) to conduct the interviews. A second workshop with the core group (as a minimum) and all of the people interviewed (as a maximum) is a good next step. The second workshop can focus on identifying themes (the subject of this third core process of AI) as well as on tasks that are covered in the next two chapters. For the purpose of illustration, we share a process that we often use.

Theme Identification Exercise

(*Note:* This process also works for topic identification from the generic interviews.)

Definition. A theme is an idea or concept about what is present in the stories that people report are the times of greatest excitement, creativity, and reward. For example, in many stories you may hear that when the topic covered by the question is at its best, people report "a feeling of success" or "clarity about purpose" or "fun and excitement." These phrases are "themes."

Instructions. First, choose a work group. Take your interview partner and join two other interview pairs, forming a group of six. (A group of as many as twelve works when the group is very large.)

Next, choose someone to keep time and someone to be the scribe.

Then each person (briefly) shares one or two of the best stories told by his or her interview partner. After hearing each other's stories, create a brainstormed list of the themes that were present in the stories—about high points, life-giving forces, ideas that "grabbed" you—ideas about what life is like when things are at their best. From your group's list, agree on and select three to five themes for your group.

Prepare a scattergram chart (see Figure 6.1) on a flip-chart sheet and write in your group's selected themes. Post your sheet close to other groups' sheets so that they can all be viewed easily. If you have several topics, for example, strong leadership, congenial work environment, etc., each covered by a separate question, use this exercise for each separate topic.

Figure 6.1. Scattergram Chart

THEMES	*'s
1.	
2.	
3.	
4.	
5.	

It is very important at every step of an AI process to be inclusive and expansive. When we deal with data, our default setting is to reduce—to place things in priority order or to sort and try to combine ideas. For this exercise, we recommend that three to five themes be selected per group, but make it clear to participants that you do not want them to be constrained by those numbers. More or less will also be fine. The idea is to capture those ideas that are most important to people. Once charts are posted, it is important not to give in to the inclination to put together similar themes or to combine charts in any way. Leave them exactly as they are. After the following steps, you can note the similar themes, which will serve to emphasize their importance.

Using the Scattergram Chart. Be prepared to answer any clarifying questions about the themes you have listed on the chart. Each person has [X] number of "dots." Working alone, decide the themes on the charts that are most important for you to be included in your dream of the future. You have five minutes to decide and place your dots on the chart. Use only one dot per theme.

(*Note:* Give each person three or four colored sticky dots. People can also use markers and make a certain number of check marks. The scattergram is more vivid if you use only one color.)

Making Sense of the Scattergram. What do you notice about the charts? What themes are most important to this group?

(*Note:* At this point the group will often notice similar themes and remark on that. Try to reinforce the idea that every theme on the wall is important to at least one group in the room. The scattergram provides a visual image of the whole group's energy for certain themes. It is important not to count or put numbers beside the clusters. We rarely put any order to the themes; this allows you to use the theme data during the next core process—sharing images of a preferred future.)

Once again, let us reinforce that the AI approach for identifying themes is different from the traditional approach. Within an AI context, something can be a theme (a life-giving force) even if it is mentioned in only *one* story. This is different from the traditional approach, governed by scientific ideas about statistical validity, for which something has to be mentioned a certain number of times before it can be called a theme.

Our focus in identifying life-giving forces uses a very *different but inclusive set of criteria. In AI, if just one person in one interview* identifies something that resonates with others in the system, then it is most likely that it is a life-giving force for that system. Of course, we also consider something a life-giving force if it is mentioned by several people. The process taps into the intuitive emotional abilities of the group members working with the data as they decide what, for them, is a life-giving force in the organization. If it resonates with members of the client system, and if people say, "Yes, I know just what she means!" then it is probably a good bet that this is a theme/life-giving force we should pay attention to. Bear in mind that this process, like much of AI, is organic and eminently dynamic. If something is missed or misinterpreted at one point, it will almost certainly be identified or restated in a clearer way at another point.

Expanding the Dialogue

Bearing in mind that AI is rooted in the theory that we create our future realities through our current conversations, the task of pulling themes from the interview data provides a marvelous opportunity to engage more people in conversations that focus on the things that give life to the organization. The group chosen to "mine" the data and select the themes can be any configuration that the AI consultant and the organization co-create. Typical choices include:

- The external or internal consultant to the process, and/or

- Members of the interview team, and/or

- Members of the senior guidance group (if there is one), and/or

- All or some significant subset of the all the people who were interviewed.

In the traditional model of OD consulting, the data is almost always collated and often analyzed by the consultant and fed back into the organization as a report or fed back to a working group for action planning. Remembering the theory that the observer always impacts and changes that which is observed, it follows that in an AI process the consultant would never be the one to analyze the data. Given that clients are used to and comfortable with certain types of processes, it may be a bit of a stretch to talk yourself out of the job of analyzing the data. We *strongly* recommend that you avoid analysis if at all possible because you will, by that act, have theoretically moved yourself and the system out of an AI process. The minimum number of participants in mining the data is the original core group. From there, add as many people as the client will allow. Working from the belief that the future is created through dialogue, it makes a great deal of sense to involve as many people as possible.

After the themes are identified, the organization is ready to move into the fourth stage of AI—*creating shared images for a preferred future.*

▶ CASE STUDY: AVON MEXICO

BY MARGE SCHILLER

Focus of the Appreciative Inquiry

Valuing gender diversity

Client Organization

Avon Mexico is among the most successful of the companies that make up Avon Products. Avon is an international direct-sales organization that serves the wants, needs, and aspirations of women around the world. Avon's vision statement is: "To be the company that best understands and satisfies the product, service, and self-fulfillment needs of women globally." Avon has been a leader in the cosmetics, skin, and hair care business. It also sells a variety of other services and merchandise by direct sales, mail order, and in retail stores. Thirty-four thousand people work as salaried employees for Avon in forty-six countries. Over 2.8 million salespeople worldwide work on commission. Avon Mexico has three thousand salaried employees in its Mexico City headquarters and a sales force of 250,000.

Client Objectives

The initial client was Avon International, a division of Avon Products located in the United States in New York City. The objective was to increase the number of senior women in the organization worldwide. Although Avon was often thought of as one of the best places for women to work, there were very few women executives and no female representation on the executive committee at Avon Mexico. The Appreciative Inquiry project described in this case study was intended to address the issue of gender equity in Avon Mexico and to be a pilot project for Avon globally.

What Was Done

This case was interesting because the consultants were hired and paid by the parent organization to serve a particular business unit. The project was analogous to a three-legged sack race: Avon International, Avon Mexico, and the consulting team were tied together at the ankle and trying to run together. If one group got too far away from the others, we would all trip and fall. Keeping all three organizations in sync was continuously challenging.

Here are the steps we took. At Avon Mexico we used the Four D Model to conduct the inquiry. Here is our roadmap.

Definition

The contracting developed a relationship with the clients and extended their understanding of Appreciative Inquiry. We began building the internal/external team with a mutual construction of the topics, the impetus for change, and the methods we could use. Later we worked together onsite to plan an upcoming AI workshop, define everyone's roles and responsibilities, consider logistics, and decide who would attend the upcoming workshop.

Discovery

The first of several two-day workshops introduced AI theory, practice, and philosophy to the people who were to conduct interviews and serve as the "pioneers" of AI. We became a learning team, developing the questions, practicing, and planning for the interviews. The internal/external team held a debriefing after the workshop. We shared our own experiences and stories, refined the interview protocol, and determined how we would manage the information that came back to us. The interviews brought best practices and compelling stories to light. We learned what gives vitality to the ways that men and women work together in Avon Mexico. The internal/external team came together again to build on what was working best and, once again, to modify the questions. We selected some of the most telling and inspirational stories from the conversations that had been held and began to construct models of exceptional practice to help us vision the ideal.

Dream

A report was written to capture the best stories and clarify the image of the organization at its very best. It presented a variety of organizational and relational possibilities. The key learnings were supported with story examples. It provided glimpses of the future based on the assumption that the ideal exists in what has and is happening already. The report articulated the best of what the interviewers found. The purpose of the report was to guide the organization to go beyond the actual data and provoke our thinking about what is possible. The next major event was a futures conference (sometimes called a summit). About one hundred of the people who did the interviews gathered together to validate and extend their collective images. The consensus around what was possible was a celebration and a clarification of collective positive energy around the topic: Men and women working together in teams.

Destination

The internal/external team produced a second report that presented the collective vision of the preferred future. It was clear and short. An internal advisory committee was formed and still continues to work. Although the words "Appreciative Inquiry" may have faded, the philosophy lives. As the director of human resources said, "This is not a program; it is a process." When we moved to the destination phase, the external consultants moved out. The client was clear how they could use what they had learned to enhance individual and organizational life. The capacity was built inside Avon Mexico because AI is in alignment with the mission, goals, and values of Avon Products.

Outcomes

- Avon Mexico's profit increased dramatically. The intervention helped a successful company become even more successful.

- Avon Mexico and Mujeres y Hombres Trabajando en Equipo (men and women working together in teams) was the winner of the Catalyst Award, given annually to a company for its policies and practices that benefit women in the corporation.

- The first woman officer was appointed to the executive committee within six months of the Appreciative Inquiry project.

- Four years after the initial intervention in 1996, the spirit of Appreciative Inquiry lives and thrives in this very successful company.

Learnings

- Appreciative Inquiry blends into the organization. It is like disappearing stitches. Appreciative Inquiry is now part of the way work gets done at Avon Mexico. I am not sure the words Appreciative Inquiry are still used, but I am sure that what the Mexicans called "the philosophia" remains.

- Because the consultants were U.S.-based English speakers, simultaneous translation of all presentations was required. This turned out to be an asset rather than a liability for two reasons: first, the consultants had to spend a good deal of time with the translators to be sure that they understood the concepts that were to be simultaneously translated. This meant that the clarity and care of communication was enhanced. Second, the resultant slowing down of the communication process and inclusion of examples to illustrate each point enhanced comprehension. People would ask for further explanation or an illustration to augment information. We went deeper because we went more slowly. This was in stark contrast to the "Yeah, sure" reaction that sometimes happens when people who speak the same language assume that they give words the same meaning.

· Mexico is a "relational" culture with a rich oral tradition. Stories are a major way of sharing and transferring information and meaning across the society. This made the Appreciative Inquiry culturally comfortable for everyone who was asked to elicit or to tell stories.

· The involvement of a powerful and thoughtful chief executive officer gave the work stability in an organization that is short-term driven because of a continuous cycle of sales drives and campaigns.

Contact

Marjorie Schiller, Ph.D.
49 Rockwood Road
Hingham, MA 02043
    (781) 749–4373
    e-mail: mrsentp@worldnet.att.com ◀

▶ CASE STUDY: DTE ENERGY SERVICES

BY MARLO DERKSEN AND TOM OSBORN

Focus of the Appreciative Inquiry

Creating a culture of choice

Client Organization

DTE Energy Services was established as a subsidiary of DTE Energy in 1994. Since its inception, the company has experienced steady growth in revenue, net income, and the number of employees. Currently, DTE Energy Services has eighty-five employees and $1.3 billion in assets. As an unregulated subsidiary of DTE Energy, DTE Energy Services offers its clients single-source financial management and technical services for energy projects. Its core business strategy is to build and operate energy projects for large industrial and institutional customers.

Client Objectives

Phase 1: Our involvement with this organization began in the summer of 1999, when we were contracted to facilitate a two-day team-building event for the executive management team. The objectives of this session were to facilitate an appreciation and understanding of different personality styles; increase the effectiveness of individual communication skills; and facilitate a dialogue around key business issues. Our interventions to address those objectives proved to be valuable to the participants; however, both the president and the human resource manager of DTE Energy Services recognized that "something more was needed" to develop a culture that they described as "inclusive, providing the opportunity for shared ownership, and driving change at all levels of the organization." It was at this time that we recommended that the entire organization engage in the AI process with the intent of creating the type of culture that they envisioned and that would support the continued success of DTE Energy Services.

Phase 2: The primary objective of the AI process was to "create a culture of choice"—embedding AI in DTE Energy Services as an approach to create the desired culture, rather than just allowing the organization's culture to evolve on its own.

What Was Done

Prior to engaging DTE Energy Services in the AI process, we met with the human resource manager. We introduced her to the AI methodology and secured her support for moving forward. The following outlines the process we presented and our rationale for using it.

1. Form an internal work group that would receive an orientation to AI and the necessary training that would allow core members to champion the process successfully. Members from this group would be responsible for conducting the interviews, reviewing the data collected from the stories told, selecting the topics for further exploration, and drafting the possibility statements that would serve as mini vision statements for the organization. We stressed the importance of selecting members for this team that represented a diverse cross section of the organization in terms of hierarchical position, functional responsibility, age, gender, and race.

2. Orient and train the internal work group in the AI methodology and interview process.

3. Conduct the first round of interviews. The intent of these interviews would be to solicit stories from members of the organization and use this data to select the topics for further exploration.

4. Meet as a group to share stories, review major themes from the data, select the topics that would be the basis for further exploration, and develop questions to collect additional data from organizational members.

5. Meet as a group to review the additional data collected and develop possibility statements for each of the topics.

6. Host a larger group event involving all members of the organization to integrate the efforts of the internal work group, finalize the possibility statements, and design next steps that would close the gap between current reality and the ideal reality reflected in the wording of the provocative propositions.

As we explained the process, it became clearer to the HR manager that our relationship and roles as client and consultants would be different with the AI process. No longer would we be the experts in diagnosis, data collection, and intervention design. Members of the organization would now be trained and ultimately responsible for this part of the process. It was our hope that this experience would increase the organization's capacity for ongoing change and continuous renewal.

Outcomes

When we first met with the internal work group that had been formed to champion the AI process, we were encouraged by the diversity of the group. We followed the outlined plan with good results at each step. As we prepared for the final one-day session with the whole system, we asked members of the internal work group for comments on their best experiences during their involvement with AI. Here are a few of their responses.

- "The interviews. I was able to create a dialogue with someone I normally wouldn't."

- "To have a conversation with someone I didn't know well, build rapport, and establish a long-term relationship with him."

- "The ease with which people came forward with positive stories. I was surprised."

- "I'm new here. The AI process allowed me to interact and educate myself in the company's history."

- "To collect all this data, hear all the positive feedback, and come up with five topics that are meaningful."

- "I learned a lot. I have in-depth knowledge about what is really happening here."

- "I enjoyed doing something different . . . out of my element, with a commitment to the process from leadership."

- "AI is out of the norm. It was fun to be so involved in the investigation and develop something for our future growth."

- "I'm new, so being involved with this group was the best experience I had. I valued the trust that senior management had in us. I thought our involvement and opinions really mattered."

Learnings

The experience of engaging DTE ES in AI provided us, as consultants, with some valuable learning and re-learning. These lessons can be summarized as follows.

1. The role of consultant changes according to the situation and the stage of client engagement. It was our experience that during the initial stages of engagement, the client was dependent on us to educate, facilitate, and coach them in AI. As the engagement unfolded, the client became counter-dependent and then inter-dependent in their relationship with us as they became more comfortable with AI and the outcomes that they desired for themselves. At this point, our role shifted to one of advisor and cheerleader.

2. With AI, organization change begins with a change in the type of conversations that people in the organization have with one another. Rather than view AI as a change event from one state to another, it can be better described as an invitation for organization members to engage continuously in inquiry with one another—seeking to find what is generative, joyful, and life-giving in the organization and how the organization can do more of those things. As organization members change the type of information they collect about the organization, they change their definition of the organization. In this way, the change that occurs is subtle yet profound.

3. It is important to trust that AI is an iterative and emergent process of change. The question asked most frequently from members of the internal work group was: "Where are we going with this?" It is more apparent to us that there is no tangible destination with AI. However, there are certain milestones that can be perceived as tangible outcomes of AI. An example of this is the creation of provocative propositions. More importantly, it is the conversations and the stories that are told that create momentum for the organization's desired future.

4. The peak experience that people describe in their stories is a powerful and energizing force. It was our observation that as people shared their stories with one another, they became energized and motivated to create a future that contained those factors that were present during their peak experiences. The image of something better is a powerful motivator in human systems.

5. Storytelling is a powerful pathway to creating images and building relationships between people. As such, it is important to reinforce

the notion of storytelling during the early stages of the AI engage-ment. Consistent with this is providing individuals with the neces-sary interview skills to listen and support others actively in their storytelling. As people engaged in their storytelling, the richness of their stories created a shared image for the storyteller and the lis-tener. Stories that were rich in detail created a clear image for oth-ers. In addition, as people engaged in storytelling, relationships were formulated and strengthened.

Postscript

Approximately four months after our engagement with DTE Energy Ser-vices, the president of the company, Barry Markowitz, was a participant in a Leadership Development Series that we were facilitating. At the break he walked over and gave us two gifts. The first was the knowledge that a group of employees had volunteered to champion initiatives to "keep AI alive" within the organization. This included the creation of an internal web page entitled "Main Street" that employees were using to share positive stories with one another. The second gift was a coffee mug with the fol-lowing words inscribed: "Appreciative Inquiry—Value the Best of What Is, Envision What Might Be, Dialogue What Should Be, Innovate What Will Be." To us, the greatest gift of all was knowing that these gifts represented the symbols of change within the organization.

Contact

Marlo Derksen
(303) 570–6020
e-mail: Marlo@osbornderksen.com

Tom Osborn
(303) 832–3343
e-mail: Tom@osbornderksen.com

Client Contact

Sharon Czekala
(734) 913–2971
e-mail: Czekals@dtees.com ◀

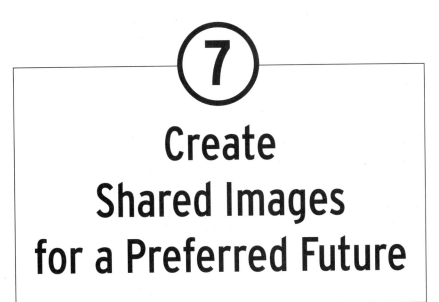

Create
Shared Images
for a Preferred Future

"One of the basic theorems of the theory of image is that it is the image which in fact determines what might be called the current behavior of any organization. The image acts as a field. The behavior consists in gravitating toward the most highly valued part of the field."

Kenneth Boulding, The Image

"A vivid imagination compels the whole body to obey it."

Aristotle

THE WORK OF THIS FOURTH CORE PROCESS of AI is to engage as many organization members as possible in co-creating a shared image or vision of a preferred future. The creation of this future image comes directly from the stories of special moments and the resultant themes or life-giving forces identified in the third core process. The invitation is to imagine an organization in which those special moments of exceptional vitality found in the stories become the norm rather than the exception.

The creation of the shared image of the preferred future often progresses through two stages: (1) articulation of the dream for the organization by creating a visual image and a written image of the most desired future for the organization as a whole and (2) generation and description of an organization structure (social architecture) that helps make the desired future a reality.

Articulating the Dream

The first stage of this process, creating the image of the most desired future for the organization, is the time for dialogue about the following questions:

- What is the world calling for our organization to be?
- What are the most enlivening and exciting possibilities for our organization?
- What is the inspiration that is supporting our organization?

To envision an organization's future collectively based on its successful past is to weave the web of meaning that endures—continuity, novelty, and transition. To engage in dreaming and envisioning is to invite organization stakeholders to go beyond what they thought was possible. It is a time for them to push the creative edges of possibility and to wonder about their organization's greatest potential. This is the time when the organization's stakeholders engage in "possibility conversations" about the organization's position, its potential, its calling, and the unique contribution it can make to global well-being.

It is this connection between past and future that makes Appreciative Inquiry different from other visioning or planning methodologies. As images of the future emerge out of grounded examples from its positive past, compelling possibilities emerge precisely because they are based on extraordinary moments from the organization's history. These stories of unique and joyful moments are used like an artist's paintbrush to create a vibrant image of the future.

In more traditional approaches to futuring, there would be an attempt at this point to reconcile differences or find common ground among the dreams of the future. Appreciative Inquiry, however, is guided not by the reductionist models of the old paradigm but by the constructionist principle and the heliotropic hypothesis. The constructionist principle holds that it is through our conversations that we create the images and frameworks that will guide the actions that create our future. The image of an organization, held in mind and conversation, both drives and limits its activities. To expand, enhance, or change an organization, its image must be reconstructed through conversations among key stakeholders. The heliotropic hypothesis suggests that people and organizations, like plants, will move in the direction of that which is most life-giving.

This first stage of articulating the dream usually focuses on descriptions of the organization's culture, how people are relating to one another, and the overall feel of the organization. The "product" of this stage is a set of expressions or visual images (songs, skits, collages, etc.) that describe the larger vision for the organization and a written statement, called a "provocative proposition" or, if that term seems too risky, a "possibility statement" that describes this macro image/vision. Begin with the dream of a shared future.

Facilitating the Creation of Shared Images

Following are two examples of ways that groups can create shared images of the future. Both of these are tested, although this is also a good point in the process to be as creative as you like!

Sample for a Guided-Image Exercise. One process that can be done in a limited amount of time is a guided imagery exercise. Someone, a facilitator or volunteer from the group, reads the following directions, or creates his or her own for the group. Turning down the lights is a good idea if you're comfortable with doing that. Pause a bit between sentences to give participants time to imagine.

"Get comfortable, close your eyes if you like, and bring one of the interview topics we have chosen into your mind. Imagine that that topic has been implemented fully in your everyday life and work. Imagine that it is your first day back at work and you are excited because you know that you'll find a workplace that has more of that topic present. Wander around your workplace. As you meet people in the course of the day, what pictures emerge that are life-giving and energizing? What are you feeling? What are people doing differently? As you head home from this day, what is life like and how has it changed? What conversations do you have with those at home? What do you tell them about the changes at work? Congratulate yourself for being a part of such a healthy and meaningful change in your work and in your life. Open your eyes and return to this room at your own speed. When ready, share a few words describing your experience."

Sample for a Dream Exercise. If you have more time, we highly recommend a process for creating visual images of the desired future. The following exercise has been especially rich for many of our clients. This is done at tables of six or more. Often the same interview pairs that identified themes will continue as a work group through the whole process. On the other hand, if one goal of the workshop is for people to meet a wider range of people, then form new groups. This exercise also can be done with simple chart paper and markers—lots of colors are nice—or with more imaginative materials for creating pictures and other visuals. It depends somewhat on the budget. When we use lots of materials, we either have packets for each table or a resource table with everything on it. We've had several hundred people do this in groups of about sixteen in about thirty minutes. The amazing thing to us is the kind of attention they pay to each other's pictures and visuals, even when there are twenty or more presentations! The energy in the room by this time is electric. Use the following instructions:

- Introduce yourselves to each other: your name and your work.

- Review the final list of themes from the scattergram exercise and ask for clarity as needed.

- Discuss what the final themes that emerged mean to those at your table.

- Create a picture on chart paper of what this organization would look like if all these themes were at their best. Be prepared to post your picture by [time] and explain it to the large group.

Creating a Macro Provocative Proposition to Describe the Dream

Once the group has created an image, either through dialogue or through pictures, their task is to write a statement that puts their vision into words poetically (see pages 138–142 for instructions on writing provocative propositions).

An example of the macro vision as described in a provocative proposition written by an international accounting firm follows:

"Our company is poised for a positive future because partners at all regions share a basic common vision in relation to the firm's core missions, intent, and direction. It is an exciting, challenging, and meaningful direction that helps give all partners a feeling of significance, purpose, pride, and unity.

The firm uses whatever time and resources are needed to bring everyone on board and thus continuously cultivates 'the thrill of having a one-firm feeling,' of being a valued member of one outstanding national partnership."

And another example from a large manufacturer of automotive parts states:

"We have created an organization where everyone experiences themselves as owners of the business—where everyone at all levels feels the organization is theirs to improve, change, and help become what it can potentially become. The organization recognizes there is a big difference between owners and hired hands. Ownership at our company happens in three ways: (1) on an economic level it happens when everyone is a shareholder and shares in the profit; (2) on a psychological level it happens because people are authentically involved; and (3) on a business level it happens when the 'big picture' purpose is shared by all, and all take part at the strategic level of business planning."

Fitting the Social Architecture to the Dream/Vision

The next stage of this core process involves generating and describing an organization structure (social architecture) that will enable the dream to become reality. This stage is a transition from free-flowing dreams about the future to interpreting those dreams and making a series of statements (provocative propositions)—guidelines for how the various elements of the sociotechnical architecture would function. These more specific provocative propositions represent a proposal by the organization to itself for how aspects of the dream would manifest themselves.

The "socio" or social system components of the organizational architecture include:

- The set of roles/jobs/relationships;
- The organizational structures and the management systems/policies; and
- The governing beliefs and assumptions that exist to support the core work of the organization.

The "technical" system components of the organizational architecture include:

- The business processes that transform inputs into outputs; and
- The technology used in those processes.

Questions at this stage are about what the structure and the processes of the organization will be, the kind of leadership structure needed, and the preferred behavior of the leaders as they do their work. What is the organization's strategy and how is it formulated and carried out? What are all of the structural elements needed?

Having reached agreement on the innovations desired in both the social and technical components and how they will function in relationship to one another and to the organization as a whole, the task of the group is to articulate those decisions in a more detailed set of provocative propositions. These statements make explicit the desired qualities and behaviors that will enable each part of the organization to function in a way that moves it toward the higher level provocative propositions articulated in the macro visions of the dream stage.

This creation of provocative propositions for the social and technical architecture of the organization ensures that everything reflects and is responsive to the dream. Both the dream and the design stages of AI involve the collective construction of positive images of the future in successive levels of clarity and translation. In practice, the two steps often happen in conjunction with each other.

Writing Provocative Propositions

We like the adjective "provocative" because a key criterion for these statements is that they elicit an "Oh, wow!" response, that is, the proposition stretches, challenges, or interrupts the status quo. Some examples of provocative propositions for the sociotechnical architecture of the organization are shown below:

Performance Appraisal. "Our organization acts on its value for high levels of trust and the belief that people are committed to high levels of personal accountability by using an appreciative performance appraisal process that focuses on employee competence and exemplary service to the organization."

Environment. "Our organization has an environment that attends to the physical, mental, and spiritual health of employees. Equipment for physical workouts and for swimming is available to all. The cafeteria offers healthy food and a pleasant atmosphere. Employees are given 'mental health' days off along with the usual time for sick leave."

Technology. "Our organization has the most efficient and user friendly technology available. Telephones, computers, copy machines, fax facilities, and so on are all available to every employee who needs access. Training is provided so that we make maximum use of our company's investment. Technology makes our work easier!"

David Cooperrider, in an e-mail to the AI listserv, offers the following thoughts on provocative propositions and how they guide the redesign of the organization:

"What is becoming increasingly clear to me is that if people do great work with [the processes of inquiry and dreaming], then rarely, if ever, do the older command and control structures of eras past serve the organization. The new dreams always seem to have outgrown the structures and systems. If we, on an ongoing basis, start sharing propositions emerging in our work, we might begin seeing patterns and connections, images of post bureaucratic forms where the future is brilliantly interwoven into the texture of the mosaic of all our inquiries.

"In my experience, which is curious to me, I have never seen people create propositions about creating more hierarchy, more command and control, more inequality, more degradation of the environment, more socially irresponsible business practices, etc. Indeed the propositions, as I've seen them written, have always moved in a direction of more equality, more self-organization, more social consciousness in terms of business practices, and the breakdown of arbitrary barriers between groups and functions. I have wondered . . .why?

"By provocative propositions (propositions that stretch beyond the status quo) we mean statements of fundamental belief and aspiration about human organizing—that body of belief of how we want to be related to one another and the ways we want to pursue our dreams. For example, every human organization must deal with questions and beliefs about power, money and distribution of resources, questions of information freedom, learning, decision making, etc. Too often we skirt these 'tougher' issues, like the sharing and distribution of resources or images of ideal power relations—and if and when we do that, then AI runs the risk of being co-opted and tremendously watered down as an approach to organization re-construction and co-construction.

"So [in this stage] of AI, we need to deal with the hard issues that are far too frequently not dealt with in OD work. Too often there are taboo areas. When we described AI to Nutrimental Foods in Brazil, for example, we asked the people bringing us in, right off the bat, if there was anything sacred about any organizational arrangement or structure that could not be opened up to all people for dreaming and designing. The first response was, 'No, everything is open to re-conceptualization.' We said, 'OK, now suppose in the 700 person meeting, people write propositions about sharing the wealth of the company? What if, in the exploration of their fundamental or constitution-like beliefs, the people articulate a vision of co-ownership and fair and equitable distribution of profits?'

"Now perhaps the managers bringing us in would balk? No, they did not. In fact they said, without hesitation, 'We are committed to creating the future together, and opening everything to inquiry and the best imagination we have.' Obviously not every leadership group would say this! It is the first project, I am honestly almost ashamed to say, that I have ever gone to this kind of depth with. But the lessons are affecting everything else I'm doing now in my work. I really feel we are at the very beginning of our learning sometimes, and its great!"

Our experience suggests that once a group has used its collective right brain to create an image of its preferred future using the visual processes described above, the translation of that image into a written provocative proposition is much faster and smoother. So we generally work with the group that created the visual to write the provocative propositions. We often use the material below, which includes a task statement for the group and an explanation of what a provocative proposition is and how to write one.

Instructions for Writing Provocative Propositions

Note: The opening statement if you are assigning specific topics or themes to the group would always end with "when leadership [or technology or the environment, etc.] is at its best."

- As a group, discuss your dream picture and decide how you will put it in writing. You will be creating a provocative proposition that describes what the organization would look and feel like when all of the chosen themes are *at their best.*

- Write your statement in *large* print on one to two chart pages. Be prepared to make a one-minute presentation to the large group to share your statement.

If there are a lot of presentation groups, we often have them present their picture and statement at the same time. Use the material in Exhibit 7.1 as a handout for your group.

Exhibit 7.1. Constructing Provocative Possibility Statements

A provocative proposition is a statement that bridges the best of "what is" with your own speculation or intuition of "what might be." It stretches the status quo, challenges common assumptions or routines, and helps suggest real possibilities that represent a desired image for the organization and its people.

By creating provocative propositions that make clear the shared visions for the organization's future, there is created a beacon, a set of unique statements that paint a picture of the group's vision of the organization's most desired future. This collection of possibility statements provides the clear direction for all of the organization's activities. Just as a stream always follows the call of the ocean, the organization will move toward its highest and most imaginative visions for the future.

Criteria for Good Provocative Propositions
(Positive Images of the Ideal Organization)

1. Is it *provocative:* Does it stretch, challenge, or interrupt the status quo?

2. Is it *grounded:* Are there examples that illustrate the ideal as a real possibility?

3. Is it *desired:* If it could be fully actualized, would the organization want it? Do you want it as a preferred future?

4. Is it stated in *affirmative* and bold terms?

5. Does it provide *guidance* for the organization's future as a whole?

5. Does it *expand* the zone of possible change and development?

7. Is it a *high involvement* process?

8. Is it used to stimulate intergenerational organizational *learning*?

Note: While the groups are writing, comments and coaching from you are in order. It is often very hard for a group to write in the active voice. Look for "waffle" words such as "aims to," "will do," "aspire to," etc. If the provocative propositions are dull and ordinary, it is a good idea to ask participants to write a few "off the wall" ones to be shared later. Also, consider showing them a few diverse examples, such as the ones below:

Guided by the Fire of Our Stories:

(Listen)   *(Listen)*

We hold hope lightly.

(Trust)   *(Trust)*

We go forward.

(Courage)   *(Courage)*

Spreading sparks of stories giving strength.

Opening the darkness.

*   *   *

Walking into our facilities you can feel the energy.

- We build on one another's strengths.
- We respond to the unpredictable with balance and passion.
- We nurture each other with challenge and understanding.
- We step out of defined roles to pursue the extraordinary.
- We seek places never imagined possible.

We build for the future while living in the present and being grounded in the past.

*   *   *

WE, the people of this organization, consistently find, express, and share

PASSION for our work.

WE are creative!

WE are appreciated!

WE make a difference!

Our PASSION invigorates every cell within us!

WE ARE AN EXCITING PLACE TO BE!

*   *   *

Finally, we refer you to the example of an AI strategic planning process, the ABC Model for Organization Design and Strategic Planning in Chapter 8, to see the application of provocative propositions to the design elements of the organization more fully.

The fourth core process can be considered complete when:

- An expression of the organization's dream for the future has been created;

- A series of provocative propositions for elements of the sociotechnical architecture have been developed; and

- There is widespread understanding and ownership of both these elements.

As with each of the five processes of AI, this process (creating shared images of a preferred future) flows into and, in practice, overlaps with the final core process (finding innovative ways to create that preferred future). The next chapter describes in more detail some of the ways in which an organization, having articulated provocative propositions for a new sociotechnical architecture, might engage its members in processes of participative design to flesh out those very same provocative propositions.

A question frequently posed by clients is, "How do we organize the inquiry process to engage large numbers of people across diverse geographies, times, and functions?" Our answer is to help each organization design a unique inquiry architecture—the structure of roles, relationships, and meetings needed to successfully bring Appreciative Inquiry to bear on their organizational processes. The following case story illustrates one company's unique inquiry architecture.

▶ CASE STUDY: BRITISH AIRWAYS NORTH AMERICA

BY DIANA WHITNEY

Focus of the Appreciative Inquiry
Whole system change

Client Organization
British Airways North America

Client Objectives
British Airways North America selected Appreciative Inquiry as a high participation process for enhancing "Excellence in Customer Service." Appreciative Inquiry was identified as a great follow on to their Pecos River Experience, an organization-wide effort that enabled all employees to participate in an experiential outdoor learning program. The employee pump of involvement had been primed. It was time to draw from the well and to put employee participation to work for the benefit of the British Airways' customer.

What Was Done
Appreciative Inquiry was introduced to a handful of executives via conference calls and meetings. They sensed merit in its positive, high participation approach to organization development, but they wanted to be certain it would "fly" at British Airways. To further introduce the concepts and practices of Appreciative Inquiry and to test its viability for BA, we conducted a two-day "core team" meeting. Forty people from all levels, locations, and aspects of the organization attended. The core team went through the process of selecting topics and drafting interview questions. At the end of two days, we asked two questions: "Shall we go forward with Appreciative Inquiry?" and "What must we do to ensure success?" By this time in the meeting, the answer to the first question was a unanimous yes. As a result, we had expanded from a small group of executives to an enthusiastic group of around forty people from throughout the company in North America.

The group listed management commitment and involvement of the entire workforce as two of its key factors for success. This led to some innovative thinking about how to best engage the entire workforce—some twelve hundred employees in twenty-two locations across the United States, Canada, and Bermuda—and how to ensure demonstrated management commitment. What follows is a brief description of the inquiry architecture designed to mobilize discovery throughout the organization, to enable data synthesis and sharing of best practices, and to foster the design of provocative propositions, principles, and appreciative practices of "Excellence in Customer Service."

A one-day management briefing was held, prior to which several core team members conducted interviews with their own managers using the draft interview guide. They explained to their managers what to expect when they attended the Appreciative Inquiry briefing. Already we had turned power relations upside down for many. During their one-day briefing, the managers heard about Appreciative Inquiry from the consultant, they heard about the British Airways process, and they heard from a subgroup of the core team who spoke about their enthusiasm for Appreciative Inquiry and the potential it held for British Airways.

During this meeting, the inquiry architecture was outlined and put in place. Each British Airways station selected an inquiry team made up of a management coach, an interview coordinator, and a group of interviewers. The goal of 100 percent interviews required that 10 percent of the workforce at each station serve as interviewers, conducting ten interviews each. Most stations decided on a self-selection process for the interviewers. Time frames were discussed and committed to—50 percent of the interviews to be completed within three months and the final 50 percent to be completed one month later.

Next Steps

After a four-month interviewing period, data synthesis meetings will be held in each of the stations. One month after the station meetings, an Appreciative Inquiry Summit will be conducted to share best practices, to dream and to design principles and appreciative practices of "Excellence in Customer Service." The inquiry teams from all the stations will attend. Best practices will be shared at weekly meetings, on the company e-mail system, and via a newsletter designed for the purpose, best practice stories will be collected and shared in a book.

At this time, it is imagined that Innovation Teams will be formed to work on projects identified during the Summit and that further Appreciative Inquiry will be organized around key success factors for the business.

Contact

Diana Whitney
Corporation for Positive Change
P.O. Box 3257
Taos, NM 87571
(505) 751–1231
e-mail: whitneydi@aol.com ◀

▶ CASE STUDY: STAR ISLAND CORPORATION

BY DAVID SANDERSON

Focus of the Appreciative Inquiry
Strategic planning for the whole system

Client Organization
The Star Island Corporation is a nonprofit hospitality organization whose mission is to "own and maintain Star Island . . . as a center for religious and educational conferences and programs consistent with the principles of the Unitarian-Universalist Association and the United Church of Christ." (Star Island is one of the Isles of Shoals, ten miles off the New Hampshire coast.) About twenty-five semi-autonomous conferences are held each summer on Star Island. The Corporation is limited by charter to three hundred members; the broader "Star Community" (conferees, staff, and membership) totals several thousand; thirteen people are on the board of directors.

Client Objectives
To update the corporate strategic plan and to obtain widespread, substantial involvement by including the Star Community in the process. The board named the process "Vision 2000."

What Was Done
After meeting and contracting around AI with the board, I designed and led a day-long meeting in November 1998 to which the three hundred corporation members were invited; about ninety attended. The day included ini-

tial discovery and design activities: the members interviewed one another and identified the life-giving qualities of Star, their values as participants in the Star Island experience, and their wishes for the future. They went on to select eight high-priority areas for further work, and in working groups they wrote "possibility propositions" about those areas and suggested possible strategies the board might pursue. (The summer of 1998 had been a bit rocky for Star Island, with a number of complaints among staff and conferees, and the board was anxious about this membership meeting. They were delighted with the results that AI brought.) Late in December, I met with about thirty-five college-age staff (called "Pelicans") at their annual reunion, and they engaged in the discovery phase and responded to the possibility propositions the membership had written.

The next step occurred in the 1999 conference season. I led a retreat in June in which the board (with nine others, including staff, Pelicans, and guests) reviewed the suggestions from the meetings held in 1998 with corporation members and Pelicans, identified external trends especially relevant to Star's future, and noted recent trends in fund raising and conference attendance (not strictly part of the AI process, but consistent with it). The major work of the retreat involved writing "visionary design statements" for six high-priority areas of Star's future.

The summer of 1999 was marked by an innovation for the Star Community. The board decided to invite people from every conference and every staff member to brief meetings to be held weekly throughout the season. I designed a two-hour meeting that board members led for each conference during the summer, and that I led for two groups of staff, Pelicans, and adults. Several hundred people directly contributed to fresh iterations of the discovery and design phases by interviewing each other, discovering the life-giving qualities of Star, and responding to the visionary design statements the board had written. The universal response to these meetings was participants' great pleasure at being included in the process in such a positive way.

In September 1999 the board held a second retreat, which began with reviewing of the conferees' and staff's suggestions from the summer. The major work was to move into delivery. The board revised the visionary design statements from June and then created strategies to follow in pursuing the vision. In a great burst of energy, the board, working as a single group, developed a set of strategies by which to pursue each of the six visionary design statements—all in about 3 1/2 hours one afternoon. I had never before seen a group sustain such extraordinary creativity over such a period.

The board completed the deliver phase in February 2000 after a small group of board members developed and proposed a set of action plans—both short- and long-term—for pursuing the vision. In March 2000, I led a review session for the corporation membership in which they responded to the completed plan and suggested a few minor changes to the board. At the corporation's annual meeting in April 2000, members ratified the complete plan, making it the formal guiding document for the next seven years.

Outcomes

- The board has updated its strategic plan with a vision around six areas for special attention and work in the next seven years. As the president of the board puts it, he has "a strong feeling of power, quality, and utility in the work."

- The board has significantly improved its relationship with the broad Star Community, especially with the staff and conferees, by demonstrating its interest in collaboration, its ability to involve others and listen, and its distinctly appreciative stance.

- A subtle cultural change has been taking place throughout the process and continues to take place across the Star Community, expressed and demonstrated in the board's visionary design statement titled "Right Relationships." The change is in the element of governance, and through the planning process the board has already gone a long way to establish new norms of collaboration and participation. Actually, Star Island's deepest values point to such norms, and the great work of this board has been to find a way to raise up those values in fresh ways and embody them in its own practice.

Learnings

- AI was perfect for this situation—conflicted by some outspoken, disgruntled members who had written long public letters of complaint—because it tapped into the deeply felt passion people have for their experience on Star Island and allowed that to surface in productive ways.

- How important it is not to rush the process, taking care to include a wide variety of people when it is most convenient for them.

- The importance of working with a small group of board members (I worked with a group of three) on all aspects of the process, including meeting design, logistics, etc., even though it is immensely time-consuming.

- The importance of having a fair-sized group of five or six (or more) write visionary design statements. (In the June retreat, two or three people worked on some of the statements and produced statements that needed a lot of revision by others in the group.)

- The usefulness of adding an identification of relevant external trends to the AI process (I took this from future search methodology rather than using the traditional "threats and opportunities" format); in this case, such trends led directly to two visionary design statements.

Contact

David Sanderson, Ph.D.
Eagle Point Consulting
107 Eagle Point Road
Lamoine, ME 04605
(207) 667–1213
e-mail: Dsand@downeast.net
www.eaglepointconsulting.com

Client Contact

Star Island Corporation
10 Vaughn Mall, Suite 8, Worth Place
Portsmouth, NH 03801
(603) 430–6272
office@starisland.org
www.starisland.org ◀

Find Innovative Ways to Create that Preferred Future

"Organizational transformation is much more than the cumulative critical mass of personal transformation. It requires macro level changes in the very fabric of organizing—the social architecture."

Diana Whitney, AI listserv, 1999

"When organizations are designed to allow members to find meaning, dignity, and community in their day-to-day lives, the benefits to society, the company, and the individuals are enormous. Unless we are engaged in helping people to redesign their sociotechnical architecture in alignment with their dream, I think we are missing a great opportunity and may even be derelict in our responsibility."

Bernard J. Mohr, AI listserv, 1999

THIS FINAL PROCESS ENGAGES (as always) as many members of the organization as possible in bringing to life on a daily and local basis the new images of the future—both the overall visions of the dream stage and the more specific provocative propositions of the architectural redesign stage. It is a time of continuous learning, adjustment, and improvisation. The momentum and potential for innovation is extremely high by this stage of the overall AI process.

For example, one organization transformed its department of *evaluation* studies to *valuation* studies, dropping the "e" and with it the accumulated negative connotations that have attached themselves to the word. Others have transformed almost every possible function of an organization: focus group methods, surveys, performance appraisal systems, leadership training programs, diversity initiatives, strategic planning, client development, quality management, business process redesign, technology implementation, union management and employee relations, as well as authority and responsibility structures, roles and information systems, changing deficit processes to appreciative ones. These changes inevitably create higher levels of excitement, enthusiasm for the work, and commitment from the people involved.

There are many stories about what happens in this core process of appreciative inquiry. One thing is for certain—and no doubt quite clear by now—there is no one way to carry this forward. There exist many good participative methods for organization design that with some adaptation can be modified to fit an appreciative orientation. Included among these methods for translating the provocative propositions into reality are:

- The Conference Method (Axelrod, 1999)
- Participative Design Workshop (Emery, 1993)
- Open Space (Owens, 1992)
- Whole System Design (Mohr & Levine, 1998)
- The ABC Model (Watkins & Cooperrider, 2000)

The key to sustaining the momentum is to build an "appreciative eye" into all the organization's systems, procedures, and ways of working. Because AI is of the new paradigm, each time you work with it will be different. It has the power of being totally unique to any group that chooses to take this route to organization transformation and renewal.

This core process is ongoing. In the best case, it is full of continuing dialogue; revisited and updated discussions and provocative propositions; additional interviewing sessions, especially with new members of the organization; and a high level of innovation and continued learning. Perhaps the most important learning that comes from this continuous process is about what it means to create an organization that is socially constructed through poetic processes in a positive frame that makes full use of people's anticipatory images and of the realization that inquiry *is* change!

Organization Design Processes

Moving from a powerful image of the preferred future to an organization that lives and breathes the essence of the provocative propositions is a process that takes many forms. The challenge is to co-create with the client a process of organization redesign, unique to the organization's culture, that avoids the trap of a mechanistic, problem-solving world view.

Two very different approaches to this challenge are (1) the "Individual Action Approach" and (2) the "Whole System Design Approach." They can be described briefly as follows.

The Individual Action Approach

In this approach (also known as the "Requests, Offer, and Commitments Approach"), participants are asked to think about the parts of the dream that they want to bring to life. Each participant is given the opportunity to state publicly a simple commitment, make an offer, or articulate a request.

Simple commitments describe actions that can be easily taken, typically within one to two weeks, and are within the existing authority and resources available to the person making the commitment.

Offers are a form of "gift." For example, a participant may "offer" access to a database he or she controls. Or someone may "offer" financial assistance to get a project started. An offer may be made in response to a request for collaboration. Offers can come in any shape or form—the more specific the better.

Requests are focused on what one person or group needs from another person or group. For example, "The western region call center requests a meeting with the chief information officer to explore upgrading of our e-mail system."

Although particularly appropriate to situations where the focus is on team or small unit development, this approach can be effectively combined with the more systemic Whole System Design approach described below.

The Whole System Design Approach

In this approach, the core group or sponsor team begins by choosing either (1) to select from among the major existing models of organization architecture, for example, the Open Socio-Technical Systems framework (van Eijnatten, 1993), the

McKinsey 7S framework (Waterman, 1982), the Weisbord 6-Box framework (Weisbord, 1978), the Galbraith Star framework (Galbraith, 1995), The Nadler/Tushman Congruence framework (Nadler & Tushman, 1988), etc., or (2) create from scratch its own framework/model of the key elements the group sees as contributing to organizational functioning. (See pages 154 through 167 for a process created by Watkins and Cooperrider that enables organizations to create a customized framework appropriate to their own needs.) Creating their own framework has at least two advantages: (1) The group has in-depth dialogue about how they want their own organization to be organized and (2) the group knows clearly what each element of the design means. This creation process avoids the inevitable debates that result when groups work with someone else's model and have no agreed understanding of what the elements mean.

Further, the second approach is more organic and in keeping with the spirit of AI.

Once group members have identified within these frameworks the key elements, such as information systems, relations with the board of directors, and work flows, they then write provocative propositions about them as described in the second part of the image-creating process in the previous chapter. This is somewhat like creating a set of design principles that are then used to guide the more detailed design and implementation of a particular element. The process of requests, offers, and commitments can then be used to move these provocative propositions/design principles forward.

Watkins and Cooperrider's ABC Inquiry Model

This organizational inquiry model is designed to inquire into the current reality of an organization and to plan its future by focusing on the successes and the life-giving forces that support the work and the people. Once those forces are located and articulated, the organization can move to affirm, expand, and increase those success factors as they imagine the organization's future. This is a departure from the traditional model of organizational diagnosis that searches for the problems and shortcomings of the organization for the purpose of "fixing" it.

The model, shown in Figure 8.1, consists of three rings. When this model is used, the organization begins by building the three rings to fit its own structure and then applies the ABC process to the items in the rings. Following are details of the model.

Figure 8.1. Model for Organization Inquiry

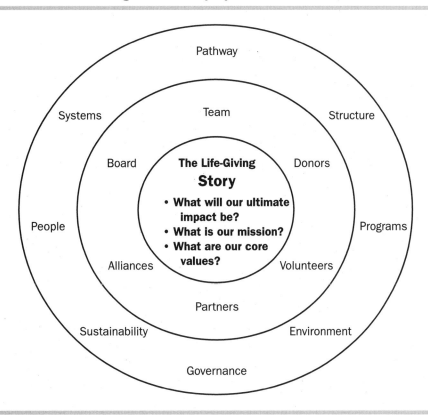

Assumptions of the Inquiry Model

The model is built on several assumptions. The first assumption (represented by the innermost ring of the model) is that the central organizing principles of organizations are the clarity about the ultimate *impact* of the work, the *core values* that are shared, and a common *mission* of a group of people who work together to meet the mission and goals of the organization. These critical ingredients provide the foundation for the organization. Without clarity and consensus on these ingredients, no amount of organizational excellence related to task and management will ensure survival. Conversely, organizations with clarity on the impact they want to make, shared understanding of their core values, and agreement on their mission can survive a great deal of imperfection and ambiguity in their organizational forms. Therefore, the premier task of every organizational member is to carry on a continuous dialogue making meaning of their work.

The second assumption (represented by the second ring) is that organizations are *networks.* What is usually called the "organization," the staff members who work in the headquarters office and in other office locations, are called the *team* and are seen as the coordinating body for the *network organization.* The organization is envisioned as a network of key stakeholders who gather around the desired *impact, values,* and *mission* to accomplish tasks that lead to social transformation. The *network organization* of a nonprofit might include the *team;* a *board; donors; partners; alliances;* and, frequently, *volunteers.* Definitions of these terms are given below. However, each organization will have a unique set of actors in this circle. This model is only one possible configuration.

Team	The core staff of the headquarters and field offices who work together collaboratively and whose central task is to provide leadership and to coordinate and sustain the work and the relationships of the organization.
Board	The group whose task is to set policy, provide guidance, and ensure that the organization has the resources it needs to sustain itself.
Donors	Those who supply the resources and whose tasks encompass providing financial resources and programmatic guidance.
Partners	Multiple groups of clients/recipients of services who are responsible for collaborating in all planning and implementation of joint programs.
Volunteers	Groups and individuals who contribute time and skills to the organization.
Alliances	Other institutions/entities who join in the work of the organization.

The third assumption (represented by the third ring) is that in addition to the core of the organization and the leadership network, there are key areas for inquiry on the ways the organization organizes its work. Inquiry into these areas enables groups to discover the life-giving forces, success stories, and generative spirit of their organizations. In this model, areas for inquiry include *pathway, governance, systems, structure, people, programs, sustainability,* and *environment.* These terms are defined as follows:

Pathway	The guiding principles, strategy, plans, and tactics for achieving the mission.
Governance	How we organize, govern, and manage ourselves; how we make decisions; how we celebrate our achievements; how our governance processes align with our values and our theory of development.
Systems	The systems and technologies that we use to manage ourselves, to communicate with each other, and to "conference" with the world.
Structure	The way we organize our work and manage our tasks.
People	The well-being, fair treatment, and empowerment of our staff team, partners, board members, alliance, and volunteers; the placement of our people in the right positions to make our work flow smoothly; how we value our diversity and celebrate our differences as organizational assets; how we relate to one another; how our rhetoric about valuing people aligns with our organizational behavior.
Programs	Our development paradigm and the theories that underlie our methods of work; the nature of our work and how it aligns with our vision and values; our programming process.
Sustainability	How we guarantee the people and resources to assure the health and survival of all of our organizational entities; how we steadily increase our capacity; how we function as a lifelong learning organization committed to continuous improvement.
Environment	Our understanding of what is going on in the world that impacts our work and our view of the organizational culture and norms that create our work environment.

How to Use the Inquiry Model

For each of the elements in (1) the core circle, (2) the network organization circle, and (3) the organization of work circle, you will use the ABCs:

A = Appreciative understanding of your organization

B = Benchmarked understanding of other organizations

C = Creation of "provocative propositions" to produce an image of your organization's future

Appreciative Understanding of Your Organization

The process begins with an inquiry into your own organization that will provide a clear picture of your organization's strengths, competencies, and life-giving forces. Using this approach, you look for those moments when your organization is at its very best. Members of your staff can interview each other in search of organizational excellence.

Questions are created for each item in each circle, for example: "Tell me a story about the best board of directors you ever worked with" or "Tell me about the best experience you ever had with a human resource department" (or some element of the department, such as health coverage; training courses, etc.). In other words, you will create questions about any and all processes, people, tasks, etc., that are included in your circle model.

Benchmarked Understanding of Other Organizations

After you have initiated the process in your own organization, you may want to seek out and understand the best practices of other organizations. This is best done as a reciprocal process in which you also share your best practices. Such mutual sharing gives both organizations a way to inform their own practices and to adapt and incorporate some ideas that can inspire innovation and improvement.

Often organizations seek out similar groups to benchmark, but there can be rich learning and exchange between even the most diverse organizations. Negotiations with potential benchmarking partners should include the parameters of the exchange and agreement on questions to be asked. Sample questions could include the following:

1. What is the most exciting and successful time you have had working with your organization? Describe for me what made it so exciting. Are there processes from that event/time that you have incorporated into your work here? Tell me about them?

2. If you had to identify the one best thing your company does when it is at its most competent, what would that be? Tell me about it. How does it work?

3. What do you value most about working for this organization?

These questions are intended as examples only. You will construct questions appropriate to the study that you want to do, many of which will focus on specific tasks: "Describe for me your organization's most innovative ways of managing communications with all parts of the system."

Creation of Provocative Propositions to Image Your Organization's Future

After you have gathered information from your own organization and have benchmarked several other organizations, it is time to make sense of that information. This process can be carried out at every level of the organization with any mix of staff and stakeholders. The process includes sharing the information and stories gathered from the appreciative inquiry of your own organization and the best practices gathered from others. This sharing is often done as a dialogue with a written report that captures the highlights.

Using this document that highlights findings, the group moves to articulate the most exciting possible future for the organization that incorporates the best that exists within, plus new and exciting practices discovered from without. Provocative propositions articulate visions for each facet of the organization and guide planning and operations in the future.

While the ABC process can be used to study every facet of an organization, at the overview level, it provides a framework for:

- The organization itself, conceived of as a network of key stakeholders that make up the decision making and operating body for achieving the mission.

- The various functions and guiding principles of the organization: impact, values, mission, pathway, environment, governance, people, programming, systems, sustainability, etc.

And this articulated framework provides a starting point for creating the dreams and images (provocative propositions) that guide the initial steps for realigning the organization's social architecture.

Finally, it is essential that some other interactive process be embedded in the organization as an ongoing dialogue, continually appreciating, reframing, and sharing the life of the people and the meaning of the work that make up the organization. It is making meaning in this community that creates a flexible, grounded, generative organization. The ABC model can be used as a framework for the ongoing conversations that will create a true learning organization. As the conversation deepens and expands, the framework itself will be changed and embellished as needed.

Sample Application of the ABC Model

The ABC Inquiry Model was used by an international organization (IO) for its strategic planning process. It was used by both the parent organization located in the Philippines and by the African Regional Office (ARO) located in Kenya. This example is from the work of the ARO. It is built around the circle diagram (shown in Figure 8.2) that the ARO created using the ABC Inquiry Model as a guide. The ARO circle was created by that organization through dialogue among members and stakeholders. It is a circle unique to the ARO.

Figure 8.2. Example of the ABC Inquiry Model

The ARO planning group was made up of nearly all of the staffs from the African Regional Office in Nairobi and of the Ethiopian office in Addis Abba, plus one member of the organization's international board and, for two days of the session, the president of the international organization. The planning group members met for a week in Addis Abba to pull together all of the preparatory work that they had done over the previous year as part of their strategic planning process.

For several months prior to the workshop, the organization used AI interviews to gather information from all of the stakeholders that they listed in the middle ring of the circle diagram (Figure 8.2). The interview questions were about the business processes that are listed in the outer ring. In other words, they interviewed a cross section of people from such stakeholders as community-based organizations (CBOs), their board of directors, donor groups, people in their programs, and so forth. The questions focused on the items for inquiry in the outer ring, programs, structures, environment, and so on. For example, some interview questions for CBO groups might be: "Tell me a story about the best ARO program you ever experienced or heard about. What excited you about the program? What part did you play? How has it impacted your life?" For each stakeholder group, the ARO asked questions relevant to the group being interviewed.

We have shown below some of the documents that the group prepared so that you can see the innovative use that was made of the ABC Inquiry Model. We have included here only a partial report of the very complex process that was carried out over a year's time. The model was used to consolidate the work into a planning document that was presented to the parent organization in the Philippines.

The following processes were identified by the organization as key areas of inquiry for the strategic planning process and are listed in the outer ring of the customized circle in Figure 8.2.

Areas Addressed in the Strategic Planning Process

- Programs:

  Training

  Collaborative Field Projects

  Documentation

  Publications

  Workshops and Conferences

- Governance:

  IO Board

  Africa Regional Office Advisory Council

- Structure:

  Management and Operations

  Communities

  Organization

  Relationships

  Teamwork

- People:

  Human Resources and Personnel Policy

  Policy and System

  Staff Development

  Equal Employment Opportunity

- Resources:

  Fundraising

  Facilities

  Materials

- Environment:

  Image

  Networking

- Systems:

  Monitoring and Evaluation

  Management Information Systems (MIS)

  Resource Management

The organization also came up with the following statement of purpose:

What We Do. In partnership with disadvantaged communities, ARO enables people to achieve their full potential. We work with other organizations (CBOs, NGOs, and governments) to enable them to help the less advantaged by building their capacity through:

- Training and mentoring;
- Technical assistance;
- Publications and documentation; and
- Collaborative field projects and action research.

ARO's priority partners include organizations involved with programs in the areas of:

- Food security rural development,
- Environment and natural resources,
- Reproductive health and HIV/AIDS prevention,
- Gender, and
- Promotion of indigenous knowledge.

Our Strategic Partners. ARO's diverse group of strategic partners includes:

- *Disadvantaged Communities:* Those hardest hit by poverty in urban and rural areas with little or no access to basic services.
- *Community-Based Organizations (CBOs):* Informal and formal voluntary groups organized around common interests and acknowledged by governments (e.g., cooperatives, self-help groups, etc.)
- *Nongovernmental Organizations (NGOs):* Nonprofit organizations that operate under the legal framework of government. These are formal organizations (as opposed to grassroots community organizations).
- *Governments:* Institutions that provide legal and policy frameworks at national and local levels.
- *Research and Educational Institutions:* Organizations of higher learning involved in research and education (universities, colleges, vocational and technical institutes, and research centers).
- *Networks:* Groups of organizations and individuals formally or informally coalescing around a common cause (associations, professional societies, consortia).
- *Private Sector:* Organizations and individuals *outside* of government. These could be for profit (e.g., business, consulting firms) or nonprofits (e.g., NGOs, foundations, and churches).

- *Donors:* Individuals or organizations that contribute funds and/or other resources. They show concern/interest in ARO's work and believe in its cause.

- *Staff:* Paid employees responsible for implementing ARO's programs and activities. Teamwork is a priority and the teams can utilize volunteers and interns.

- *Board:* A voluntary group with overall responsibility for policy and fiscal accountability. It helps generate resources and enhances the image of ARO.

Governance for ARO. ARO's management and programs are governed by a global IO board and board committees. IO's board should be diverse, and trustees should enjoy a reputation and status that will enhance the credibility of the organization.

It is recommended that the IO global board appoint an African Advisory Council. The council will be comprised of Africans or African residents from the countries where the IO works and who have an understanding of regional issues and challenges.

The council's purpose will be:

- Fundraising;
- Enhancing IO's image in Africa; and
- Assisting IO-ARO to establish partnerships in the private sector.

The council will be limited to a maximum of five men and women from diverse backgrounds, including the private sector, government, and international agencies.

To create a close link between the global board and the council, the council's chair should have an automatic seat on the global board.

ARO's Program. In the next five years, IO-ARO will provide capacity-building support to community-based organizations, small local NGOs, and government through training, mentoring, and collaborative field projects. Priority countries will be Kenya, Ethiopia, Uganda, and Tanzania. Field operational research and process documentation will be key components of the field projects. Figure 8.3 illustrates the relationships and flow of information among the networks of partners that work with IO-ARO.

Figure 8.3. Flow of Information

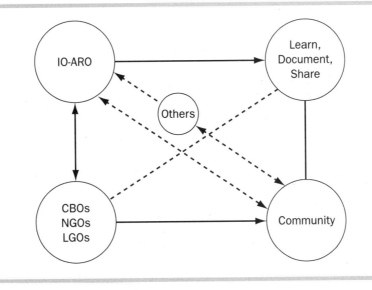

The top-left circle, IO-ARO, represents the African division of the international organization. The top-right circle describes the work of the organization, to learn from their work, document what works, and share both the ideas and the documentation. The bottom-left circle defines the working partners with IO-ARO: CBOs—community-based organizations; NGOs—nongovernmental organizations; and LGOs—local government organizations. The bottom-right circle describes the core beneficiary group for the work, the community itself, with community being a broad description of the groups that are identified as needing the kind of projects and services that IO-ARO has to offer. The center circle, "others," refers to the multiple and diverse partners and people who work with IO-ARO—donors, other groups and organizations, educational institutions, etc. The solid lines represent continuous working partnerships and constant, sustained communication. The dotted lines represent relationships that develop on an as-needed basis.

IO-ARO will also document and disseminate best practices from its own experiences and those of other organizations through workshops and conferences and other means.

Specifically, IO-ARO will:

- Develop a comprehensive training policy;
- Review curricula and develop training materials; and
- Conduct fifteen regional courses in project design, program monitoring and evaluation, and development management. Customized courses in these areas as well as in strategic planning, gender, and organization development will be conducted as necessary.

Seven collaborative field projects will be undertaken:

- Gender in Leadership and Decision-Making (Ethiopia);
- Kenya Micro-Fund;
- Kenya CBO/NGO Capacity Enhancement and Technology Transfer project;
- Integrated Watershed Management (Ethiopia);
- Watershed Management (Uganda);
- Learning Our Way Out (LOWO/Family Planning in Ethiopia); and
- Nairobi Urban Gardening Project (status to be determined).

In addition, IO-ARO will explore the potential for establishing other projects, for example:

- Partnering with universities and other academic institutions in training and field projects; and
- Exploring the possibility of a training program for youth (needs further discussion).

Ten IO-ARO publications are planned, five on best practices, and five manuals, two on gender and three on training.

IO-ARO will provide technical support to other organizations willing to document their own experiences. Efforts will be made to develop local capacity in documentation.

IO-ARO will plan and conduct eleven workshops, eight of which are related to gender and three of which are exploratory workshops addressing themes of concern. Two conferences are planned, one on gender and the other on a theme to be determined.

People. In the next five years, IO-ARO will have standard personnel policy with clearly defined salary structure, benefit packages, performance appraisals, and staff development.

Image and Networking. IO-ARO will create an identity and image that reflects the organization's vision/mission/values to promote our work in Africa.

IO-ARO will develop a sound public relations strategy to reflect an excellent and accountable program and to facilitate continuous dialogue with our partners in Africa's development.

We will formulate a PR policy; develop and implement an effective strategy; and train staff in PR skills. We will establish a fellowship fund to promote participation of women in development.

IO-ARO will strengthen its networking through publication of a newsletter to share information. We will make use of the Internet and networks and actively participate in forums that promote our work, such as conferences and workshops.

The IO-ARO was part of a year-long whole-system planning process that led to major shifts in the program, policies, and practices, as well as in the social architecture of the organization. Implementation met with a minimum of resistance because of the whole-system involvement in the process. It is ideal when the whole organization is involved, especially if the process is focused on both strategic planning and a commitment to redesign the organizational architecture. The chance to do such a complete process is relatively rare, but opportunities are increasing as Appreciative Inquiry becomes known and understood by potential clients and by organization development practitioners.

Along with the whole-system processes, there are many other kinds of innovative uses for AI system-level interventions. In our practices, we have had the opportunity to design an AI-based (e)valuation process for a large pharmaceutical company, parts of which we have shared in various parts of this book. Several times we have used AI with survey feedback data in a large communications company. Although there was a time when we might have seen AI and survey feedback as incompatible, we are now convinced that almost any traditional management or organization development method can be applied in an AI-based process. In this case, the survey data is fed back to the employees as successes and opportunities. A large group of representatives from the division involved in the survey come together to create dreams and designs of what they want to do to increase their successes and meet the challenge of those "opportunities."

In each of these cases—the valuation project and the survey feedback summits—we have gone through lengthy design processes with internal groups to fit AI theory and practice to the organization's goals. In both cases we were fortunate enough to have excellent internal HR and OD people to work with. In one case the group was already highly skilled in AI and in the other we began with the AI training workshop. In both cases we also had line people who were intimately involved in the work of the divisions to help with the design and occasionally with the delivery as well. In both cases we are seeing the impact of AI in many other related projects and activities in those companies.

The more comfortable we become with the requirements of the emerging paradigm and with the social constructionist basis for the work, the easier it becomes to trust the organization and the people to know what they want and how to get it. Our work becomes both easier and more fun! And we believe that our best successes are those organizations who have taken on the AI process and made it their own. The old consultant "saw" about working ourselves out of a job can be a reality with AI. And the best part is that there always seem to be new challenges and new clients on the horizon.

In the final chapter of this book, we write about the process that is near and dear to the hearts of those who cling to the hope that there really is a best way to do a job or a task—evaluation.

▶ CASE STUDY: GROUP HEALTH COOPERATIVE

BY DIANE ROBBINS AND SCOTT CALDWELL

Focus of the Appreciative Inquiry

Performance Improvement

Client Organization

Like most health care organizations in the hyper-competitive environment of the 1990s, Group Health Cooperative, a large nonprofit HMO in Seattle, has had to make extraordinary changes in a short period of time in order to remain a major player in the marketplace. One of the things we have realized is that the organization needs both focused, decisive leadership and high levels of employee involvement. Creating and managing this apparent paradox, we believe, will be critical to our success.

As the competitive pressures in the health care marketplace have increased, so have the challenges at Group Health Cooperative. In the autumn of 1995, several conditions existed that left an opening for some major organizational learning to occur:

- Group Health Cooperative's performance in the major areas of service and cost were not where leadership thought they needed to be in order to be competitive in the market;

- The organization had been through a protracted period of restructuring and downsizing. People throughout the system appeared confused about the overall direction of the organization and generally not hopeful about the future; and

- Leaders were at a stage where they clearly recognized both that the organization was not meeting its performance targets and that people seemed more demoralized than ever. They had a sense of urgency about making things better and were therefore open to trying some new ways of approaching these issues.

Client Objectives

The project goals had to be focused on improving the performance of the delivery system in the areas of cost, quality, and service. But underlying the performance issues, we believed, was an inability of the various stakeholders to take concerted, timely action together on behalf of the whole system. In a highly "professionalized" culture such as health care, members of the various subsystems often feel more allegiance to their profession than they do to the organization. In Group Health, as the pressures and changes of recent years accumulated, we saw these subsystems increasingly disaggregate—pulling away from the whole and spending more and more time talking primarily among themselves. It was as if Group Health Cooperative, once a one-room apartment, had grown into a huge mansion, where various groups lived in their own separate rooms, rarely coming together in the common space. And when they did come together, they brought with them a range of assumptions and understandings increasingly different from one another. Although there was widespread agreement that performance had to be improved, common ground about how to do that, as well as the cause of our poor performance, was slipping away.

To address the business issues as well as the underlying process issues, we proposed a project that would combine Appreciative Inquiry and Future Search in a year-long process designed:

1. To build alignment around a common vision for the delivery system, and

2. To develop specific actions for improvement based on the vision.

In addition to these business goals, we also had three primary process goals. These were:

1. To build strong, aligned leadership, including senior, mid-level, and front-line leaders;

2. To create a high level of effective employee involvement in organizational planning; and

3. To change the "internal dialogue": we wanted to change not only the nature of the conversations but also to shuffle who was talking with whom.

Finally, we wanted to achieve these goals guided by some key principles. First, we wanted to involve as much of the system as possible. Second, we wanted to create a process that would be both thorough and time-efficient. Our plan was to use an Appreciative Inquiry process to gather data from a large portion of the system and then use that data in a multi-search conference designed to develop specific proposals for action.

What Was Done

First Steps: Sponsorship and Leadership Alignment: The sponsors of the work were the COO (the operational leader of the Group Health delivery system) and the medical director (physician leader of delivery system). They asked our internal OD team to develop a proposal initially designed to address the issues of morale and delivery system performance. After some discussion, we realized that improved employee morale ought to be an outcome of the work, but not the goal.

Our project, called "Building Bridges," began in earnest in the spring of 1996. Our internal OD group has been strongly influenced by Darryl Conner's (1993) Sponsor-Target-Agent model. Our first step, then, was to build strong sponsorship for the project with the COO and medical director. With our consultation, they defined a statement of vision that came to be known as the Principles and Values Statement. In this document, the sponsors outlined, first, what would *not* change, that is, those values, principles, and goals that Group Health would always strive to preserve. This is what Cooperrider refers to as "continuity." Second, they said that, in order to preserve these values, the delivery system would have to change in ten key areas and, in a series of from/to statements, they described at a more specific level what would have to change. These from/to statements addressed what Cooperrider calls "novelty" and "transition." Creating this document was a key first step, and the document provided an ongoing frame and reference point over the course of the entire project.

Next, both to build strong sustaining sponsorship for this work and to begin the process of developing alignment among senior leaders, the sponsors created a steering committee. This eighty-member leadership group was comprised of all senior leaders in the delivery system and other parts of the organization. The role of the steering committee was to understand the work, support the work by communicating with staff, provide resources when needed, and help design some pieces of the process. In a two-day session, this group made revisions in the Principles and Values Statement and came to agreement that it described the broad vision and direction for the delivery system. They also learned the principles of Appreciative Inquiry

(AI) and determined the major areas of inquiry to be used in the AI inter-view protocol.

Key Activities: Employee Involvement: Having brought the leadership of the delivery system to a satisfactory level of alignment around direction and to an increasingly strong level of sponsorship, we were ready to begin those activities that would more directly and actively involve employees.

The first of these was the "kickoff event." On this day, nearly three hun-dred participants gathered to be oriented to the project and trained in AI so that they could interview other members of the delivery system. These participants reflected almost every type of diversity imaginable: profes-sion, level in the hierarchy, race and gender, geographical, and attitudinal (we wanted the cynics as well as the cheerleaders). These participants interviewed a minimum of five other people over the course of two months using the AI interview protocol that the steering committee and the con-sultants had developed over the summer. By the end of November, inter-viewers had conducted approximately eleven hundred interviews containing nearly fourteen thousand pieces of data. Many of them described the AI interview process as fascinating, enlightening, and energizing.

To consolidate the data into a comprehensive and comprehensible report, the consultants developed a process for coding, analyzing, and reporting the data that was gathered. In creating the report, we organized the data around key sections of the Principles and Values Statement, and we sent the report to all the interviewers three weeks prior to the Futures Conference at the end of January 1997. Our intent was to have all eleven hundred voices represented in the room at the Futures Conference, so we asked participants to read the report before they came and to bring it with them to the conference.

We modeled the Futures Conference on the design developed by Marvin Weisbord and Sandra Janoff (1995), but we added AI approaches in some areas and adapted the design so that people were forced to con-verge on specific actions by the end of the conference. In addition, instead of a single conference, we designed a multi-search conference that included six separate and simultaneous conferences spread over three days. The four hundred participants included all those internal stakehold-ers who had been at the kickoff event, the steering committee, and approx-imately one hundred external stakeholders. These included patients, consumer activists, brokers, employers who buy Group Health Cooperative's services, and labor leaders.

By the end of the third day, all participants had agreed on four key action proposals and established two additional support groups having to do with communication and how to utilize ideas not chosen in the convergence process. All six action teams—each made up of a cross section of the organization—were to do more extensive planning and come back to a follow-up day in May having identified key actions to take.

That describes the work. What it doesn't describe is the affective changes that came as a result of the conference. Participants' reactions ranged from ecstatic to merely enthusiastic, although some skeptics remained. A great number of folks reported how stimulated they were by the opportunity to hear all the different perspectives that existed in and around the organization. What most people discovered—and said they were surprised by—was just how much common ground there was. While excited, most said they retained some healthy skepticism about the organization's ability to follow through with action.

Follow-Up Activities: In our follow-up activities, we wanted to do two things: (1) identify the work to be done and establish clear accountability for it and (2) "widen the circle," gradually involve more and more of the organization in the work.

Outcomes

In our follow-up activities, we wanted to ensure that the action teams developed plans for accomplishing specific work and followed through with those plans. The action teams continued to meet during the next nine months and presented their results at a final conference meeting in November.

No one change effort stands by itself. This effort took place in the midst of several large changes—new leadership, the beginning of a major affiliation, and ongoing structural changes. It is difficult, therefore, to know precisely what intervention created which results. But looking back from fall of 1999, it is remarkable how far we have come in fulfilling many of the provocative propositions that resulted from the Appreciative Inquiry interviews in the fall of 1996. Key results include the following:

- There is strong leadership alignment around a common, positive vision and purpose for the organization;

- The organization is making hard but good decisions leading to improved financial performance;

- It has established performance management systems that are improving accountability and clarity of expectations;

- It has improved reward and recognition systems;

- Its decision-making structures are simpler, clearer, and more functional;

- It has established a way to honor and reward employees who provide outstanding customer service;

- It has established a way to evaluate and implement employee suggestions for improvement;

- It has identified leadership competencies—identifying skills and attributes the organization wants and needs from employees and finding ways to evaluate, reward, and develop these.

- There is an increased organizational competence in how to engage in appreciative discourse to access and use the intelligence of the whole system.

Learnings

Although it is clear to us that creating and sustaining both strong leadership and high involvement in a professional culture is key to a humane and effective workforce, it is less clear how to hold both of these qualities on a daily basis. There has been much written in recent years about developing the capacity to hold the tension of the opposites and the need to change our mental models from "either/or" to "both/and." Certainly those are essential operating principles for us as we continue this work.

For example, we have found that to the degree a sense of hope, enrollment, and expectations increase in one group (employees), chances are good that anxiety and confusion will increase in another (leaders). We have also found that high involvement tends to be quite messy, and therefore requires an increased level of skill in dealing with (and sometimes even encouraging) messiness. We are learning about the power of making public promises to each other and the challenges of staying true to those promises. We're learning about the collective trances we've been in and how much they limit our capacity and inherent wisdom. Two that come to mind are:

- Our deeply ingrained habit of paying attention to, being drained by, and trying to fix all that's wrong with us/our organizations instead of noticing, appreciating, and amplifying all of the ways in which things are going remarkably well, and

- The habit of staying separate from one another. Although having the "whole system" in the room is risky and invites a certain degree of increased conflict, the rewards are well worth the price. What we've seen is that people's sense of isolation and disenfranchisement dramatically decrease, their mental models get stretched and challenged, their judgments of each other tend to disappear or at least decrease in potency, and their ability to think about the good of the whole is expanded.

The environment around us continues to change wildly as we write this article. Because structures, people, and circumstances will continue to be fluid, we believe that developing our capacity to hold the tension of these opposites is the key to keeping us on the right path.

References

Connor, D.C. (1993). *Managing at the speed of change.* New York: Villard Books.

Weisbord, M., & Janoff, S. (1995). *Future search.* San Francisco, CA: Berrett-Koehler.

Contact

Diane Robbins
D.B. Robbins Consulting
2330 30th Avenue, South
Seattle, WA 98144
(206) 890–0465
e-mail: dbrobbins@mindspring.com

Scott Caldwell, Consultant
Group Health Cooperative
Seattle, WA ◀

► CASE STUDY: HUNTER DOUGLAS WINDOW FASHIONS DIVISION

BY AMANDA TROSTEN-BLOOM

Focus of the Appreciative Inquiry

Creating a shared vision

Client Organization

Hunter Douglas Window Fashions Division is a one-thousand-person manufacturing company in Broomfield, Colorado. The largest and most profitable division of Hunter Douglas International, the Window Fashions Division (WFD) innovates, manufactures, and fabricates high-end window covering products.

Having experienced off-the-chart growth during its first ten years of business (going from twenty-seven people in 1985 to nearly one thousand in 1998), the division made the decision to reorganize into separate business units—one per product.

At the same time, the WFD lost a number of key players to other parts of the HD organization, as HD North America promoted several high-level leaders with extensive knowledge of the WFD business.

The result of these concurrent events was a seemingly sudden and unexpected confusion over the WFD vision; lack of experienced leadership at the top; reduction of "bench strength"; and more noticeable communication gaps (from leadership to the general workforce, as well as across business units and functions). All of this was accompanied by diminishing levels of initiative in the workforce, increasing turnover, and a decrease in employee satisfaction and productivity.

Client Objectives

Leadership sought the following:

- To create a *collective vision* for the future of the organization that could engage and excite the entire organization and its stakeholders;

- To re-instill the *creativity, flexibility, intimacy, and sense of community* that had contributed to the division's original success;

- To build leadership within the organization (that is, to enhance the skills of existing leadership and build bench strength by identifying and training future leaders); and

- To transcend the silos that had recently emerged between management and the general workforce, across business units, and between operations and support functions.

What Was Done

Following an introduction to AI for leaders, we sent a handful of leaders through the week-long AI training at the Taos Institute. This group became the Focus 2000 Advisory Team for the intervention.

We initially introduced AI to the workforce through a series of "town meetings"—ninety-minute interactive presentations to cross-shift, cross-function, and cross-level groups of up to one hundred fifty people. These meetings used storytelling and videos to introduce "Focus 2000" (our name for the Appreciative Inquiry effort), its purpose, how it would work, and why it was different from what we'd done in the past. We solicited volunteers and nominations for participants in a one-hundred-person offsite session, the purpose of which was topic selection and protocol design.

After developing the protocols, we initiated a system-wide inquiry. Two hundred fifty people were trained, and nearly one hundred fifty of those served as interviewers for the first five hundred interviews (employees, customers, suppliers, and community members), all of which were conducted prior to our first Appreciative Summit. At the summit, we revisited what we had learned during discovery and moved through the last three phases of the 4-D process to dream, design, and deliver the WFD of the future.

Even as we began implementing what surfaced at the summit, we continued our inquiry. In the end, a total of one thousand employees, customers, suppliers, and community members participated in our process for re-imagining the organization. Feedback from the second wave of interviews was included as background data for our first-ever Strategic Planning Summit—an appreciatively based, whole-system, strategic planning process that has now become an annual part of the company's business planning process.

Outcomes

Looking back over the first two years of the cultural change process, Rick Pellett (general manager) and Mike Burns (vice president, human resources) reflect on just a few of the more striking changes they've experienced:

"Our production and productivity have both improved, largely as a result of people's increased participation in problem-solving and decision-making activities. Turnover is the lowest it has been for six years, despite extremely low unemployment in our local job market. Our operations improvement suggestions are up over 100 percent. This, in turn, has had a big impact on both our quality and our internal customer service.

"Relationships between the WFD and other divisions of the company have really grown over this same time frame, largely as a result of changes that were initiated as part of the Focus 2000 effort. Cross-divisional collaboration that was initiated by the WFD during Focus 2000 has resulted in an integrated, streamlined customer communication process. Under the WFD's leadership, the larger organization is starting to build relationships between quality and our customer service functions throughout North America, again using the tools that were learned through the division's work with AI. In 1998, employees from all levels and functions in the division participated in creating the company's ten-year strategic vision and five-year strategic plan; the planning process was repeated and deepened in 1999 and is scheduled for annual review in the future."

Also in 1998, the company undertook the challenges of ISO 9001 registration and conversion to an enterprise resource planning system. Says Pellett of both experiences, "These changes have transformed the way we do business by raising the bar on standards for supplying quality products and services. They were infinitely more doable because of Appreciative Inquiry." Says Burns:

"Perhaps the most telling change in our division is demonstrated by people's ongoing increased involvement in personal and professional development activities—both on and off the job. This includes such things as formal course work, training programs, mentoring and career development activities, and peer support groups. For example, our Dale Carnegie enrollment soared within six months of our having started the intervention. First one—and then several other—Toastmasters chapters formed and 'graduated.' Both programs were largely filled with employees from the hourly/non-professional ranks, particularly from the production areas of the company."

In fact, research conducted within this organization in early 1998 confirmed positive changes since commencement of the cultural change effort in such areas as:

- Employees' understanding of organizational goals;
- Employees' understanding of how their work fits with the organization's goals;
- Employee commitment to the organization's goals;
- Employees' sense of ownership for their work; and
- Employees' motivation to be productive, innovative, and creative.

In July 1999, the Focus 2000 Advisory Team voluntarily disbanded, to re-form (with new membership) around a *new* AI-based business initiative that was identified over the course of the original inquiry. In their closing meeting, members of this team reflected back on the overall accomplishments of the Focus 2000 effort:

- "By trusting in people's capacities to be bigger than their job, and to act on behalf of the organization as a whole, we *created leaders* and gave them confidence that they could lead."
- "We proved that you don't have to be an executive to get things accomplished."
- "We engaged lots of people in creating a common vision."

Learnings

Feedback from the final meeting of the Focus 2000 Advisory Team provided us with much learning:

- "Training is an important component in any cultural intervention. Lots of training, provided early on (which includes participation by mid-level leadership), will make future culture change processes even more successful than this one."
- "Create an infrastructure that supports people in participating in future 'convener groups' (if you intend to engage employees in this way). For example, be sure that the issues that are identified are of strategic importance to the organization. Then create a way

to find the people who are passionate about the issue or project and give them time and resources with which to do the work. If possible, tie their involvement in the group to their performance reviews and incentives."

- "Representation from multiple levels, multiple disciplines, and multiple viewpoints is critical—both in the Advisory Team and in related culture-change gatherings."

- *"Large events work.* When they are purposefully planned for maximum diversity, they help fertilize and cross-pollinate the organization, level the hierarchy, and send 'out of the ordinary' signals. They create safety and build relationships. They provide a container in which people can volunteer to become involved in things that stretch them."

- "[Advisory teams] don't have to do much! We just provided guidance and the green light for people. We helped build confidence that people's ideas and plans made sense."

- "Make future Advisory Teams *even more diverse* than this one was (including by shift, race, gender, function) and be sure to include first-level supervisors."

Contact

Amanda Trosten-Bloom
Clearview Consultants
2070 Foothills Road
Golden, CO 80401
(303) 279–2240
e-mail: Clearcons1@aol.com ◀

9

Evaluation

"We inhabit a world that is always subjective and shaped by our interactions with it. Our world is impossible to pin down, constantly changing
and infinitely more interesting than we ever imagined."

Margaret Wheatley, Leadership and the New Science

THIS CHAPTER COVERS THE MAJOR IMPACT that the shifting paradigm, particularly the new sciences and social constructionism, have on our concepts and practice of evaluation. It describes AI as an approach to evaluating AI
interventions as well as an approach to evaluating any process or situation.

Classical Evaluation

The encyclopedia defines evaluate as: "To ascertain or fix the value of." Whether it
is a performance appraisal for one's job, an evaluation of a project, feedback from a
colleague, or criticism from a significant other, the feelings evoked by having one's

"value" fixed, one's faults, short-falls, and limitations pointed out, are troubling and unsettling.

In most situations, evaluation carries the burden of "judgment." Even though these days most traditional evaluations point out successes as well as failures uncovered in an evaluation process, it seems to be human nature to focus on, if not to obsess about, those things that others declare (or that we ourselves fear) do not measure up to some standard assumed to define "perfection." Furthermore, no matter what kind of intervention one makes in an organizational system, the conversation will, at some point, get around to the subject of monitoring and evaluation. Volumes have been written. Methods have been formulated and tested. Millions of dollars have been invested. We yearn to know how our inputs determine outcomes; whether our carefully crafted goals have been achieved; how much return we got for our investment.

We would argue that applying the scientific methods of the Newtonian paradigm to human systems is flawed at best, if not actually a useless endeavor. It is one thing to count the number of vaccinations given in an area and relate that to the incidence of the disease in the area covered by the vaccination program. It is quite another to try to determine the impact of any person or group on the performance of a large and complex system.

Evaluation from an AI Perspective

Evaluation from the Appreciative Inquiry perspective works from the assumption that the uncountable number of variables in any human system makes it impossible to determine the one or even several best ways to do any human process. Nor is it possible to replicate what works in one group and assume that it will work the same way in the next. Indeed, working in human systems requires a flexible, open, creative stance that embraces ambiguity and innovation. In any human interaction, each person has an experience unique to that individual and substantially different from the experience of every other person.

Appreciative Inquiry as a perspective for an evaluation process is grounded in several basic beliefs. The first is the *belief that the intervention into any human system is fateful and that the system will move in the direction of the first questions that are asked.* In other words, in an appreciative evaluation, the first questions asked would focus on stories of best practices, most successful moments, greatest learnings, successful processes, generative partnerships, and so on. This enables the system to look for its successes and create images of a future built on those positive experiences from the past. Appreciative Inquiry enables organizations to carry out evaluations that move organizations toward their highest aspirations and best practices.

Second, the theory that we are all connected, as the new sciences demonstrate, suggests that there is *no such thing as an objective observer.* This implies that every evaluation in a system needs to be understood and planned as a powerful intervention into the system with the power to alter and shape the future of that system.

Finally, an AI evaluation process gives the additional *benefit of continuity.* There is no implication that the past is deficient or wrong, simply that we look back for those life-giving forces, those moments of excellence in which we can take pride, and use those as guidance to move us into a positive and generative future.

Following is an example of an AI evaluation process.

An Appreciative Evaluation Example*

During 1998, the Research and Development Division of a large multinational pharmaceutical company undertook an evaluation of a major and innovative simulation-based training program.

This training program had been designed to help scientific leaders and key contributors work effectively within the new drug discovery process. Over the course of three intensive days, participants worked in research teams utilizing a dynamic computer model simulating the drug discovery process. The aim was to create a realistic learning environment in which a drug company attempts to maximize its portfolio of research efforts over a ten-year period.

At the time of this evaluation process, 480 people from the pharmaceutical company in the United States and the United Kingdom had attended the program—a critical mass of the original target population. End-of-course evaluations were conducted for each program. The data collected was largely favorable, with participants reporting an increase in knowledge and understanding in a number of areas. Suggestions for improvements were acted on wherever appropriate, so that the program was continuously refined during the rollout.

The OD group, which had led the design and delivery of the simulation in conjunction with senior research scientists, was satisfied up to a point that the simulation now worked well and consistently elicited positive responses from those who

---

*From an article by Bernard J. Mohr, Elizabeth Smith, & Jane M. Watkins (2000).

attended. However, they had made a major investment in this program and decided it was important to conduct an in-depth evaluation study to ascertain whether it had made a lasting impact on the organization. If such an impact could be demonstrated, they also wished to determine how to further capitalize on this investment.

To find an outside evaluator, the company put out a request for proposals to several consulting groups that the company knew would offer different approaches, but still with the expectation that they would conduct a reasonably traditional evaluation process in which the consultants would interview people in the company, compile the data, and give the client a report of their findings. The usual report includes the strengths, weaknesses, and outcomes of the simulation and recommendations from the consultants for next steps.

One of the companies that received the invitation to tender was The Synapse Group, Inc., a consulting firm based in Portland, Maine. The Synapse consultants responded with a proposal that turned traditional evaluation thinking on its head. The proposal suggested the use of Appreciative Inquiry to conduct a "valuation process," sometimes called "embedded evaluation." They believed that this approach could give the company information about the strengths of the program in ways that would create positive forward momentum by taking the best of what had happened and using it to create a collective image of a desired future as a basis for moving the program in the direction of its best practices.

Following the usual AI process, the consultants and the company team designed an interview protocol, conducted one hundred and nine interviews, created provocative propositions, and created five different reports, each tailor-made for a part of the system.

To give readers an example of the kinds of information that result from an AI process of valuation, we offer a truncated version of one chapter in one of the reports from the pharmaceutical company. In this "Findings" chapter, the report highlights major themes and supporting data that emerged from the data set of interviews, each approximately one hour in length, conducted over a two-month time period. A wide range of participants who attended a session of the simulation workshop during 1996 or 1997 were interviewed.

The team of interviewers (five members of the company's human resources staff; one senior research chemist formerly employed by the company; and two Synapse consultants) reviewed the aggregate data to discover the major themes that describe primary learning from and impressions of the simulation. In a two-day work session, the data was categorized and discussed, and the themes were formulated. The data fell into three major categories:

1. *Transfer of Learnings:* What participants learned in the workshop that they now use in their work.

2. *The Use of Simulation Technology:* The reactions to the simulation experience of those who participated.

3. *The Organization:* How the participants felt about the organization itself.

Themes were then identified within from the collated data. A summarized version of the data in each category is presented below.

Topic 1: Transfer of Learnings

One of the major purposes of the simulation workshop is to provide participants with an experience of learning skills that will be useful to them in their work. The experiential learning methodology that is the basis for the simulation provides an environment and tasks that closely resembles the real work of the company's drug research process, also known as the *discovery process.* The interview data describes many ways that participants have been able to use what they learned through the simulation.

The data about transfer of learnings falls under six major themes:

1. Discovery System. As a result of attending the simulation, participants have a detailed understanding of how research progresses from initiation to pre-project. They have greater clarity about their own role and those of others within the process. They also have a much greater appreciation of how the wider discovery system operates and of working within the context of the overall discovery port-folio. They are applying this knowledge and as a result are more efficient and effective in the workplace.

2. Self-Development and Confidence. Through their experience with the simulation, many participants have learned to place a greater value on their personal expertise and to recognize the important contribution they can make to drug discovery. They have increased self-confidence; they are more proactive in making contributions in team meetings; and they are more ready to take the initiative. They are also seeking out further ways to develop their knowledge and expertise.

3. Teamwork. Almost 100 percent of the participants interviewed cited the opportunity for teamwork with colleagues from different departments and disciplines as being a major highlight of their experience. This has translated back to the laboratories, where participants are now using their collective expertise more effectively to make decisions and make progress on their research efforts.

4. Networking. The interactions with other disciplines that took place during the simulation began a process of networking that has continued after the program. Participants have been proactive in establishing new and broader links with individuals in other departments and are using these networks to assist themselves in developing and bringing out new ideas more quickly and effectively.

5. Leadership and Development of Others. Many of the organization leaders who have attended the program have an increased appreciation for the responsibilities of both their own and their managers' roles and have taken steps to evolve their leadership style for improved effectiveness. Some have also recognized and addressed additional developmental needs for their staff as a result of their involvement in the program.

6. Research Planning and Decision Making. Participants in the simulation are now more purposeful in planning their research efforts, including identifying critical activities, estimating timelines, and building in key check points and go/no go criteria. They are also more effective in requesting and allocating appropriate resources for specific activities. This has increased the efficiency of their research activities and is enabling them to make more timely decisions, including decisions to terminate.

Topic 2: The Use of Simulation Technology

The second area of inquiry was about the key elements that were present when the use of simulation technology was most effective in promoting learning and application to the workplace. The data drawn from the interviews fell into five major themes, described below.

1. Real-Life Business Process. The great majority of the participants interviewed commented that the simulation closely mapped the actual discovery process from ERP through to pre-project, including drug target selection, planning, resourcing, data assessment, and phase changes. It provided an opportunity for people to experience the complexity of real life in compressed time, while at the same time producing the excitement and involvement of real-life drug discovery. This meant there was a direct application to their everyday work.

2. Learning Design. In addition to providing a realistic environment, the simulation enabled participants to engage in the full challenges of drug discovery in a nonthreatening, stimulating, and enjoyable way. By experiencing the system in this manner, people have shown commitment to the workshop and have had fun while learning about drug discovery. In addition, the learning process design and format, which was spread over three days, allowed people to learn from and reflect on the various stages of their experience.

3. Team Formation. By virtue of the ability of the simulation technology to parallel real life, the workshop has attracted participants with broad and varied levels of experience from a mixture of scientific and other disciplines. More importantly, it has promoted their effective interactions throughout the program, allowing the less experienced people to learn from the more senior members. In particular, participants work in cross-disciplinary, self-managed teams that learn from each other by sharing knowledge and opinions and making joint decisions. Almost 100 percent of interviewees cited the teamwork as being one of the most valuable features of the workshop.

4. Decision Making. By condensing the time frame of the discovery process, the simulation technology allows participants to make decisions and examine the consequences of their actions in compressed time. This contrasts markedly with real life, where it may never be possible to gain this important perspective. In this way people can learn from their experiences in a benign environment and so reduce the chances of making poor decisions in their day-to-day work.

5. Business Strategy. In addition to modeling the discovery process, the simulation technology and workshop format emphasizes the ultimate purpose of drug discovery—to produce marketable products fulfilling both humanitarian and business needs. It develops a strong awareness of the business context of the work and facilitates managerial role playing.

Topic 3: The Discovery Organization

The third area of inquiry during the interview focused on the organization itself. The purpose of the simulation was to influence the behavior of people working in or working with drug discovery. In that context, interviewees were asked what they valued about working in the organization, what they believed to be the core value of discovery, and what wishes they had for its future. Almost without exception, the interviewees conveyed both excitement and pride in being part of the organization.

The following four themes emerged from the data:

1. People. People like working for the organization and they like and respect the people they work with. They are given freedom and opportunity to develop independent ideas and to manage the direction of their work. They feel valued for their contributions and expertise and work to highest standards of scientific excellence.

2. The Discovery Process. The discovery process and system are robust—strong, consistent, reliable, and well-funded. They are understood and utilized at all levels. The system is also focused and targeted toward the ultimate goal of getting good drugs to market. As a result, discovery puts good compounds into development.

3. Good Science. The organization is known for its commitment to pioneering science, its investment in technology, and the high caliber of its scientific research.

4. Collaboration. The organization works collaboratively across functions, matrix teams, and levels—both within and outside drug discovery. There is a spirit of openness and willingness to share experience and assist others. People leverage and learn from one another's expertise to reach organizational goals jointly.

And what has happened as a result of the original purpose of this evaluation? The HR department not only learned a great deal about the strengths and assets of the simulation that enabled them to improve it even further, but they also received widespread support from the people of the company and firm support from the leadership to use simulation technology in future training. At our last check-in with members of the team, they were also using their AI skills in their organization development work.

Learnings, Innovations, and Reaffirmations

Some months after the final report had been distributed and its recommendations were being implemented, the external consultants sat down with the company project manager to explore our own learning about using Appreciative Inquiry for the purpose of "evaluation." We wondered, in retrospect, what we had learned from this work. What were the innovations? What was reaffirmed for us? We began this reflection by making individual lists, followed by sharing and dialogue. The two perspectives—client and consultant—are listed in Table 9.1.

Table 9.1. Learnings, Innovations, and Reaffirmations

Client's List	Consultant's List
Joint partnership between consultant and client generates a synergy not present when the consultants and clients relate to one another in a more traditional manner (for example, the consultant as expert or vendor).	Joint partnership with the client and ongoing adaptation to the local conditions is key to using innovations successfully
AI does work for evaluation purposes, particularly at level 3 of Kirkpatrick (identifying behavioral changes).	The scale of a project does not necessarily correlate to the quality of organizational learning.
AI is not antithesis of problem solving.	External consultants may tend to underestimate the client's interest in the theory and constructs underlying the intervention approach.
Things that from a traditional evaluation process might be considered impure are helpful within an embedded evaluation/AI process, such as the use of leading questions, the use of data from the pilot, the use of people who have a vested interest in the outcome as interviewers/data collectors.	By participating as interviewers, the external consultants were able to contribute more to the data compilation and were also able to become more a part of the team. We all had similar stakes in the learnings/outcomes.
The "core AI" questions were the ones that produced the richest data.	Before the client can receive innovative assistance, innovation must be present in the world view of the consultant. And innovations are more likely to come from an outside source who doesn't have a set picture of how things ought to be.
The experience of AI interviewing is so positive that it affects the interviewer as well as the interviewee.	HR/OD professionals who have been trained in traditional interviewing styles may find it harder to use the more flexible dialogue protocol approach of AI.
Because the data generated are in a qualitative/narrative form, the amount of time for digesting the volume of data is significant (particularly in evaluating applicability/applications).	Management trusted their internal HR/OD group to conduct the evaluation without a steering committee, and the project was completed just fine without one.
The richness of the data allows many more questions to be answered than might be answerable with a more traditional quantitative model of evaluation.	Making assumptions about what clients will or will not be comfortable with can lead to unnecessary constraints on the project.

As we chatted about our lists, we realized once again the power of partnership—for what constituted innovation for the consultants was a new learning (but not necessarily an innovation) for the client. A case in point was the inclusion of the consultants as part of the interview team. From the consultant perspective this was "innovative." Appreciative Inquiry practice suggests the importance of limiting the active role of the consultant in interviewing/data collection in order to minimize consultant dependency. The client's learning that a partnership between consultant and client generates a synergy not present when the consultants and clients relate to each other in a more traditional manner (the consultant as expert or vendor) was not a new learning for the consultants. It was a reaffirmation of deeply held beliefs.

As we shared the things that we had learned, the things we saw as innovations, and the things that we felt were reaffirmed for us, we recognized once more the criticality of our partnership that enabled the consultant and client to build a shared world, a shared language with which to make decisions and conduct the work. Not only did the data reflect a generative and creative picture of the simulation itself, but it also told a powerful story of the pride, loyalty, and commitment that the employees felt for their company. As with all Appreciative Inquiries, it is the innovative, generative, and creative processes that are co-created by client and consultant that become a life-giving force for the organization. We realized that we were sharing a reflection about our work together that was, itself, an AI evaluation process.

AI Evaluation As an Integral Part of the Process

In the early 1990s the Global Excellence in Management (GEM) Initiative ran a series of institutes for the leadership of international development agencies. The process included a workshop to help each client system develop a customized interview protocol; time for the clients to conduct the interviews; a six-day residential institute to work with the data and do strategic planning; consultant time over the following year; and formal evaluation visits twice over the next two years to do an appreciative evaluation of their work. The evaluation questions included such subjects as the most exciting stories of events following the institute; positive changes in the organizations in alignment with their strategic planning process; unexpected positive outcomes for their organization; and so forth. The evaluation interviews were part of a full day's workshop with the clients and consultants, all participating in the dialogue about best and most exciting outcomes. These dialogues became guidance for the ongoing work of the agency. Most of the clients incorporated this practice of appreciative review for their organizations.

This was a major example of the ongoing and iterative nature of AI. A colleague once asked what to do when an AI process had been very successful over a long period of time but was running out of steam. My cryptic answer was, "Do more AI!" What I was actually referring to was the process of continually evaluating with AI questions how the AI process itself is going—questions like: "Let's share some stories of our most successful and exciting experiences using an AI approach in our company. What have we liked most? What changes are apparent as a result?" and so on. Once again, the image of the stream comes to mind. It is through the constant shifting and changing of our organizational dialogues that we flow toward our imagined future. Using AI as an evaluation process on a regular basis assures that the imagined future will be positive.

And so we end this book repeating our mantra: Appreciative Inquiry is a way of seeing and being in the world. It is based on the belief that we can create what we imagine when we open our minds and our social processes to the widest possible dialogue among the largest number of people who are involved and invested in our enterprise. Appreciative Inquiry applied, whether as a planning process or an evaluative process, becomes empowering and life-affirming in any human system.

The two-cup tumbler filled with one cup of water is, indeed, both half empty and half full. How we describe it is our choice to make. We wish for each of you the image of half full; a life lived, like the sunflower, turned toward the sun; and days full of powerful and positive images of a future that is generative, creative, and joyful.

Postscript:
FAQs About
Appreciative Inquiry

THE FOLLOWING LIST OF QUESTIONS came from several sources: those solicited from the subscribers to the AI listserv,* those we have collected from participants in our workshops and from our clients, and those we have asked ourselves as we work with AI in multiple settings and situations. We offer the reader our answers to these questions, aware that in the context of AI as a co-creative process there are many possible answers to them.

We have put the questions into two categories: theory-oriented and technique-oriented. These categories are vague at best, but offer what we hope is some sense of order.

---

*The AI listserv (The Appreciative Inquiry Discussion list) is hosted by David Eccles School of Business at the University of Utah. For subscription information, go to: http://lists.business.utah.edu/mailman/listinfo/ailist

Theory-Oriented Questions

1. Can you describe AI in four bullet points? How do we put the ideas of AI across in, say, one hour, to give people a taste of the process? What really should be included? What can be left out?

- Appreciative Inquiry assumes that every living system has untapped, rich, and inspiring accounts of the positive. It holds that these stories, these experiences, when systematically explored and shared, release positive energy and innovative insight into how a system functions and that this kind of energy and insight is vastly superior to the kind of energy and insight achieved through the negation, criticism, and spiraling diagnosis associated with problem- and deficit-based approaches to change.

- Appreciative Inquiry is both a *practical philosophy* of being in the world at a day-to-day level and a highly adaptable *process for engaging people* to build the kinds of organizations and world that they want to live in. As a practical philosophy, AI invites people to choose to seek out and inquire into that which is generative and life-enriching in their own lives and in the lives of others and to explore the attendant hopes and dreams for the future. As a process for *engaging* people to build the kinds of organizations and world that they want to live in, AI involves systematic discovery of what gives a system "life" when it is most effective and capable in economic, ecological, and human terms and weaving that new knowledge into the fabric of the organization's formal and informal infrastructure.

- Appreciative Inquiry is the art and practice of asking questions that strengthen a system's capacity in positive ways that enable the system to re-conceptualize its purpose, principles, and design and that enhance its most generative forces.

- Communication patterns, roles, processes, systems, strategies, and structures shift during a formal AI process of organization development as people learn more about what contributes to times of energy and excellence.

As far as putting the ideas of AI across in one hour, we would offer the following: We live in a world in which we have historically made things better by identifying problems and dissecting them. Thus, until people have experienced AI, the ideas, assumptions, and language used to describe it seem abstract and sometimes counter intuitive. Therefore, whenever possible, introductions to AI should incorporate the experience of an appreciative interview (and, if possible, a micro dream and design activity) very early in the process.

In Chapter 4 you will find a design for a forty-five-minute introduction to AI.

2. How is this any different from all the other "change processes" of the last decade (and then some)? What difference can it possibly make in this organization?

Appreciative Inquiry is very different from current OD practice in two ways: (1) It focuses on inquiry into the life-giving, generative aspects of organizational functioning, rather than using the traditional pathology-oriented focus, and (2) AI is a more holistic/systemic approach to inquiry, rather than the separating-into-parts analysis of Newtonian physics. These two distinguishing features are congruent with what we describe as the emerging paradigm in which (a) language is seen as a powerful force for creating social reality, rather than just for describing it, and (b) we understand the simultaneity of inquiry and change.

3. In what ways is AI more than simply "thinking positively"? Are AI and positive thinking the same thing?

Because of its focus on finding that which is life-giving in human systems, AI is often confused with positive thinking. Two factors that make AI fundamentally different. First, AI has its conceptual roots in the philosophy of social constructionism, which essentially says that reality is constructed during the social interactions of people, rather than in the mind of an individual. Secondly, AI is about inquiry, about asking questions. It engages people in building the kinds of organizations that they want to live in. It is a highly relational approach to systemic and structural change in human systems that, although not incongruent with positive thinking, is totally different from it.

4. What about our *problems* then? When can we talk about them? How does AI deal with problem solving? Does AI solve real problems? Isn't AI just putting a brave face on things and ignoring reality?

AI can be used to solve problems; it just approaches problem solving with a different perspective. Traditional problem solving looks for what is wrong and "fixes" it, thereby returning the situation to the status quo. Appreciative Inquiry solves problems by seeking what is going *right* and building on it, thereby going beyond the original "normal" baseline.

The term "problem solving" carries a set of assumptions based on the paradigm that treats human systems like mechanical ones. We have all been taught to solve problems in human systems based on the following assumptions:

- There is some ideal way for things to be.
- If a situation is not as we would like it to be, it is a "problem" to be solved.
- The way to solve a problem is to break it into parts and analyze it.
- If we find a broken part and fix it, the whole will be fixed.

The process for solving problems in the current paradigm follows:

- Identify what is wrong.
- Analyze the causes.
- Decide on goals to fix these causes.
- Make a plan that will achieve the goals.
- Implement the plan.
- Evaluate whether we fixed the problem or not.

If we embrace the concept of a socially constructed reality, we can look at the same "problem" from the Appreciative Inquiry perspective based on these assumptions:

- The way things are is socially constructed by our system and can be changed.
- In any situation, we can find the seeds of excellence to build on.
- We build on excellence by seeking out examples and sharing stories throughout the system.
- As we create images of excellence, our system will move toward that image.

The process for solving "problems" in the emerging paradigm follows:

- Let's look at our experience in the area that we want to improve in order to discover the times when things were going well—times when we felt excited, successful, joyful.
- From these stories we can collectively create a description for what we want (our image of the ideal).
- We can go out and ask others how they have successfully dealt with a similar situation.

- We can share our images, discover the images that others hold, and continually re-create a generative and creative future throughout the system.

Both approaches are based on the belief that we can make things better. The first suggests a finite process that will find, fix, and return things to baseline status. The second recognizes that both problems and resolutions are social constructions, created by our dialogue and generalized into social norms and beliefs. In this situation, resolution is generalized throughout the system and builds in the potential to move continuously toward our highest image of ourselves and our systems.

We suggest that—far from ignoring the "negative" and putting a brave face on things—an AI approach has real potential to create a learning organization with the capacity to correct its course continuously in its journey toward its mission, purposefully choosing to move toward those images of the system at its most creative and innovative.

To the question, "Does AI ignore reality?" we say, "Whose reality?" In our culture, we often consider the negative as "real," while calling hope and joy and love such names as "touchy-feely" or Pollyanna. We live in a time when critical analysis, even cynicism, is considered the hallmark of intellect. We suggest that someone is cynical and the reply is, "I'm just being realistic." Appreciative Inquiry suggests that there is a positive and generative view of reality that is equally real. We do not deny that "bad" things happen. We do believe that we get more of what we focus on in human systems. The AI choice is to focus on what we want more of!

5. If AI only looks at the positive, how does it deal with power, oppression, and injustice? What is the role of the shadow, the "negative" in AI?

AI suggests that *whatever* the situation, we can search for a time when we felt proud and excited about how we handled a particular dilemma. Suppose you have some hidden shame. What happens if, instead of trying to bury the memory as quickly as possible, you ask yourself what you can value about the situation? What lessons have helped you build a more generative and exciting life for yourself?

Try this. Think about a time when your whole organization or a significant part of it acted in a way that violated your values. Perhaps there was even a time when there was public humiliation. Tell a story about that time of trouble when you felt excited and proud of your organization and its actions in the midst of much that you did not feel proud about. We can use AI to help an organization recover from a time of trouble, not by rehashing what was done wrong or by looking for a scape-goat, but by looking for the triumphs of the human spirit and for organizational resilience in hard times. Appreciative Inquiry isn't about focusing on the positive and denying the negative. It is about seeking the life-giving forces in *any* situation.

So what about power, oppression, injustice? These are the areas of real challenge! It goes against the current paradigm to take incidents of misuse of power, oppression, and injustice and search for the generative and creative stories in the situation. However, our experience has convinced us that, even in these most challenging situations, AI works. We have come to believe that looking for the downside of any situation really does lead to more downside.

In a previous project, we worked on gender issues in a country that we might be tempted, from our U.S. perspective, to think of as highly macho. Our current paradigm suggested that we confront the offenders, point out their sins, and admonish them to stop it—a clear no/not situation! (No, don't think of a red brick wall. No, don't pay women less than men for the same job.) We could look for and find many incidents of real injustice, oppression, and misuse of power by men toward women. Instead, we suggested to the client that they begin a search for the "solutions" embedded in even the most egregious inequitable situations.

The questions in the interview protocol were along the lines of: "Can you tell me a story about a time when you were working, men and women together, that was exciting, successful, and creative? What happened?" Also included in the interview protocol were questions about values and about three wishes for men and women working together in the company. The organization eventually interviewed all three thousand of its employees. Several years later the company won an award in that country for doing the most to achieve gender equity. The organization believes that Appreciative Inquiry made that possible. It is something of a "no brainer" to notice that putting the offending "oppressors" on the defensive will not speed up change. Finding, highlighting, and holding up instances of success really does breed more success.

6. This stuff is too much process—too "touchy/feely." Where's the action?

Once you understand the concept of social construction, you realize that the action happens in the dialogue. The first question you ask is fateful, and the whole system will turn in that direction. Furthermore, given the heliotropic effect (remember that the sunflower always turns its face to the sun), the system will turn toward its most positive images of itself. Those first interviews *are* the action! Add to that the principle of simultaneity which posits that change is simultaneous with the first questions we ask, and you have a process that recognizes the power of human language to create our reality. We create what we imagine.

Given the power of our current paradigm and the prevalence of OD interventions that focus on action plans and deliverables, it may be hard to get a client to buy into the idea that the system will change in the direction of conversations, even if you never write down a plan or a deliverable. We suggest that you co-create with your client the process you want to use to document, plan, and implement. Often this will look like a pretty standard planning process but *you* know that the change is already happening from the first word you speak.

7. How do we help ourselves and others be appreciative?

We think this stuff is contagious! The more you try it, the more satisfying your relationships become and the more pleasant your environment. It doesn't take long to see the impact of appreciation on your personal relationships. We hear stories about marvelous transformations of children's self-images and attendant shifts toward more positive behavior when they experience appreciation from their parents or other authority figures in their lives. If we believe that people move toward the images that they create, it makes sense to hold out positive and appreciative images for those we work with and live with day-to-day. We have found it immensely liberating to give up the notion that there is a "right" way to be or a "perfect" path to follow. We recommend it!

8. Do people really follow through on their commitments? And what is the AI approach to following up on those who do not follow through?

In an unpredictable and rapidly changing environment, following through on 100 percent of our commitments may not be realistic. Actually, it may not even be necessary given the rapidly changing environment and shifting realities. We find that, in an AI environment, people are proactive in collaboration with the network of relationships that have been created through their conversations. In other words, when the daily dialogue between people is appreciatively oriented, more people follow through with many more of their commitments than they do in organizational cultures that are based in the language of deficit.

Consistent with AI philosophy, when people do not follow through on their commitments, we would inquire into what progress *has* been made (and how) and what sort of support they now need to fulfill their commitments.

9. But how do we change the way people work? How do we really improve performance? What does this process do to measure it?

The AI process of asking people to share stories about their most exciting, creative, and life-giving experiences creates an environment of trust and mutual respect. We observe that people begin to work together more collaboratively, valuing their different contributions and perspectives. Most of what we know comes from anecdotal data, which is appropriate in a paradigm that encourages people to move toward their highest and best images, rather than assuming some *ideal* way to perform that people can be measured against. There are studies of this new paradigm that do make an effort to do some quantitative measures. There are many papers available through the Taos Institute web page and from Case Western Reserve's School of Organization Behavior, where many students are researching and writing about AI. There are also people on the AI listserv who will generously share their experiences with AI in client systems.

10. What are the advantages of shorter versus longer AI sessions? Some workshops go several days, while other practitioners are completing the process in a few hours. When is longer better? When is shorter better?

You can introduce AI in forty-five minutes (see Chapter 4 for an example). You can teach a client to create and use the interview protocol in about a day (unless there are multiple languages in use, in which case it will take more time just to ensure understanding). You can do an AI team-building session in a day or two. Or you can embed AI in a system so that it becomes a way of thinking and informs all of the systems processes. If you think, as we do, that Appreciative Inquiry is a radically different way of approaching change and that the challenge is to help people think and act from a radically different set of assumptions, then it may well take a considerably longer time for the whole system to "get it."

So there is no easy answer to that question except to say, "It depends." It depends on the purpose, your client's willingness to invest, and how long you have to do the work. The remarkable thing about working from an AI perspective is that you can do no harm! Although your client may not understand much more than the good energy that an AI process generates and may see this as "just making nice," the fact that they are trying it, discussing it, and find it interesting is a good start.

If you want to equip people to facilitate AI processes in their workplace or with clients, our basic workshop is six days long and is designed as a first step for grounding participants in the basic theory and practice of AI. It is designed for OD practitioners and senior managers who want to use AI in a wide variety of applications throughout a system. We stress that AI takes a real commitment to continuous learning, largely because of the challenge of shifting our own paradigms and the time it takes to identify our own "stuckness" in a dichotomous, hierarchical, and often cynical world view.

We recommend, at the very least, that an AI practitioner needs to be grounded in knowledge about human behavior in groups and about organization development theory and practice. To learn how to use an AI approach, we think it is helpful to have experienced a session introducing AI, to have tried it in some limited arenas, and to have spent at least a week in an intensive workshop focused on the theoretical basis of AI. To embed AI in a system requires knowledge of how to work with people in the system to co-design and co-create an ongoing process appropriate and unique to that system.

This kind of work with AI requires a great deal more than a superficial knowledge of how to apply AI as just another OD intervention. The 4-D Model is not, strictly speaking, an intervention model. It is a guide that can help you work with a system as you co-create a process for that system. With a comprehensive grounding in how and why AI works, you can design any kind of organization change intervention—strategic planning, team building, executive coaching, project planning, conflict transformation, evaluation, organizational re-design, and some interventions that don't have names! Every time it looks different.

Further, in our own development we have intentionally been part of a learning community of AI practitioners and theoreticians who share their experiences with applications in a wide variety of systems. We believe that learning to think, to do, and to be "AI" is likely a lifetime endeavor!

Technique-Oriented Questions

1. How do you sustain the energy after provocative propositions?

The answer will differ from client to client and from situation to situation. If the dream process is generative and exciting, the provocative propositions that result will be lively and will have real meaning for the group. (We often use both right-brain activities—pictures, symbols, skits—to create an image of their ideal, followed by a left-brain activity of using words to describe that image. We encourage poetic words!) Because we can't control the environment that people return to, we usually talk about what it is like to return to business as usual with such different (perhaps even threatening) energy and ideas. For more answers to this question, check out the AI listserv. People have wonderful examples and ideas to share.

2. Why ask about what people value about themselves as individuals (outside of a work context)? I don't think my people will go for that sort of question.

Unlike other approaches to organization development, AI values the co-construction (by the client and the consultant) of the questions to be asked. Other than the imperative around asking questions that are non-analytical and that search for the generative forces in a given situation, there are no immutable laws of AI requiring us to ask what people value about themselves outside of the work context.

Having said that, we would always engage the client in a dialogue about our rationale for the values question, which is, quite simply, our belief that it will reveal the fundamental life-sustaining forces for that individual, both within and outside of work. We believe that people are complex beings who bring their home world to work and their work world home. We would also invite the client to test out this concern in some sort of low-risk setting. If in fact people responded negatively to the question about what they value about themselves outside of the work context, we probably would encourage the client to omit the question.

3. What about goals? Doesn't strategic planning need goals and objectives? What if we don't know where we want to go? Can AI help? How about assessing external trends, threats, opportunities? Does AI allow for that?

It is our current paradigm that says we can plan for a future that is predictable. Goals and objectives are useful if you see them from a constructionist view, knowing that what we know in the present will change soon and often. In AI we talk about dreams and images of the future and plan for how to bring those dreams into reality. We engage clients in dialogue about flexibility and the image of an organization as a "stream" (as Margaret Wheatley suggests) that knows it is going to the sea and knows that it follows the law of gravity. Beyond that, it has the capacity to reorganize itself instantaneously and regularly. As so often in AI, it is the process of *how* we choose and move toward our goals/dreams that is important, and that is often a much more organic and less systematic process than traditional objective setting and action planning. As for assessing external trends, threats, and opportunities, we'd suggest that the threats be articulated as "wishes," for example, "War could break out" is a threat; "We wish for a tranquil and peaceful environment" is an image of what you want. Remember that we create what we imagine, so we suggest that imagining peace rather than war is a good idea! When all is said and done, we are strong advocates for the idea that almost *anything* you have done as an organization intervention in the past can be done from an AI perspective.

4. Appreciative Inquiry has really worked well for us in our planning project. How can I sustain this approach as we move into implementation?

The way to sustain AI is with more AI. Often we suggest to clients that they build into their next steps a process for reconnecting with each other formally or informally and asking questions such as: "What's the most exciting thing that's happened for you as you have (whatever task that person chose to implement)?" If you find people being pulled back into the current paradigm (either/or thinking; one right way, etc.), get together and ask some AI questions about what is going on. Say: "We seem to be a bit stuck in our implementation process. Let's share some stories about where we are being really successful, where we are feeling excited and creative." Above all, try not to analyze why it's not working!

5. Regarding visioning from AI, I wonder whether we might at times constrain ourselves by focusing on what is/has been and thus restrict ourselves from truly innovative ideas. What do you think?

This is an important question. We don't want to get stuck at the level of trying to do again what has been successful in the past. Remember that the importance of those stories is two-fold. First, they provide a way for organizations to value their past so that they do not feel that everything before now is devalued. Second, those stories hold the qualities—topics or themes—of things that are present when people are feeling excited, energized, and successful. It is these qualities, the essence of the exciting and successful experience, that become the inspiration for our images and visions of the future. We are using "right-brain" activities in the dream phase that seem to capture and embed those qualities in the system. For example, suppose the stories are shared; the group identifies several qualities/topics such as trust, reward for good work, a challenging task, feeling connected to others; you move into the dream phase and ask the groups to create a visual representation of the organization as it will be when all of those qualities are present in everything that the organization does. After they create the picture, we ask them to write a provocative proposition to capture in words what they have represented visually. When they move into the design phase, they have an image based on past successes around which they can create innovative ways forward.

One more thing. We more and more view the vision as something to be revisited and reaffirmed again and again. In order to avoid reductionism, it is fun to go with the reality that people are motivated by many different visions. Unless your task is to create a twenty- to fifty-word vision statement, we've had great success in helping clients be comfortable with multiple provocative propositions that guide the design and implementation process.

6. Why does the literature suggest that it is unnecessary to assess the readiness of an organization before attempting AI? What characteristics must an organization have to be successful with AI?

Appreciative Inquiry is an essentially inclusive, democratic process of change that places high levels of responsibility on members of the system to move the process forward. Because of this, it is prudent to explore with the people who have accountability for the organization's future any parameters that they know in advance must be respected as givens. What makes AI unique is the power of its questions that can alter and shift the very fabric of thinking within the organization. In other words, AI sees organizations as a moving stream where one can never step into the same water twice. Therefore, any attempt to assess readiness is better conceived of as: "What is the strategy we can co-construct with our client to help them participate in building the best and highest future for their organization based on the identification and enhancement of the best of their past?"

We have found our AI work to be particularly useful to the client when there is evidence of the following factors:

- A *reverence for the mystery of life* is truly present as the underlying motif, for example, when the sponsors of the inquiry process are really curious about some critical aspect of the system's functioning.

- A *profound knowledge of the system's capabilities* is an essential requirement for progress forward. Those inside the system are truly curious about how the system works and how it can improve.

- *Time to achieve outcomes is short,* so the period available for exploration, goal setting, and implementation is compressed.

- *Quantum rather than incremental change is sought,* for example, total elimination of greenhouse gasses versus a 5 percent reduction of the gasses.

7. How will the success of an AI intervention be evaluated?

First, let us say that evaluation in the traditional sense would not be congruent with the theory of Appreciative Inquiry. That is, it would not be congruent with an appreciative process to evaluate it by looking for what didn't work or how something failed. Furthermore, because AI is not a one-time intervention, but rather a shift in how the organization understands the process of change and renewal, formative "valuation" rather than summative evaluation would be appropriate. (If there is no end point, summative evaluation couldn't be done anyway.) So formative valuation done periodically to ask the question: "How are we doing?" could easily and profitably be done from an appreciative perspective. At any point in time, the system could ask itself: "What are the most exciting and creative outcomes from our AI approach to our work?" And, of course, they might also want to ask: "What wishes do we have for our future work with AI?" In formal evaluation language, this kind of process would fall into the qualitative methods category.

This kind of inquiry was done by the pilot project called the Organization Excellence Program (OEP) that was the precursor of the Global Excellence in Management (GEM) program that has spread AI throughout the international development community. Following a discovery process done by a development organization, the OEP gathered a team from several organizations together for a one-week institute that guided the organizations through a process that grounded them in AI theory and facilitated their use of the discovery data to do strategic planning. The consultant was available to each organization for several days over the following year. Also, the OEP provided "valuators" who visited each organization and conducted a meeting with members of the organization to ask the questions above. In essence, the valuation process stimulated further Appreciative Inquiry that, as we now know, was a major change intervention in itself. It follows the concept that the first questions we ask are fateful. By doing an Appreciative Inquiry to inquire into how the organization is using the AI process, we foster more AI in the organization.

In this transitional time when organizations and their leaders are rooted in the paradigm that puts high value on counting and measuring, there are ways to adapt evaluation methods using AI. One large corporation that we work with uses questionnaires. However, because they are grounded in AI, the questions are generally seeking positive information. As an innovation, this corporation has run AI summits to feed the questionnaire results back to large groups using an AI process to look at the successes and challenges that came out. At the summit, we applied a full 4-D model (see Chapter 3). The outcomes of the summit are provocative propositions and plans for building on their successes and achieving excellence in the areas of challenge.

8. What does a failed AI intervention look like and how does one recover?

There have been times when an intervention did not go as we expected, but even if only a few people really understand the power of the first question and the importance of dialogue, a seed has been planted. Failure is a concept from a paradigm that believes there is a "right" way to do something. Appreciative Inquiry is a world view, a way of seeing and understanding the world that is open to endless possible outcomes. We might feel that we have failed if nothing we thought about or designed for lived up to our hopes and dreams for that event. However, in the spirit of AI we would hope that we could do an Appreciative Inquiry into what happened and what we learned.

9. What do you do when people bring out the negatives and you can't get to the positives? What if we can't find an example where things worked or it seems as if we're searching for something that isn't really there?

If people are unable to identify a good experience in their own organization, ask them whether they can identify one from their experience in other work environments. If the answer is still "no," ask them to imagine what it would look like and feel like if it were present. Say to them: "When we say that things are wrong, broken, unworkable, it means that we have images in our head of how things would be if they were right, whole, and working well. Can you describe your image of that?"

Another alternative is to invite negatively focused people to participate in a benchmarking visit to a place that you know has stories and examples of successes similar to ones that you are searching for in their organization. In this case, it is important that the negative people participate in the spirit of Appreciative Inquiry, seeking to explore the contributing factors to the "success" that is being described to them.

Remember, you are looking for the exceptional moments of excellence, excitement, and creativity. Even in the most dire and distressed situations, there are moments of hope and generativity. So coach the interviewers to delve deeply, while also assuring those being interviewed that they are not ignoring things that need to change. Point out that in the wish question there is an opportunity to identify those things that they want to see improve.

10. So what happens when you start a process like this, and the leadership changes and we start all over again with a new administration, new leaders, new consultants, and the newest management fad?

It is tempting to say "It depends." Your first job is to ground yourself and your client in the theory of AI so that it isn't seen as a management fad. A major factor would be how long and how widely you have worked with AI in the system and how well you have embedded it with the internal HR/OD people. If you have had lots of time in the system and have seen the internal people think AI and turn to it for all kinds of organizational processes, then there is a high likelihood that much will survive. If, on the other hand, AI has been seen as just another intervention and the system has remained dependent on outside consultants, then your strategy would have to be to sell it to the new system.

11. What happens if you want to do something small, such as a pilot in one department of an organization or agency where there isn't support for a full-scale approach or even the commitment to an approach like this? What difference can you make?

Although AI probably has more of a chance to spread beyond a pilot situation than a traditional deficit-based approach, paying attention to boundary-crossing opportunities is always important. Engaging people from other parts of the organization in the early educational sessions on AI can help, as can the development of an explicit diffusion strategy early rather than later. Perhaps the most powerful way to foster diffusion is to have members of the pilot department interview key stakeholders from other parts of the organization as well as from outside—suppliers, customers, and regulators—and then to demonstrate with action that they have listened and are shifting their way of operating to be more in line with the messages from their key stakeholders.

Although it is always advantageous to have the support of the leadership of an organization, it is also possible to spread AI from the bottom up. In one large corporation, the first AI work was done with the "front line," the part of the organization that interfaces with customers. The success of that first work has since spread throughout the organization with many of the HR and OD staff trained in AI, which is now regularly requested by departments throughout the company. The most exciting result of this process has been the innovative and creative ways that AI has been used, and it continues!

12. How can AI be applied to appraisal systems in companies that feel appraisal just must deal with weaknesses?

Many traditional organization processes can be done from an AI perspective. That is a far greater challenge for processes that are fully grounded in the belief that there is a best way to do a thing, and when evaluation/appraisal is the process used to determine how we measure up. The previous innovations in this process—Management by Objective (MBO), 360-degree processes, and more dialogic methods—are all responses to our realization that it is impossible to determine an ideal behavior for a human being, let alone a human system, and to judge each other against that ideal. We struggle with how to measure innovation, quick thinking, good judgment, creativity, and all those qualities that help us do good and useful work. If you can get an organization to do a performance review that looks for strengths and is based on stories that describe successes and high points, you will have made an inroad into a process that is at this time firmly grounded in deficit-based thinking.

13. When we put the provocative propositions together, will we have a coherent vision or a lot of specific visionary statements that don't hang together?

A shared vision in the traditional sense is a useful beacon for the organization only so long as it is revisited, enlarged, shifted, and re-imagined at the level and speed of the changing environment. To have power, organizational visions must be agile and impermanent—capable of meeting the challenges and opportunities that are continually and endlessly emerging.

We have reached the point in our practice at which we urge clients to embrace multiple possibilities (provocative propositions/possibility statements) that any human system has for re-creating itself. One of our clients insisted on writing provocative propositions for all twenty themes that they gleaned from the interview stories. And they did not try to combine them!

Another client, after deciding on five themes that were especially important, had small groups of eight write provocative propositions (PPs) for each of the five themes. For this group of eighty people, there were ten PPs for each theme. And they left it at that! As they moved into the "Making It Happen" phase, the group members recognized that they had multiple dreams (PPs) about how to bring a theme to its highest and best potential, but they didn't want to limit images to one shared statement.

We believe that the process often used to reach a consensus statement about what should happen actually takes a great deal of the energy out of the process. And the statement that results from the effort to find something that everyone can agree on often captures very little of the dynamics of the original dialogue. To have many possibilities is advantageous and actually captures the multiple realities and images of a group. However, if you need to create a single comprehensive statement, try to do it in the least reductionist, least "wordsmithing" way, and make sure that it is seen as a work in progress.

14. The discovery and dream phases seem redundant because of the telling of stories. What is a good way to distinguish between these two phases?

We think of discovery as having two phases: the initial paired interviews and the subsequent sharing of stories told. The story sharing here is different from the longer and more comprehensive sharing in the paired interviews, in that these stories are briefer and identified by the interviewer as particularly exciting. The purpose of this phase is to listen to those stories in order to identify topics and/or themes that are present when things are at their best.

The next step is to have the group that shared stories brainstorm a list of topics and select several that they all want to inquire into in the larger system (creating a customized interview protocol) or that they want to write provocative propositions about to guide their future actions. After the topics are chosen, the group begins the dream phase, a process of imagining how the organization will be when all of the topics are at their best.

References
and Bibliography

Axelrod, E. (1999). *The conference model*. San Francisco, CA: Berrett-Koehler.

Barker, J.A. (1993). *Paradigms: The business of discovering the future* (2nd ed.). New York: HarperBusiness.

Beckhard, R. & Pritchard, W. (1992). *Changing the essence: the art of creating and leading fundamental change in organizations*. San Francisco, CA: Jossey-Bass.

Beecher, H. (1955). The powerful placebo. *Journal of the American Medical Association, 159*, 1602–1606.

Berger, P.L., & Luckmann, T. (1966). *The social construction of reality: A treatise in the sociology of knowledge* (7th ed.). London, England: Pelican Books.

Boulding, K. (1966). *The image*. Ann Arbor, MI: University of Michigan Press.

Burr, V. (1995). *An introduction to social constructionism*. London: Routledge.

Bushe, G.R. & Coetzer, G. (1995). Appreciative inquiry as a team development invention: A controlled experiment. *Journal of Applied Behavioral Science, 31:1*, 19-31. Washington, D.C.: NTL Institute of Applied Behavioral Science.

Capra, F. (1984). *The Tao of physics: An exploration of the parallels between modern physics and eastern mysticism.* New York: Bantam Books.

Capra, F. (1988). *The turning point: Science, society, and the rising culture.* New York: Bantam Books.

Capra, F. (1996). *The web of life: A new scientific understanding of living systems.* New York: Anchor Press/Doubleday.

Cooperrider, D. (1990). Positive image; positive action: The affirmative basis of organizing. In S. Srivastva & D. L. Cooperrider (Eds.),*Appreciative management and leadership, 91-125.* San Francisco, CA: Jossey-Bass.

Cooperrider, D. (1995). Introduction to appreciative inquiry. *Organization Development, 5th Ed.* New York: Prentice Hall.

Cooperrider, D., Barrett, F.J., & Srivastva, S. (1995). Social construction and appreciative inquiry: A journey in organizational theory. In D. Hosking, P. Dachler, & K. Gergen (Eds.), *Management and organization: Relational alternatives to individualism, 157-200.* Aldershot,UK: Avebury Press.

Cooperrider, D., & Passmore, W.A. (1991). The organization dimension of global change. *Human Relations, 44(8),* pp. 763-787.

Cooperrider, D., Sorensen, P., Whitney, D., & Yaeger, T. (Eds.) (1999). *Appreciative inquiry: Rethinking human organization toward a positive theory of change.* Champaign, IL: Stipes.

Cooperrider, D.L., & Srivastva, S. (1987). Appreciative inquiry in organizational life. In W. Pasmore and R. Woodman (Eds.), *Research in organizational change and development, Vol. 1.* Greenwich, CT: JAI Press.

Cousins, N. (1981). *Human options.* New York: Berkeley Books.

DeBono, E. (1982). *DeBono's thinking course.* New York: Facts on File.

DeBono, E. (1991). *I'm right, you're wrong.* London: Penguin Books.

Drucker, P.F. (1980). *Managing in turbulent times.* New York: HarperCollins.

Eisler, R. (1994). *The chalice and the blade.* New York: Harper & Row.

Elliott, C. (1999). *Locating the energy for change: An introduction to appreciative inquiry.* Winnipeg, Manitoba, Canada: International Institute for Sustainable Development.

Emery, M. (1993). *Participative design for participative democracy.* Centre for Continuing Education. Canberra: Australian National University.

Ferguson, M. (1982). *The aquariam conspiracy: Personal and social transformation in our times.* New York: HarperCollins.

Freire, P. (1994). *Pedagogy of the oppressed.* London: Penguin.

Galbraith, J.R. (1995). *Designing organizations.* San Francisco, CA: Jossey-Bass.

Gergen, K.J. (1991). *The saturated self: Dilemmas of identity in contemporary life.* New York: Basic Books.

Gergen, K.J. (1994a). *Realities and relationships: Soundings in social construction.* Cambridge, MA: Harvard University Press.

Gergen, K.J. (1994b). *Toward transformation in social knowledge* (2nd ed.). Thousand Oaks, CA: Sage.

Gergen, K.J. (1999). *An invitation to social construction.* Thousand Oaks, CA: Sage.

Gleick, J. (1987). *Chaos: Making a new science.* New York: Penguin Books.

Goleman, D. (1996). *Emotional intelligence: Why it can matter more than IQ.* London: Bloomsbury.

Hall, N. (Ed.). (1992). *The new scientist guide to chaos.* London: Penguin Books.

Hammond, S.A. (1996). *The thin book of appreciative inquiry.* Plano, TX: Thin Book Publishing.

Hammond, S.A., & Royal, C. (Eds.). (1998). *Lessons from the field: Applying appreciative inquiry.* Plano, TX: Practical Press.

Hampden-Turner, C. (1990). *Creating corporate culture.* Reading, MA: Addison-Wesley.

Hampden-Turner, C. (1994a). *Charting the corporate mind.* New York: Macmillan.

Hampden-Turner, C. (1994b). *The seven cultures of capitalism.* New York: Doubleday.

Handy, C. (1989). *The age of unreason.* London: Arrow Books.

Handy, C. (1994). The empty raincoat: Making sense of the future. London: Hutchinson.

Heisenberg, W. (1930). *Physical principles of the quantum theory.* Dover Publishing.

Hollinger, R. (1994). Postmodernism and the social sciences: A thematic approach. *Contemporary social theory, Vol. 4.* Thousand Oaks, CA: Sage.

Jaworski, J. (1996). *Synchronicity: The inner path of leadership.* San Francisco, CA: Berrett-Koehler.

Jessum, C. (1986). Self-fulfilling prophecies: A theoretical and integrative review. *Psychological Review, 93*(4), 429–445.

Johnson, B. (1992). *Polarity management: Identifying and managing unsolvable problems.* Amherst, MA: HRD Press.

Kuhn, T.S. (1970). *The structure of scientific revolutions* (2nd ed.). Chicago: University of Chicago Press.

Land, G., & Jarman, B. (1992). *Breakpoint and beyond: Mastering the future today.* New York: HarperCollins.

Mann, A.J. (1997, Summer). An appreciative inquiry model for building partnerships. *Global Social Innovations, 1*(2).

Marshak, R.J. (1993, Summer). Managing the metaphors of change. *Organizational Dynamics.*

Marshall, I., & Zohar, D. (1997). *Who's afraid of Schrodinger's cat?* New York: William Morrow.

Mintzberg, H. (1994). *The rise and fall of strategic planning: Reconceiving roles for planning, plans, planners.* New York: The Free Press.

Mohr, B. (1999). AI listerv.

Mohr, B., & Levine, L. (1998). Whole system design: The shifting focus of attention and the threshold challenge. *Journal of Applied Behavioral Science, 34*(3), 305–326.

Mohr, B.J., Smith, E., & Watkins, J.M. (2000). Appreciative inquiry and learning assessment: An embedded evaluation process in a transnational pharmaceutical company. *OD Practitioner, 32*(1), 36–52.

Morgan, G. (1994). *Images of organizations.* Thousand Oaks, CA: Sage.

Nadler, D., & Tushman, M. (1988). *Strategic organization design: Concepts, tools, and processes.* New York: HarperCollins.

Owens, H. (1992). *Open space technology: A user's guide.*

Pasmore, W., & Woodman, R. (Eds.). (1989). *Research in organizational change and development, Volume 5.* Greenwich, CT: JAI Press.

Peters, T. (1992). *Liberation management: Necessary disorganization for the nanosecond nineties.* New York: Fawcett Columbine/Ballantine.

Peters, T. (1994). *Thriving on chaos.* New York: Harper & Row.

Pritchett, P. (1995). *New work habits for a radically changing world: 13 ground rules for job success in the information age.* Dallas, TX: Pritchett & Associates.

Rosenthal, R., & Rubin, D. (1978). Interpersonal expectancy effects: The first 345 studies. *Behavioral and Brain Sciences, 3,* 377–415.

Rukeyser, M. (1994). *Out of silence: Selected poems.* (K. Daniels, Ed.) Evanston, IL: Northwestern University Press.

Rushdie, S. One thousand days in a balloon.

Senge, P.M. (1994). *The fifth discipline: The art and practice of the learning organization.* New York: Doubleday.

Senge, P.M., Kleiner, A., Roberts, C., Ross, R.B., & Smith, B.J. (1994). *The fifth discipline fieldbook: Strategies and tools for building a learning organization.* New York: Doubleday.

Sheldrake, R. (1994). *Seven experiments that could change the world: A do-it-yourself guide to revolutionary science.* London: Fourth Estate Limited.

Sheldrake, R. (1995). *A new science of life: The hypothesis of morphic resonance.* Rochester, VA: Park Street Press.

Simonton, C., et al. (1992). *Getting well again.* New York: Bantam.

Srivastva, S., & Cooperrider, D. (1986). *The emergence of the egalitarian organization.* London: Tavistock. Human Relations.

Srivastva, S., Fry, R.E., & Cooperrider, D.L. (Eds.). (1990). *Appreciative management and leadership: The power of positive thought and action in organizations.* San Francisco, CA: Jossey-Bass.

Toffler, A. (1970). *Future shock.* New York: Random House.

van Eijnatten, F.M. (1993). *The paradigm that changed the workplace.* Stockholm, Sweden: Van Gorcum.

Waldrop, M.M. (1992). *Complexity: The emerging science at the edge of order and chaos.* New York: Simon & Schuster.

Waterman, R.H., Jr. (1982, Winter). Strategic organization. *The Journal of Business Strategy, 2*(3).

Watkins, J.M., & Cooperrider, D.L. (2000a). Appreciative inquiry: A transformative paradigm. *OD Practitioner, 32*(1), 6–12.

Watkins, J.M., & Cooperrider, D.L. (2000b). Organizational inquiry model for global social change organizations. In D. Cooperrider, P. Sorensen, Jr., D. Whitney, & T. Yaeger (Eds.), *Appreciative inquiry: Rethinking human organization toward a positive theory of change* (pp. 249–263). Champaign, IL: Stipes.

Weisbord, M.R. (1978). *Organizational diagnosis: A workbook of theory and practice.* Reading, MA: Addison-Wesley.

Weisbord, M.R. (1991). *Productive workplaces.* San Francisco, CA: Jossey-Bass.

Weisbord, M.R. (Ed.). (1994). *Discovering common ground.* San Francisco, CA: Berrett-Koehler.

Wheatley, M. (1994). *Leadership and the new science: Learning about organizations from an orderly universe.* San Francisco, CA: Berrett-Koehler.

Wheatley, M.J., & Kellner-Rogers, M. (1996). *A simpler way.* San Francisco, CA: Berrett-Koehler.

White, L., Tursky, B., & Schwartz, G. (Eds.). (1985). *Placebos: Theory, research, and mechanisms.* New York: Guilford.

Whitney, D. (1999). AI listserv.

Zohar, D., & Marshall, I. (1994). *The quantum society: Mind, physics and a new social vision.* New York: William Morrow.

About the Authors

Jane Magruder Watkins is a past chair of the NTL Institute for Applied Behavioral Science and, with David C. Cooperrider and others, a founding member of Appreciative Inquiry Consulting. She has worked in the field of organization development (OD) for thirty-five years. She is an innovative consultant who pioneered the use of OD and Appreciative Inquiry in nongovernmental organizations across the globe. She has worked in nearly fifty countries on five continents. This global perspective has led her into an interest in transformational processes for organizations that are facing the realities of an environment that is always shifting and changing. She has been at the forefront of the development of Appreciative Inquiry, an organizational transformation process that enables creativity and generativity within systems and results in the kind of agile organization needed to succeed in the emerging environment.

Although most of Ms. Watkins' work has been in the capacity of a consultant, she has held director-level positions in two international development agencies, served on the director's staff of the Action Agency, and has owned her own business. This substantive experience in the private, government, and nonprofit sectors has led her to innovate with Appreciative Inquiry in a wide and varied range of organizations, including Avon, GTE, Detroit Edison, SmithKline Beecham, and ScottishPower in the corporate sector, several government agencies, a wide range of nonprofit organizations in the United States, and over one hundred international development agencies.

She has taught management and organization development to senior-level managers from agricultural ministries in Asia, Africa, and Latin America for the U.S. Department of Agriculture, was an adjunct professor at the American University, and has taught Appreciative Inquiry courses at Pepperdine and Antioch. Her favorite work today is teaching AI through the Taos Institute, NTL, in client organizations, and for graduate programs.

Ms. Watkins holds master's degrees in English literature and organization development and has done post-graduate research and study at the Judge Institute of Management Studies at Cambridge University in the United Kingdom.

After ten years as a manager and consultant in the professional and financial services sector, Bernard Mohr founded The Synapse Group, Inc., an international consultancy in the fields of socio-technical systems, organization evaluation, and organization transformation, in 1979. Because of his belief that organizations are the primary social institutions of our time, he has always sought to collaborate with his clients in developing agile workplaces that are both more equitable and more capable at mission fulfillment. His strategy is the creation of cultures, structures, and systems that are ecologically sound and economically sustainable, and that are worthy of commitment from their employees.

Some of Mr. Mohr's work is described in *The Emerging Practice of Organization Development* (Sikes, Drexler, & Gant, 1989, NTL), *Reengineering Management* (Champy, 1995, HarperBusiness), *Empowered Teams* (Wellins et al., 1991, Jossey-Bass), *Inside*

Teams (Wellins et al., 1994, Jossey-Bass), and *Whole System Design* (*Journal of Applied Behavioral Science*, 1998). His clients have included AT&T, British Airways, BP Amoco, Arthur D. Little Co., Bell Atlantic, Canadian Pacific Rail System, Coca-Cola USA, EXXON, ITT/Hartford, L.L. Bean, R.R. Donnelley and Sons, and SmithKline Beecham Pharmaceuticals, as well as not-for-profits such as the Executive Council of the Episcopal Church, the Internal Revenue Service, and the Canadian Department of National Defense.

Mr. Mohr completed his undergraduate studies in organizational psychology at the University of Waterloo, Ontario, and his graduate work in organization change at the University of Toronto and organization design at Columbia University. He served between 1984 and 1988 as an elected member of NTL's Board of Directors and chaired NTL's professional development committee. He is a founding member of Appreciative Inquiry Consulting.

About the Editors

William J. Rothwell, Ph.D. is professor of human resource development in the College of Education at The Pennsylvania State University, University Park. He is also president of Rothwell and Associates, a private consulting firm that specializes in a broad array of organization development, human resource development, performance consulting and human resource management services.

Dr. Rothwell has authored, co-authored, edited, or co-edited numerous publications, including *Practicing Organization Development* (with R. Sullivan and G. McLean, Jossey-Bass/Pfeiffer, 1995). Dr. Rothwell's latest publications include *The ASTD Reference Guide to Workplace Learning and Performance*, 3rd ed., 2 vols. (with H. Sredi, HRD Press, 2000); *The Competency Toolkit*, 2 vols (with D. Dubois, HRD Press, 2000); *Human Performance Improvement: Building Practitioner Competence* (with C. Hohne and S. King, Gulf Publishing, 2000); *The Complete Guide to Training Delivery: A Competency-Based*

Approach (with S. King and M. King, Amacom, 2000); *Building In-House Leadership and Management Development Programs* (with H. Kazanas, Quorum Books, 1999); *The Action Learning Guidebook* (Jossey-Bass/Pfeiffer, 1999); and *Mastering the Instructional Design Process*, 2nd ed. (with H. Kazanas, Jossey-Bass/Pfeiffer, 1998).

Dr. Rothwell's consulting client list includes thirty-two companies from the *Fortune* 500.

Roland Sullivan has worked as an organization development (OD) pioneer with nearly eight hundred organizations in ten countries and virtually every major industry.

Mr. Sullivan specializes in the science and art of systematic and systemic change, executive team building, and facilitating Whole System Transformation Conferences—large interactive meetings with from three hundred to fifteen hundred people.

Mr. Sullivan has taught courses in OD at seven universities, and his writings on OD have been widely published. With Dr. Rothwell and Dr. McLean, he was co-editor of *Practicing OD: A Consultant's Guide* (Jossey-Bass/Pfeiffer, 1995).

For over two decades, Mr. Sullivan has served as chair of the OD Institute's Committee to Define Knowledge and Skills for Competence in OD and was a recent recipient of the Outstanding OD Consultant of the World award from the OD Institute.

Mr. Sullivan's current professional learning is available at *www.RolandSullivan.com.*

Kristine Quade is an independent consultant who combines her background as an attorney with a master's degree in organization development from Pepperdine University, and years of experience as both an internal and external OD consultant.

Ms. Quade draws from experiences in guiding teams from divergent areas within corporations and across many levels of executives and employees. She has facilitated leadership alignment, culture change, support system alignment, quality process improvements, organizational redesign, and the creation of clear strategic intent that results in significant bottom-line results. A believer in whole systems change, she has developed the expertise to facilitate groups ranging in size from eight to two thousand in the same room for a three-day change process.

Recognized as the 1996 Minnesota Organization Development Practitioner of the Year, Ms. Quade teaches in the master's programs at Pepperdine University and the University of Minnesota at Mankato and the master's and doctoral programs at the University of St. Thomas in Minneapolis. She is a frequent presenter at the Organization Development National Conference and also at the International OD Congress and the International Association of Facilitators.

Index

This Page Constitutes a
Continuation of the Copyright Page